The Complete Book of

PASTA

JACK DENTON SCOTT

The Complete Book of
PASTA

An Italian Cookbook

With photographs of Italy by *Samuel Chamberlain*
& drawings by Melvin Klapholz

GALAHAD BOOKS · NEW YORK

ACKNOWLEDGMENTS

My appreciation for the vision and the knowledge of my editor, Narcisse Chamberlain; and my thanks to staff members of the National Macaroni Institute and to Robert M. Green, its Executive Secretary; to Maria Luisa Scott, una tifosa di pasta who was there at the birth and with her knowledge of language and cooking really made this book possible. Thanks also to my friend Fanny Graef for her help in research; to Lucia Balsamo Contessa di Loreto (Mrs. Frank Abbot) for her skillful help in translations; and to the professional Italian chefs for their conversations with a convert—and, not least, my gratitude to friends and acquaintances who shared their recipes.

Design by Lynn Hatfield

*For my mother-in-law, Maria Cifelli Limoncelli,
who taught me that the kitchen is the true place
of creation, and for her daughters who carry on
the tradition, Maddalena Altman, Maria Luisa
Scott, Palmina Thompson*

AREZZO—Tuscany

Contents

LAKE ORTA, *the Island of San Giulio—Piedmont*

Foreword

Why does a writer spend time on a cookbook? In my case there were three reasons: Knowing that cooking, especially of pasta, was my hobby, the publisher trapped me into doing it. Then, with a cookbook, a writer perhaps has closer communication with a reader than in any other type of writing; this is good for the writer, as is the precise language he is forced to use. A cookbook, lastly, and to use a worn and weary word, comes as a challenge in today's world. I am faced with the fact that my fellow man is rapidly becoming less and less interested in *cooking* food, rapidly coming to depend almost completely upon those frozen meals requiring only the effort to remove them from the packages and place them in a saucepan; some are even heated in the packages! So, in essence, writing a cookbook is like writing history. I had the urge to hurry and get this one between covers so that someday (perhaps tomorrow) a person can take it from a bookshelf (if we still have them) and say: "Look! A *cook*book. Those were the days when they had to work to eat." Such is the stuff of history.

But that does not explain why, exactly, a book about pasta. "I could write a better book about cookery than has ever been written," remarked Dr. Samuel Johnson. "It should be a book about philosophical principles."

Indeed it should be, and Dr. Johnson could have found such a book lying in wait for him in the subject of Italian pasta. For the Italians, acknowledged masters of the art of pasta manufacture and cookery, are nothing if not philosophical about their favorite food. For example, I was sitting in George's Restaurant in Rome one day with an Italian travel expert, a pasta devotee and trencherman of the first order. We both had just polished off a noodle dish tossed with sweet butter and heavy cream and laced with that superb ham from the hills of Parma, prosciutto, and sat watching a heavy-set Italian, wearing pince-nez and a worried expression, set about demolishing a dish of spaghetti in tomato sauce. He seemed to be having trouble in the winding and in finding his mouth.

"A lawyer," said my friend. "He has a case now of a young woman accused of impairing the morals of minors. Now she is in the majors. It is said that he has fallen in love with her. A difficult case. I can tell that he truly has become smitten. Look! See how the spaghetti uncoils before he can eat it. See that spot of tomato on his tie. Poor man! He is in trouble!"

Italians believe that they can read a man's character in the way he eats his pasta, are certain that they can quickly tell if a person is parsimonious or generous, in control or in emotional trouble, a good husband or a playboy, an honest worker or lazy, an epicure or a greedy clod. And it could be that they have something, for pasta is much more than food in the land of its birth. It is a way of life.

Pity the foreigner who travels Italy and treats pasta poorly. He is immediately relegated to the lowest type of unappreciative tourist, an insensitive boor who can never understand the glory that is Italy. For pasta is taken

LORETO, *the Santuario della Santa Casa—The Marches*

seriously. Not only is it a healthful food eaten at least once daily. It is also almost an art object, brought to its highest expression differently in each region, each with its own imaginative forms and inspired sauces. Ranging from the spectacular to the poetic, pasta is Italy: creative, colorful, historic, dramatic.

Use your fork properly on pasta in Italy and you are in. You are *un tifoso di pasta* (a dedicated enthusiast) and a member of the club. Misuse it, or fail to show the proper respect for pasta, and you might as well pack your bags and go home.

THE COMPLETE BOOK OF PASTA is the result of my using a fork with enthusiasm and dedication. It led much further afield than expected. Italy is the true pasta paradise and needs no assistance on this from anyone. But pasta is a remarkable substance; it commands respect in other countries, too. No one can come near the talent of the Italians, but others do have a knowing way with pasta. So the pasta story could not be "complete" without interesting dishes from around the world that appear in the Appendix to this book.

These international vagaries are only a bonus, however. The exploration of purely Italian pasta led into such nether reaches of Italian cookery as a whole that something exceedingly interesting emerged. *All* of the style, tradition, regional flavors, ingredients, techniques of Italian cooking must

xiii

at least be touched upon if pasta is one's subject. The Table of Contents sounds as though pasta were hardly the topic at hand at all. Soups, Seafood, Meats, Poultry, Game, Vegetables—these are normally the backbone of a "general" cookbook. The pervasive affinity that pasta has for almost everything else that is good to eat makes it about the most general "specialized" topic in cookbookdom. The subject is almost too big. Perhaps that is why no comprehensive book of pasta has ever been written before.

Lastly, and importantly, what I have learned about cooking pasta I could not know had I not eaten it almost daily during repeated travels throughout Italy. After a while, the panorama of the country itself proved to be involved, like an ingredient, in her cooking. Would not Dr. Johnson have suggested this very idea as a philosophical principle of national cuisines? Samuel Chamberlain, with his photographs, brings concretely to this book the ingredients that mere words cannot adequately describe—Italy herself, like her incomparable national dish, spectacular and poetic, creative, colorful, historic, dramatic—in pictures to which the same glowing adjectives apply.

J.D.S.

The Complete Book of

PASTA

"No man is lonely while eating spaghetti—it requires too much attention . . ."

Christopher Morley

Chapter I

ROME, *the Bernini Fountain, Piazza Navona*

A PASTA a Day

$\mathcal{E}$very book has its moment of inspiration, often in a conversation, a song, a sight or a memory. This one began in Rome in 1960, in one of Italy's finest restaurants, George's, where my wife and I were sitting with the Italian Tourist Office's United States director and an official of CIT, the leading travel agency in Italy. We were gathered for lunch, talking about a travel book I was researching, just before taking off for an exploratory drive through the little-known southern section of Italy.

The Tourist Office lady had a dish of tuna and white beans to start; the CIT man suggested that we instead have *spaghetti all'amatriciana* and spoke glowingly of that favorite dish of Rome before it arrived, describing it as a

3

sauce of sweet red peppers and ripe tomatoes simmered with young pork cheek, served over *bucatini*. It finally came, hot and sending up steam as I like it, in soup bowls. Before we started, the CIT man straightened in his seat, looked severely at us and said: "Please, as a favor, do not disgrace the pasta and use a spoon!"

When I told him that we never used a spoon (a lesson taught by my mother-in-law many years ago), he brightened and smiled. "*Grazie,* thank you. I am happy."

In many restaurants in Italy, the waiter, when he sees that you are a foreigner, brings a big tablespoon and fork, knowing that most visitors use the spoon as the base on which to twirl their spaghetti. But the proper way is to use just the fork. Push a small portion away from the rest of the pasta on your plate, then twirl it until a reasonable amount is nicely entwined on the fork. This is comparable to the etiquette of spooning soup away from you, or not trying to eat an entire piece of bread without first breaking it into pieces. This fork technique is not, however, so easy as it sounds and takes practice. I am told that the reason many Italians, especially the Romans and the big city types, look down on those who use the spoon as a crutch is because the lower classes usually do eat pasta that way. I am not certain, however, that the spoon in some cases isn't preferable to the manner in which many supposedly sophisticated Italians handle their pasta: somewhat like the Chinese with chopsticks, they push their faces close to the plate, sending in a continuous stream of pasta. A most unappetizing sight, even if it is done with gusto.

But I mentioned none of these thoughts that day in George's. I didn't have the chance, for the CIT man was in full control of the conversation.

"We are proud of our pasta," he said. "Only in this country is it served properly, a delight to the palate, a thing of beauty when it comes to the table with its many shapes and variety of sauces. We make poetry with our pasta—flowers, stars, seashells, beautiful twirls and elegant twists."

He stopped then and gave me a searching look. "Did you know, for example, that we can serve a different pasta every day of the year? Without repeating ourselves?"

There it was. The inspiration, even a possible title for a book. A pasta a day! And research has proven the CIT man right, even conservative. My years of wandering about Italy, fork in hand, have since produced evidence that the Italians probably could serve two different pasta dishes a day without repetition all year long.

Italians do not hold grand opera in higher regard than they do their national dish. They have even raised a museum in its honor. Called the *Museo Storico degli Spaghetti,* it is located in Pontedassio, not far from the Ligurian Sea and the Italian Riviera. I discovered much about pasta there that should be passed on.

The *museo* is in a huge old house, the family seat of the Agnesis, who, it is believed, began the Italian pasta industry in an old mill in Pontedassio in 1824. Vincenzo Agnesi, the remaining scion of these spaghetti pioneers, spent many years assembling the items in the museum. I spent two days wandering there, taking notes and becoming educated.

A few of the facts I discovered: Pasta was not discovered by Marco Polo in China and brought back to Italy, for *ravioli* was being eaten in Rome in 1284, almost twenty years before Marco Polo's famous travels. *Fettuccine,* that tasty dish of noodles, cheese, butter, cream and raw egg yolk, was not created in Rome by a restaurateur named Alfredo for Mary Pickford and Douglas Fairbanks, but was eaten by the Romans much as it is now in 1200 and was known as *lagano cum caseo.*

CAMOGLI—Liguria

ROME, *the Spanish Steps*

In the museum are ancient and modern machines and instruments used in the manufacture of pasta, from long, gleaming Sicilian "knitting needles" used to dry spaghetti in spirals to the mechanical monster, the continuous-extrusion press, that forms and sends out pasta in a swift stream. Paintings are everywhere, etchings, prints—showing pasta being made in huge sheets, peasants dancing in the streets eating it in long streamers from their hands, nobles daintily eating it as it is brought by servants; cartoons showing foreigners having difficulties (such as winding the strands around their necks) eating pasta. There is a puppet show with Chinese characters in pigtails eating spaghetti while Marco Polo stares in astonishment.

Museum books and ancient documents attest to pasta being one of the oldest and most revered foods, eaten as early as 5,000 B.C. Boccaccio paused in his salacious attack on the Church long enough to create the country of Bengodi where people live on a mountain of cheese and do nothing but make, cook and eat pasta. Rossini, Rabelais, d'Annunzio, Goldoni rave about pasta each in his own inimitable way; the poet, Merlin Cocai, created a book of poetry, glowing odes to pasta. I leafed through a cookbook, *De Honesta Voluptate* by Platina, published in 1485, which gave excellent old pasta recipes, plus several intriguing ways to serve those ancient necessities, larks' tongues and hummingbirds' livers.

And for the first time I found, at the museum (and more in Rome), a list of pasta names with English translations. As I have never seen them elsewhere, I think they are worth recording, even though many of these names are not the ones best known commercially in this country. The illustrated Glossary, which begins on page 22, includes the names on this list, to which have been added many more—translated or described to the best of my own ability—of other pastas I have eaten in Italy and as many as I could find of the names that are familiar on the shelves of American grocery stores and supermarkets.

A few times, when in doubt concerning the list, I consulted D. Maldari & Sons in Brooklyn, die makers for the pasta industry in the United States, men with a vast knowledge of the myriad forms pasta takes. But even these experts couldn't give me a complete list.

"Must be a thousand different shapes," the senior Maldari said. "Who can list all the ways of the imagination?" Who indeed, especially of the Italian imagination? There are enough different kinds of pastas to keep most of us busy at the boiling pot for the rest of our lives. Unfortunately, in America manufacturers have taken the color from many of their names. Spaghettini has become "thin spaghetti"; *vermicelli,* "fine spaghetti"; *fusilli,* "nonskid spaghetti," etc.

This leads into what else we have done with pasta in the United States. Much has happened since Thomas Jefferson introduced it here in 1786, after he returned from a long stay abroad as Ambassador to France. He brought back one spaghetti die from Italy and used it to make small amounts of pasta, serving it only to family and friends. It did not appear commercially until 1848, and didn't begin to catch on until fifty years later when Dr. Mark Carleton of the U. S. Department of Agriculture introduced durum wheat to our tables. World War I planted us firmly in pasta production when all Italian imports were cut off.

According to statistics of the mid-1960's, if all the pasta consumed by Americans in one year had been spaghetti, rather than the 150 forms recognized by our National Macaroni Institute, it would have reached 4,425 feet per person, or more than four-fifths of a mile for every citizen of our country. Our total consumption would have stretched to the moon and back 270 times.

We averaged about 7.4 pounds of pasta per person (this later went up and presumably is still climbing), making us fourth in the pasta parade. First, naturally, was Italy with each person annually eating 62 pounds; Switzerland was second with 20 pounds; France, which oddly enough seldom mentions pasta when talking up its famed cuisine, was third with 14 pounds per person.

Despite this evident love of pasta, few of us in the United States have learned to cook and serve it properly. We overcook, serve too much, don't approach it the way they do in the land of its birth. It too often is the main course and rarely comes as a slender, tempting first offering. Prime movers in this incorrect way of handling pasta in our homes have been home and women's magazines, which offer outlandish recipes that would make any pasta-respecting Italian give up eating it for the rest of his life. We goo it up in long-cooked casseroles; we mismate it with inappropriate ingredients to

create oddities such as spaghetti Stroganoff, mix it in meat loaf, drown it in the sauce of another dish. I am not saying these ideas are all wrong, but they should have to do only with leftover pasta, which can be used in many interesting ways. The key word here is "leftover," otherwise these are not fit recipes for pasta.

It is also a sad fact that few Italian restaurants in the United States offer pasta worth eating; most serve it poorly, overcooked, in huge portions that accompany the entrée. There are avaricious reasons for this, of course. Served this way, the diner must pay the full price for the pasta, usually equaling or nearly equaling that of the entrée. Expense aside, the custom is barbaric. Few Italians in their own country will take more than a small portion of pasta before the main course except in unusual circumstances. Larger portions are served only when a special pasta is presented as an entrée, such as *lasagne* or one of the wide noodles that are stuffed and prepared for a hearty main dish.

Properly, pasta comes in a warm bowl, two or three ounces per person (more details on this later when cooking methods are discussed), and it is used to fan the appetite for the next course—not to kill it.

Why, then, is it served the wrong way in homes and in most restaurants in the United States? And why are meatballs and spaghetti always in tandem, when it is difficult even to find them on a restaurant menu in the place of their supposed birth? Why are the sauces always made of tomato and tomato paste and long cooked to a heavy and indelicate consistency? Most Italians I have talked with who visit this country flee back to their homeland distressed at what their countrymen have done here.

My research divulged that the answer may lie in the fact that most of the immigrants who came to the United States in the early days were poor, mostly from the southern section of Italy. If they were lucky, they had meat once a week, usually on Sunday. As the meat was always a cheap cut of beef, pork, or mutton, it was cooked all day in tomato, to make what is called a *ragù*. Thus the sauce was heavy. The pasta was served first. And as this was the day to eat heartily, it came to the table in the thick sauce, in a huge bowl or platter. The meat was then properly served next. Sometimes the beef would be so tough that it was perforce chopped and fashioned into meatballs or *polpette*. These received the same treatment: long hours on the stove. Now there are good and tasty *ragù,* and these are classic dishes of Italy, cooked for special occasions. They don't happen to be among my favorites, for I lean toward the light and the delicate in flavor. But that weekly *ragù* was a memory that the immigrants brought to the promised land, and they spread the prac-

BAGNAIA—Latium

tice in their homes and restaurants to the point where pasta here is not good propaganda for their country and has become what their visiting countrymen refer to as *indelicato*—indelicate, a heavy food that is far from inspired.

I don't want to engage in that favorite game of many who visit and think that they know Italy, disparaging the southern people and their food. Much good pasta is prepared in the South. The seafood sauces are superb, among the best in the country. But generally speaking, the poor immigrant's *ragù* offers the best explanation of some of the inferior pasta dishes in the United States.

And the practice of using tomato paste in so many sauces, where did that originate? Probably also as an economic necessity. The poorer grade of tomatoes that weren't used immediately during the season were sundried into a conserve and during the winter months became the base for sauces. For my taste, tomato paste kills the sauce; it overwhelms it, the heavy, almost chemical flavor drowns the other seasonings and flavors. Of the many Italian chefs whom I have met, they almost all condemn the use of tomato paste in anything.

Two more subjects should be discussed: portions, and weight (your weight). One report has it that a very hearty spaghetti dinner when stretched straight out would be 150 feet long, half the length of a regulation football field. I am not going to suggest that you eat 150 feet of any kind of pasta at a meal. To repeat: a small dish of pasta should precede the main course and its purpose is to whet the appetite. Some concerned pasta manufacturers in Italy are even sending emissaries around the world, showing how properly to prepare and eat their products. As yet, America hasn't been graced by their presence. But those of us who have learned know that the perfect pasta should leave you wanting more, not loosening your belt and thinking uncomfortably about the weight you are putting on by twirling that fork so dexterously.

Eaten as it should be, pasta is not a weight builder. It is one of the world's perfect foods. To begin with, it is a low-fat food. Statistically, the National Macaroni Institute assures us that the fat content of pasta averages no more than 1.4 per cent. (Egg noodles are slightly less innocent, averaging 4.5 per cent fat.) The famed nutritionist and physiologist, Dr. Ancel Keys, who has traveled the world over delving into the diets of people everywhere to find the basic reasons for overweight and heart disease, advocates a low-fat diet. His only cautions regarding pasta are to eat small portions and not to load it with oil or butter.

The National Macaroni Institute can further supply you, if you really want to know, with copious scientific, nutritional details concerning pasta. Two ounces of uncooked macaroni, for instance, contain only 200 calories, the amount in two small apples. Pasta products are valuable providers of protein, and protein contains eight essential amino acids. Now pasta, it must be owned, is not very strong on a couple of those amino acids. But many of the ingredients of good pasta sauces *are*. In fact, I note that a general list of such ingredients reads like a nutritionist's dream of what's good for you— meat, seafood, fresh vegetables, cheese, eggs, fruit (tomatoes are fruit)—a balanced diet if ever there was one, with every amino acid in place. The Institute can tell you a great deal more, too, about energy-giving carbo-hydrates (pasta is far superior to potatoes in this respect and has more protein as well), pasta as an economical source of good nutrition, pasta as a satis-fying food that discourages between-meal nibbling, and so on. The informa-tion is very encouraging and, knowingly or not, the Institute's advice is true to Italian tradition. Pasta products should indeed be served in small portions.

To further pass on the good word about pasta being the perfect food, not long ago no less an authority than the *Journal of the American Medical Association* reported on a town in Pennsylvania, Roseto, whose 1,600 resi-dents are mostly Italian (first-, second-, and third-generation immigrants from Roseto, east of Rome near the Adriatic). It seems that on a diet high in pasta of all kinds, washed down with much wine, the "vigorous and fun-loving" Rosetons had a strikingly low death rate from heart attacks—not one such fatality to anyone under 47 during the entire seven-year study—a rate up to four times better than was found among the people of mainly Welsh and German descent in neighboring towns. The team of doctors who made the study reported that the most impressive factor in their observations was the way people enjoyed life.

The people of Roseto found (or did they know all along?) that a pasta a day keeps the doctor away.

Chapter II

CHÂTEAU DE ST. PIERRE—Valle d'Aosta

PASTA: What Is It?
& a Glossary
of Pasta Names

*W*hat is pasta? Many Americans, if they haven't visited Italy or eaten in one of the few good Italian restaurants in this country, are confused by the word (an Italian word, obviously, but now part of the English language). Spaghetti, macaroni, or noodles, fine, these are no mystery. But they are only a small part of the pasta picture. Actually, pasta is the generic term for all the multitude of products made from semolina and water. Semolina is the golden, sugar-fine flour made from the heart of durum wheat. This is the hardest and purest of all wheats.

Pasta products are also called macaroni products, which is inconvenient, as macaroni also means a particular type of pasta. However, Webster uses that term to define the subject: Macaroni is "a paste, composed chiefly of wheat flour, dried in the form of long, slender tubes, and used, when cooked, as an article of food . . ."

Simple enough. In fact, too simple. In the land of its birth, pasta is much more than that. As my CIT travel-agency friend said, "We Italians make poetry with pasta." And indeed they do. Each region of Italy has its special shape, the variations limited only by the imagination. The Romans cut theirs in long strips; the Bolognese like ribbons of various widths; in the South some places specialize in pasta shaped like seashells, others the clam or star shape; in Naples they prefer the "little worms," *vermicelli*; in Sicily, spirals dried on knitting needles are popular.

In addition to taste, pasta passes another test of all excellent foods—it is pleasing to the eye. Its graceful twirls and twists, slender reeds, shells, butter-flies, and ribbons appeal to others than chefs and diners. One of the most successful window displays that Tiffany's, the famed jewelers on New York's Fifth Avenue, ever had was one that used pasta as its theme. Every window had it, hanging from the ceiling suspending a diamond ring; piles of it, looking like wheat sheaves, displaying a single watch; *rigatoni* and *ditalini*, *linguine* and *bucatini*, *fettuccine* and spaghetti were arranged in patterns that stopped passersby in their tracks. I saw the windows a few years ago; never has the imagination of the Italians in designing their pasta forms had a more glittering showcase.

But I still prefer to admire pasta at the table. Unless it is made at home (by far the tastiest), all first-class pasta is made the same way: just a healthy mixture of fine semolina and water (eggs are added for noodles and many *pastine,* the tiny pastas used in soups), kneaded into a smooth dough that will pass through dies (pierced metal discs). As the dough goes through the dies, it comes forth as solid rods, spaghetti. When a steel pin is placed in the center of each die, the dough emerges as hollow rods known as macaroni. For the short elbow style, a notched pin is used, allowing the dough to move through more quickly on one side, curling it somewhat.

The long strands of spaghetti and macaroni are placed on racks and put in drying ovens. The shorter varieties go on trays, then into drying cabinets. Pasta is not baked. It is slowly dried while filtered air constantly passes over it. Timing is all important. If it dries too quickly, then it breaks easily; if it dries too slowly it may spoil.

Egg noodles are made the same way except that, rather than the dough passing through dies, it is pressed through rollers in sheets, then cut into the desired shapes.

No matter what the form, pasta emerges as an almost magic substance that has the ability to carry and pass on a range of other flavors that is remarkable. A commercial tomato-grower near Pompeii pulled this power of pasta into perspective for me. "Pasta," he said, "absorbs and magnifies anything it is mated with. Even a simple thing like olive oil becomes magnificent when warmed and tossed with pasta. . . ."

Right. But pasta achieves these results by taking many forms and by being used in many ways. The subject of how pastas are used in cooking can be confusing. For my own purposes, I take the complication out of pasta dishes by separating them into categories and then noting how these overlap.

For instance, a first group of four categories includes pastas that are . . .

> . . . *boiled,* and served with all manner of sauces, such as spaghetti, *linguine,* etc.
> . . . *boiled,* too, are noodles such as *fettuccine,* but usually tossed with simple sauces
> . . . *baked,* with their sauces, such as *lasagne* or *ziti*
> . . . *stuffed,* first; then boiled and sauced, such as *ravioli;* or sauced and baked, such as *cannelloni*

The baked and stuffed-baked categories above are a special group unto themselves, *pasta in forno,* which means that this pasta is not usually served onto the plate and the sauce then added, as with most of the others, but is a dish cooked in the oven (or partly cooked in the oven; the pasta itself is parboiled before the dish is assembled and baked). *Lasagne* is the queen of this variety. *Pasta in forno* is important because it is about the only pasta the Italians, who know how to handle it better than anyone else, consider an entrée or main course.

Or, a different kind of distinction can be made by placing pastas in just two classifications . . .

. . . *pasta in brodo,* pasta in broth; in other words, soups
. . . *pasta asciutta,* literally "dry" pasta, but simply meaning all the
pastas *not* served in broth; in other words, all the pastas in the four
initial categories

Pasta in brodo is an important classification because of the fantastic range of sizes and shapes made to be used just in broth. Dies for at least eighty-four shapes are available to American manufacturers. These pastas run from tiny golden kernels and *pastine* much smaller than a grain of rice to snails just under the size of a golf ball. Cockscombs, sparrows' eyes, stars, shells, butterflies, nuts, cloverleaves, tubes, sausages, baby chicks, wheels, little hats, flowers, horseshoes, umbrellas—the list is limitless. They are usually served in a rich chicken broth. Often only the pasta floats in the clear broth; sometimes vegetables and meat are added. Most of us are familiar with the thick, lusty meal-in-itself, *minestrone.* This is *pasta in brodo,* despite the fact that in addition to curved tubular pasta it also has tomato, beans, meat, and sometimes potatoes.

Pastas used for *pasta asciutta* are not quite so fanciful but they still have a wide range of sizes and shapes, and it is with these that the huge repertory of pasta sauces are served.

You can now start all over again with *pasta asciutta* and divide *it* into two categories . . .

. . . *pasta fresca,* which is fresh or homemade pasta
. . . *pasta secca,* which is dried or commercial pasta

Fresh pasta, at least in Italy, is usually made at home, although it can be purchased in many shops. It can run to any shape or size the cook knows how to make, or has the equipment to make—spaghetti, noodles, *cannelloni, ravioli,* just about anything. *Ravioli* are always *pasta fresca* and are best homemade. Technically, they should be stuffed with a mixture of vegetables, cheeses, and eggs. If they are filled with meat, they are larger, often round, and become *agnolotti. Pasta fresca* is often used for *pasta in forno.*

Pasta secca, that is all the commercial dry pastas we usually buy, can run from the thickness of a hair to the size of your thumb, can be flat like *linguine* and *fettuccine* (my favorite), thick and grooved like *rigatoni,* curled, twisted, or just smooth and straight, and these all come in several thicknesses, as does spaghetti.

Both *pasta secca* and *pasta fresca* are used *in brodo*.

Finally, in connection with meal planning and the way that Americans will use this book, pasta recipes can be classified—in a non-Italian way and depending on the circumstances—into first course and entrée, both of which should be labeled *use your better judgment*.

You will see on reading some of these recipes that it is not those for *pasta in forno* exclusively that have the hearty ring of a main dish. Some others are so clearly entrées that the recipes specifically state this. But then still others, with elaborate sauces or numerous ingredients, are more ambiguous—substantial dishes that, as first courses, certainly will serve at least six people or even more if the entrée to follow is also substantial. Though I consider almost all pasta dishes as first courses in spirit, I do not always go on to the conclusion that an entrée *must* necessarily follow. A modest dish of pasta, salad, cheese, and fruit are quite enough for most of us, at luncheon, supper, or at times of weight-watching in general. Consider, if you will, that such a meal is to have only a first course and no entrée, and you will still be serving pasta as it should be.

Though this is an heretical American view, I would even suggest that The Complete Book of Pasta is one of the best possible places to look for interesting recipes when you want to plan very small and simple meals—and that for this purpose many of the very easy recipes made with few ingredients can even be the best.

A Glossary of PASTA Names

This glossary is an informal affair, designed to help you find your way around the tangle of pasta terminology but by no means claiming to be the authoritative last word on the subject. It is, nevertheless, a larger compilation of terms than I have seen in any one place before.

The list has been assembled from four sources and it can be used as a dictionary to look up any pasta word you find in this book and a good many more besides. First, I have included the entire translated list that I found at the *Museo Storico degli Spaghetti* in Pontedassio. Just a few of these pastas I have never seen, and this fact is indicated by an asterisk preceding their names. These are not used in the recipes in this book. Most of the items on the Pontedassio list, however, are available in this country, or counterparts are available that are easy to recognize.

Second, all the pastas I have used in the book are listed here. Many, though well known, were not on the museum list. Wherever necessary, the English titles of the recipes give an informal literal translation of the Italian name of the pasta used. But some clarification is often needed in addition, so this glossary provides a description when the literal translation cannot do the job. All the pastas used in the recipes are available in this country, though it is a question, as explained below, whether you will always find them sold under the same names.

Third, some of the most-used pastas do fall into definite categories, such as spaghettis, macaronis, noodles, which have variations in size, length, surface texture, etc., that can be quite systematically classified. I have turned for this information to the catalog of one of the largest suppliers of the dies that American manufacturers use in making pastas. The die manufacturer has neatly summarized the categories and suggested an orderly Italian nomenclature, which I repeat here, for most of their possible variations. Not all these variations are in fact produced, but they could be.

There is no guarantee that the American pasta brands will use this nomenclature, however. Each manufacturer has his own idea of how to explain the nature of the product to his buying public. As I mentioned before, "non-skid spaghetti" proved to be one saleman's idea of how to identify *fusilli*,—a description neither accurate nor appetizing but it must be owned it does stick in the memory. I have listed here hardly any of these highly variable American terms. Happily, though, the pasta manufacturers *do* use much Italian nomenclature, if not in very standardized fashion. Differences in size in one product, such as the several sizes of spaghetti, they indicate by numbers, but as these are not the same for every brand I have not referred to them here. However, when you find a pasta you like, those numbers are worth remembering for future reference.

Besides the basic forms of pastas, there are all sorts of unclassifiable shapes which the pasta industry refers to, somewhat helplessly, as "specialty products." They are not necessarily obscure; some, such as pasta shells, are well known indeed. I have listed many here by their Italian names.

The selection of pastas available varies widely from one part of the country to another. In fact, it even varies disconcertingly from one Italian specialty shop to another in the same city. Nevertheless, nowadays, any self-respecting supermarket carries two or three dozen or more different pastas and noodles. You may not always get exactly what you want, but you cannot often complain of lack of variety. My fourth source of information for this glossary was an all-day shopping trip to the downtown Italian section of New York City where the grocery stores carry what may very well be the widest selection of pastas, both American and imported, to be found in the country. Here I unearthed many more names, often for pastas I already knew by other names. The glossary points out many of these duplications to you and lists names found usually only on imported brands for which there are nevertheless counterparts in American brands.

Which brings us to the most important use of this glossary. Each recipe in this book calls for a particular pasta. It is the one which in size, shape, thickness, texture, is the best suited to the particular sauce and method of cooking and serving. But this is not to say that *no* other pasta will do, let alone that the name has to be exactly the same. The point is to know what the pasta called for is like, and then to find a counterpart or an approximation if exactly that pasta by exactly that name is not to be found.

The illustrations in the glossary are drawn life size. They show forty widely available shapes, some of which can have more than one name (in which case we give you a cross-reference). None of the many long straight pastas are illustrated, but the listings explain the variations in their dimensions. Armed with this information, you should be able to tell what you are looking for for any given recipe. Then you should certainly be able to find either the right pasta by some name or a similar one that will do quite as well.

ACINI DI PEPE "peppercorns"— (for soup)

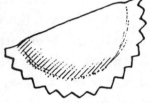

AGNOLOTTI round *ravioli* filled with meat; they are also made as semi-circles, like tiny turnovers. Though these should be made fresh (see page 196), there are good frozen brands in some specialty shops.

*ALPINI "mountains" or "Alpines"

AMORINI "little cupids" (for soup)

ANELLI "rings" (for soup)

ANELLINI "little rings" (for soup)

ANELLINI RIGATI "grooved rings" or "gears" (for soup)

ARANCINI "little oranges" (for soup)

AVENA "oats" (for soup)

BAVETTE translated as "steel castings" in the list at the Italian spaghetti museum, this is an oval (rather than round) spaghetti, thinner than *linguine* (which is also oval). See *Linguine*.

BAVETTINE very narrow *linguine*

BOCCONCINI "small mouthfuls"; this pasta is quite a mouthful, being a grooved tube ½ inch in diameter and 1½ inches long before it is cooked. It is similar to *rigatoni*.

BOWS the American versions of these are usually made of egg-noodle dough and there are many sizes. *Farfalle* ("butterflies") are the Italian version, likely to be plain, not egg, pastas, also of many sizes.

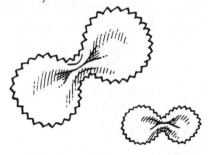

BUCATI "with a hole"; an adjective applied to some pierced or hollow pastas

BUCATINI pierced hollow pasta, like macaroni, but thinner than spaghetti; see Macaroni

CANNELLE "small reeds" or "pipes", i.e., hollow. This is, however, quite a large pasta; see Macaroni.

CANNELLINI "tiny reeds"; a small version of *cannelle*

CANNELLONI "large reeds", i.e., large and hollow, though *cannelloni* are usually flat squares of pasta rolled around a stuffing. To make, see pages 42 and 43.

CANNERONI "large reeds"

CANNERONI LISCI "large smooth reeds"; see *Zitoni* to which these are similar

CANNERONI RIGATI "large grooved reeds"; see *Zitoni rigati* to which these are similar

CANNOLICCHI small pasta tubes

*CANNONI "cannons" or large tubes

CAPELLI D'ANGELO "angel's hair" (for soup)

CAPELLINI "fine hairs"; very fine pasta, as fine as soup noodles but round. See Spaghetti.

CAPPELLETTI "little hats" that are stuffed; to make, see Index

CAPPELLI DI PAGLIACCIO "clown's hats" (for soup)

CAPPELLI DI PRETE "priests' hats"

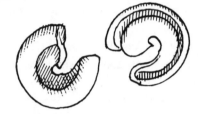

CAPELVENERE "maidenhair fern"; fine noodles for soup

CAVATELLI a short curled noodle; to make, see page 335. The Italian commercial version illustrated here is like a narrow, ripple-surfaced pasta shell. The American commercial version is larger and less well shaped.

CHICCHI DI RISO "grains of rice"; see also *Orzo*

CHIOCCIOLE "snail shells"; see *Lumache*

CHITARRA see Spaghetti *alla chitarra*

CONCHIGLIE "conch shells"; these are usually called simply "shells" and are the same as *maruzze* (see). They are often made grooved or *rigati*. See also Giant shells.

CONCHIGLIETTE "tiny shells"; *maruzzelle* is another diminutive for the same thing. *Conchigliette piccole* is a term for very tiny shells for soup.

CORALLI "coral"; one of several names for very small pasta tubes used in soup. There is also *corallini*, even smaller, and both versions are also made *rigati* (grooved). See *Tubettini* which is very similar.

*CRAVATTE "bow ties"

CRESTE DI GALLI "cockscombs"

*DATTERI "little dates"

*DI NATALI Christmas pasta

*DI NATALI RIGATI grooved Christmas pasta

DITALI "thimbles"; macaroni cut in short lengths, even shorter than elbow macaroni to which it is related

DITALINI "little thimbles"; small macaroni cut in very short lengths

ELBOW Familiar to all in the term "elbow macaroni," elbow pastas are small semicircles that can be made of any of the hollow tubular pastas. The die manufacturer lists almost all the macaronis in elbow form, some in large as well as small semicircles. The diameters range from the size of spaghetti to over ½ inch . . .

Elbow *bucatini*
Elbow *perciatelli*
Elbow *maccheroncelli*
Elbow *mezzanelli*
Elbow *mezzani* or macaroni
Elbow *ziti*
Elbow *zitoni*

These are followed by grooved or *rigati* forms, of which, theoretically, there could be more than those listed . . .

Elbow *mezzanelli rigati*
Elbow *mezzani rigati*

24

Elbow *ziti rigati*
Elbow *zitoni rigati*

Combining the number of dies for elbow and elbow-*rigati* pastas, in both small and large semicircles, these 11 names could account for 28 products, providing the pasta manufacturer does not invent still more sizes for the semicircles!

In actual practice, not too many elbow names are used, but the American passion for elbow macaroni per se has led the Italian importers to use the English word elbow on their packages of this pasta.

*ELENA named after an Italian Queen Elena

*ELETTRICI RIGATI "grooved electric wire"

FARFALLE "butterflies"; usually called "bows" in this country. There are many variations in size and design. American bows are likely to be made of egg rather than plain pasta dough.

FARFALLETTE "little butterflies"

FARFALLINE "tiny butterflies"

FARFALLONI "big butterflies"

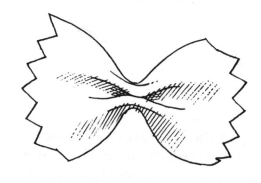

*FAVORITI "favorites"

FEDELINI "the faithful," according to the museum list; this is one of the thinnest of the spaghettis, thinner than *vermicelli*

FETTUCCINE "small ribbons"; one of the best-known Italian noodles (the other is *tagliatelle*). Commercially, they are sold both as straight rods and loosely bent and curled, as illustrated. They are about ¼ inch wide. *Fettuccine* are often made fresh; see pages 42 and 43. Directions for how wide to cut them vary in recipes for homemade *fettuccine*.

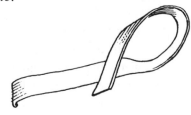

FETTUCCELLE "little ribbons"; a narrow version of *fettuccine*

FETTUCCE "ribbons"; the widest of this noodle family, about ½ inch

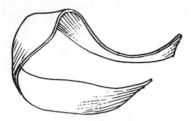

FETTUCCE RICCIE "curly ribbons"; noodles with a rippled edge. See *Riccie,* and see *Margherita* which is about the same as *fettucce riccie.*

*FIORENTINI small pasta of Florence

FORATINI "small pierced" pasta (for soup)

FORATINI FINI "tiny pierced" pasta (for soup)

FUNGHINI "little mushrooms" (for soup)

FUSILLI "twists"; spaghetti twisted like a corkscrew in a long form. Quite different but given the same name is a tight short spiral that looks like a machine part; this version is given yet another name, *rote,* or "wheels."

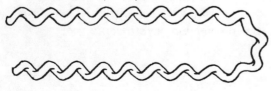

FUSILLI BUCATI "twists with a hole"; i.e., *fusilli* made of thin macaroni

GEMELLI "twins"; these look like two short pieces of spaghetti twisted together like rope. An Americanized name for them is "twists Napoletani."

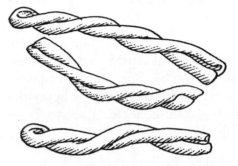

GIANT SHELLS these are very popular in this country and are served stuffed. They come grooved (*rigati*) and plain. Italian words for shells are *conchiglie* and *maruzze.*

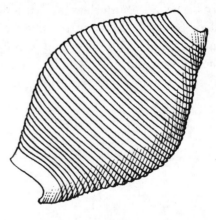

GNOCCHI "dumpling"; there are Italian dishes in which this word does indeed mean a type of dumpling. But

it is also used by Italian manufacturers as a pasta name, and variations of the name apply to quite different pastas.

Gnocchi itself is used for a pasta similar to *cavatelli. Gnocconi* looks like a short piece of *mafaldine.* (See illustrations under these names.)

GNOCCHETTI "small dumpling"; some short forms of pasta tubes may have their names changed to *gnocchetti* if they are cut even shorter. An example is *canneroni lisci* (see), which also has a *rigati* (grooved) form. These become *gnocchetti lisci* and *gnocchetti rigati* when they are cut about 1½ inches instead of 2 inches long. *Mezzi gnocchetti lisci* is the same tube cut about ½ inch long. All these tubes are roughly the diameter of *zitoni* (see).

GNOCCHETTI DI ZITI these are shorter forms of cut *ziti* (see illustration under *ziti*) and there can be four: *gnocchetti di ziti,* both smooth and *rigati,* only about ½ inch long and very like *ditali* (see illustration under *ditali*); and *gnocchetti di ziti lunghi* ("long"), also both smooth and *rigati,* about an inch long.

LANCETTE "small   spears"   (for soup)

LASAGNE a word, according to the Italian spaghetti museum list, that means "pots" (derived from the Latin, *lasanum*). Be that as it may, *lasagne* is the familiar, very wide flat pasta used

most often in baked dishes. To make, see pages 42 and 43.

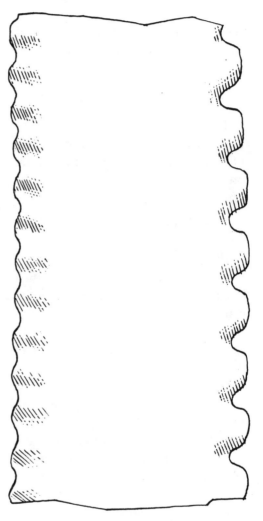

LASAGNE RICCIE *lasagne* with one or two sides "curly" or rippled, sometimes called *lasagne riccie un lato* if rippled only on one side; see *Riccie.* Ripple-edged *lasagne* is often sold without the word *riccie* appearing on the label at all.

LINGUE DI PASSERI "sparrows' tongues"; similar to *linguine* but a little bigger (see below)

LINGUINE "small tongues"; this is really a spaghetti, but it has the shape of a narrow, thick noodle. The American manufacturer's dies produce *linguine* that are actually oval rods, a sort of flattened spaghetti. He gives for these products (which are all long) the following names, ranging from quite fine to somewhat oversize . . .

> Bavettine
> Bavette
> Linguine
> Lingue di passeri

With variations in die sizes, these 4 names can actually cover 6 sizes of oval-rod pastas.

LINGUINE FINE a smaller version of *linguine*

LISCI "smooth"; the adjective applied to pastas made with a smooth surface to distinguish them from the same pastas also known in grooved (*rigati*) versions

LUMACHE "snails"; a shell shape, of which there are several sizes

LUMACHINE "small snails"

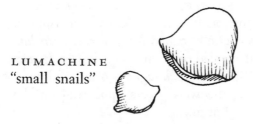

MACARONI our general term for hollow or pierced pasta products. The possibilities range from a macaroni no larger than spaghetti to *tufoli*, a very large tube, a good inch in diameter, which is served stuffed, somewhat like *manicotti* or *cannelloni*. The die manufacturer gives them these names . . .

> Spaghetti bucati
> Bucatini
> Perciatelli
> Maccheroncelli
> Mezzanelli
> Mezzani or Maccheroni (see below)
> Ziti
> Zitoni
> Occhi di lupo
> Cannelle
> Tufoli

Pastas by these 11 names can most of them be made with dies of several different sizes, for a possible total of 20 sizes of hollow pastas.

Through sizes as large as *ziti* or *zitoni*, some brands, especially the Italian, are made long like spaghetti. The very thick ones are cut shorter. However, for all except the thinnest hollow pastas, short lengths (1 to 2 inches or sometimes more) are the ones you are most likely to find. The American brands sometimes call them "cut to cooking size." Some of these short forms are often curved rather than straight; see *Magliette* and Elbow. They are also made with surfaces grooved rather than smooth; see *Rigati*.

In addition, there are numerous

other Italian names for hollow pastas of various sizes and lengths that are listed throughout this glossary.

MACCHERONI   the Italian spelling of macaroni; the diminutive for a smaller size is *maccheroncelli*. See also *Mezzani*. You will often find these in either long or short forms without a distinction being made in the names ("*tagliati*" would indicate the short form).

MAFALDA or MAFALDE   a broad noodle rippled on both edges; *mafaldine* is the diminutive for a smaller version. See also *Riccie*.

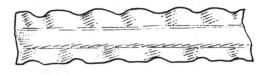

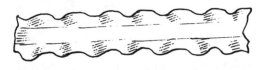

MAGLIETTE   "links"; the word is used for rather short and slightly curved sections of pasta rods whose names indicate the original long forms, such as . . .

MAGLIETTE MEZZANI   "medium links"; curved sections of medium-size macaroni

MAGLIETTE RIGATE   "grooved links"; curved sections of grooved pasta tubes

MAGLIETTE SPACCATE   "split links"; curved section of split pasta tubes

However, the total number of pastas that could be cut and curved in *magliette* form as suggested by the die manufacturer is much more imposing than the few above that I have most often used. They are all based on macaroni, i.e., hollow forms, from a thickness of less than ¼ inch up to a diameter of about 1 inch . . .

> *Magliette maccheroncelli*
> *Magliette mezzanelli*
> *Magliette mezzani*
> *Magliette ziti*
> *Magliette zitoni*
> *Magliette occhi di lupo*
> *Magliette cannelle*

Pastas by these 7 names can most of them be made with dies of more than one size, for a total of 14 sizes of *magliette* pastas, and then the entire list can be repeated grooved, or *rigati*. The *rigati* forms can be made on so many sizes of dies that there is a conceivable total of 28 of these.

But finally, note that the word *magliette* is often omitted in the naming of both American and Italian pasta brands. The reason may be that in actual manufacture the straight short forms of hollow pasta tend to come out of the dies not really straight but also slightly curved, so that the distinction between straight and curved becomes largely theoretical. At any rate, you will often see pastas that certainly look as if they should be qualified as *magliette* referred to merely by their basic names.

MANICOTTI "small muff", i.e., a tube. However, *manicotti* is usually fresh homemade pasta cut into large flat squares and rolled around a stuffing; to make, see pages 42 and 43.

A commercial form of *manicotti* is a giant tube, at least 4 inches long, over an inch in diameter, with the ends cut on the diagonal. The tube is often grooved. See *Mostaccioli rigati,* as this form of *manicotti* is just like it in over-size form with oversize grooves.

MARGHERITA "daisy"; this does not look like a daisy, however. It is a moderately narrow noodle rippled along one side, similar to *fettucce riccie.*

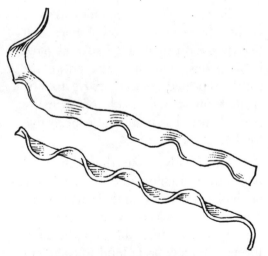

MARGHERITINE "small daisy"; this does look a little like a flower. See *Funghini; margheritine* is almost exactly the same shape and about three times the size.

MARUZZE "seashells"; there are at least 7 sizes, including the giant shells that are served stuffed. See Giant shells. And see *Conchiglie*; these are the same thing as *maruzze* and there are several names for the several sizes.

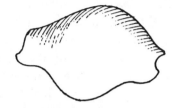

MARUZZELLE "small seashells"

MARUZZINE "tiny seashells"; the smallest of the pasta shells

MEZZANI "medium"; this word is often used for the standard middle size of macaroni, or *maccheroni.* You will find both long and short forms by the same name.

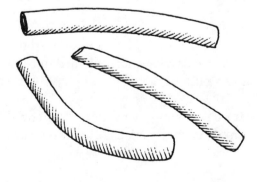

MEZZANI TAGLIATI medium-size macaroni cut into short lengths; *tagliati* is often left off the name of the pasta

*MILLEFIORI "one thousand flowers"

MILLE RIGHE "one thousand stripes"; see *Rigatoni,* as the two are almost identical. This pasta is cut a little shorter (about 1½ inches) and has finer grooves.

MOSTACCIOLI "small moustaches"; but these do not really look like moustaches. They are medium-size pasta tubes, 2 inches or so long, with diagonally cut ends. See also *Penne,* which are the same thing.

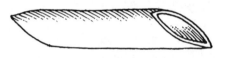

MOSTACCIOLI RIGATI "grooved small moustaches"

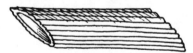

MOSTACCIOLINI "tiny moustaches"; see also *Pennine*

MUGHETTO "lily-of-the-valley" (for soup)

*NAPOLEONI "Napoleons"

NASTRINI "ribbon" or "tape"; the name is not very descriptive, as this pasta is a small bow with a zig-zag edge all the way around, like American egg bows. See also *Farfalle.*

NOCCIOLE "hazelnuts"; a shell shape of which there are several sizes as well as *rigati* (grooved) forms

NOODLES there are many names for noodles of many widths, manufactured or homemade. The range of widths available commercially goes from less than ⅛ inch to over 1 inch and the die manufacturer gives them these names, with corresponding English terminology . . .

Trenettine	Extra fine
Trenette	Fine
Fettuccelle	Medium
Fettuccine	Medium
Fettucce	Medium
Lasagnette	Broad
Lasagne	Extra broad

Lasagne, of course is also made much wider than the inch or so the die manufacturer suggests when it is used for baking. Starting with *fettuccelle,* noodles may be rippled on one or two sides; see *Lasagne* and *Mafalda,* and see *Riccie.* See *Tagliatelle* for another important noodle family.

The 7 names above cover 14 sizes of dies with which noodles can be made and even more widths than that are surely made. In addition, noodles are sold as long straight rods, in folded form, and loosely bent and curled. The width of the noodle has more bearing on the texture and flavor of the cooked pasta than the form in which it is packaged. In theory, noodles are always made with egg dough, which make a definite difference in flavor.

OCCHI DI LUPO "wolf's eyes"; these are large tubes; see Macaroni

OCCHI DI PASSERI "sparrows eyes"; tiny circles (for soup)

*OCCHI DI TROTA "trout's eyes"

*ONDULATI pastas "that wave"

ORZO "barley"; small pasta that looks more like rice and is cooked in much the same way (see page 209)

*PANIERINI "small baskets"

PAPPARDELLE broad noodles; in Italy this noodle is often served with hare.

*PARIGINI small pasta of Paris

PASTA FRESCA fresh pasta or pasta dough; to make, see page 46

PASTA FRESCA ALL'UOVO fresh pasta or pasta dough with egg (for noodles); to make, see page 42

PASTA GRATTUGIATA grated fresh pasta (for soup); to make, see page 87

PASTA VERDE green pasta or pasta dough; to make, see page 45

PASTINA "tiny dough"; very small pasta for soup. The labels, American and Italian, usually recommend it for baby food as well, but don't let that put you off.

PENNE "pens" or "feathers"; pasta tubes cut diagonally at both ends, like a quill pen, into short lengths. See *Mostaccioli*, which are the same thing. Most of the *penne* family is also made *rigati* (grooved).

PENNINE small *penne*; there are also *pennette* which are quite tiny

PENNONE large *penne*

PERCIATELLI "small pierced" pasta; long, hollow like macaroni, and about twice the thickness of spaghetti. See Macaroni.

PERCIATELLONI a larger version of *perciatelli,* it is about equivalent to a slim macaroni such as *maccheroncelli* or *mezzanelli*

PERLINE MICROSCOPICI "tiny pearls" (for soup)

PIPE see *Lumache; pipe* are not quite the same thing, but they are very similar. There are *lisci* (smooth) and *rigati* (grooved) forms.

PULCINI "little chickens" (for soup)

QUADRETTINI "small squares"; flat, like noodles. Other forms of the word are *quadrucci* and *quadratini.*

RAVIOLI the well-known pasta squares, stuffed with eggs, vegetables, or cheese; to make, see page 44. See also *Agnolotti.*

RAVIOLINI small *ravioli*

REGININI "little queens"; small short pasta tubes

*REX "king"

RICCI if you come across this, it will look like the short spiral form of *fusilli;* see *Fusilli.*

RICCIE "curly"; the adjective applied to noodles of various widths when one or both sides are wavy or rippled. The ripple-edged noodle family is large, including widths from about ¼ inch to 1¼ inches, rippled on one side only, 4 names covering 11 possible widths . . .

Fettucelle riccie
Fettucce riccie
Lasagnette riccie
Lasagne riccie

Un lato, meaning "one side," can be added to these names to distinguish them from the noodles rippled on *both* sides. The latter the die maker lists in widths from about ½ inch to about 3 inches. Five names cover 9 sizes . . .

Mafaldine
Mafalda
Lasagnette riccie
Lasagne riccie
Lasagne large riccie

All these pastas are long. The illustration shows only fragments, but full-width; the larger is *lasagne large riccie,* the smaller is *mafaldine.*

RICCINI another type of small "curl" or twisted pasta, this one is shown in a grooved (*rigati*) form

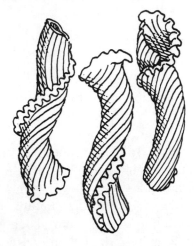

RICCIOLINI "little curls"

RIGATI "grooved"; the adjective applied to various pastas when their surfaces are grooved or ridged. Hollow pastas, pasta shells (nut and conch), and some decorative soup pastas are made *rigati*.

The die manufacturer lists for hollow or macaroni pastas, ranging from less than ¼ inch to over 1 inch in diameter . . .

Perciatelli rigati
Maccheroncelli rigati
Mezzanelli rigati
Mezzani rigati
Ziti rigati
Occhi di lupo rigati
Cannelle rigati
Rigatoni

The pastas by these names can be made on so many different sizes of dies that there is a theoretical total of 41 grooved, hollow-pasta forms. And then, this list is only for the straight and more or less long forms of *rigati* pastas; see *Magliette* and Elbow for others.

Seashells (*maruzze* is one name) can be made *rigati* in at least 7 sizes, nut shells (*nocciole*) in 4.

RIGATONI "large grooved" pasta tubes, actually the largest of all except for commercial *manicotti*

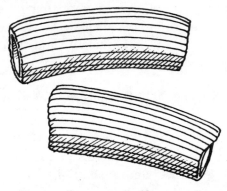

RISINO "tiny rice" (for soup)

*ROSA MARINA "rose of the sea"

ROTE "wheels", complete with hub, spokes, and grooved rim; there are also square wheels! However, the same name is used for an entirely different form, a spiral also called *fusilli*; see *Fusilli*.

ROTELLE "small wheels"

ROTINI "tiny wheels"; you may also find *rotelline* which are very small and used in soup

SALAMINI "tiny   sausages"   (for soup)

SEMI DI MELA   "apple seeds" (for soup)

SEMI DI MELONE   "melon seeds" (for soup)

SHELLS see *Conchiglie, Maruzze,* and Giant shells

SPACEMEN AND ASTRONAUTS believe it or not, there are such, obviously aimed at the juvenile trade. They serve fairly well as a substitute for pasta wheels; see *Rote.*

SPAGHETTI "a length of cord or string" is the metaphor that describes the most famous pasta of all; it is a solid round rod, as distinguished from the macaronis (round but hollow), *linguine* (solid but flattish or oval), and noodles (flat).

The list of spaghettis for which American pasta manufacturers can buy the dies, ranging from fine as a hair to slightly oversize is . . .

Capellini
Fedelini
Vermicelli
Spaghettini

Spaghetti
Spaghettoni

Pastas by these 6 names can each be made with dies of several different sizes, for a total of 16 sizes of solid-rod round pasta. These are all made long; the die manufacturer suggests only one short and probably rare form, elbow spaghetti.

In addition to the straight-rod form, the very thin spaghettis (*capellini, fedelini, vermicelli*) may be found in folded form similar to the folded forms of noodles. American manufacturers give these such names as "*vermicelli* clusters."

SPAGHETTI   ALLA   CHITARRA "guitar-string" spaghetti. In reality a long, thin-cut noodle, it may be rolled into a nest, a variation of the folded spaghettis mentioned above. You may find this pasta called *maccheroni alla chitarra,* but it is nevertheless as thin as the one called spaghetti. A wire cutter that looks very like a musical instrument is used to make it.

35

STELLE "stars" (for soup)

STELLINI "little stars" (for soup); you may also find this spelled *stellette*

STIVALETTI "little boots" (for soup); a small elbow macaroni

STORTINI "small crooked" pasta (for soup); these look a little like tiny wriggling fish

TAGLIATELLE a word derived from the verb *tagliare*, "to cut"; there is an entire family of these noodles, which are really no different from the *fettuccine* family except that this first one, *tagliatelle,* is wider, about ¾ inch in the homemade version (see page 43). The flat pasta called *lasagnette,* which name some manufacturers use, is a noodle about this same width.

The 4 names in the family, progressing from ¾ inch to ⅛ inch, are . . .

Tagliatelle
Tagliolette
Tagliolini
Tagliarini

TAGLIATI "cut"; an adjective applied to short versions of some pastas

TORTELLINI "small twists"; to make these stuffed pastas, see page 45.

Some specialty shops carry good frozen brands and dried *tortellini* are also made but these are not very satisfactory.

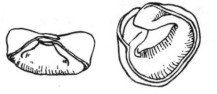

TRENETTE narrow noodles; see Noodles

TRIANGOLI "triangles"; flat, like noodles

TRIFOGLI "cloverleaves" (for soup)

TRIPOLINI little pasta bows, named in honor of the conquest of Tripoli

TUBETTI "little tubes"; these are very short as well as small. You may also find *tubetti lunghi* ("long") which are 1-inch lengths of slim macaroni; there is a *rigati* (grooved) form of these.

TUBETTINI "tiny tubes"; a smaller version of *tubetti* for which there are also long and/or grooved versions

TUFOLI very large pasta tubes; they are served stuffed

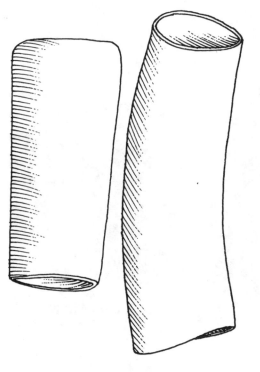

VERMICELLI "little worms"; a very thin spaghetti. Like a number of the thin pasta products, *vermicelli* are sold not only as straight rods but also in folded or "cluster" form.

VONGOLE "clam shells"

VONGOLETTE "little clam shells"

ZITI "bridegrooms"; a large macaroni, really a tube. See Macaroni. This word alone means the long form, as long as spaghetti. *Ziti tagliati* ("cut") is the correct name for the short form illustrated. This is the form you are most likely to find, but very often the qualifying *tagliati* is left off the name. American brands sometimes say "cut in cooking lengths" on the package. Long *ziti* are often broken before they are cooked.

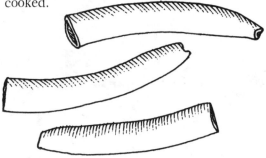

ZITI RIGATI "grooved bridegrooms"; a version of *ziti* with ridges

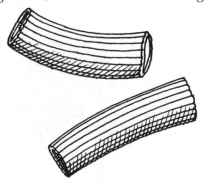

ZITONI "husky bridegrooms"; a large version of *ziti* that also has a *rigati* form

Chapter III

PASTA:
How to Cook It
How to Make It

Books and recipes probably have instructed you to use four quarts of boiling water for a pound of pasta, stir with a spoon, drain in a colander, usually rinsing in cold water afterward. I believe all of this to be wrong, designed to convert pasta into a gooey mess, and so do the professional Italian chefs I have turned to for advice and technique.

Never use a spoon for stirring pasta while it is cooking. A spoon brings it together, and togetherness is not part of pasta cookery. Separate but equal is the way here. Use a wooden fork and gently separate the strands as they cook. A successful dish of pasta begins in the pot of water in which it is boiled.

Providing it is a good *pasta*. So let us start with the pasta itself, then take it in steps until it reaches your table.

As most commercial pastas are made with semolina, it is virtually impossible to get a bad one, but some are better than others, and a few American manufacturers are now delving into so-called "starch-free, instant-cooking" varieties. I say beware of these. But most made-in-America pastas are very good, even though I have found some of the imported ones superior, both in flavor and in standing up to cooking without becoming too soft too fast. Most better stores carry at least one of the imported brands. I won't go into their names here, but I do suggest that you try one. Perhaps your taste buds won't agree with mine, but it is definitely worth the experiment.

Of course the prince of all pastas is that made at home. Once you've eaten it, I believe you'll feel that the extra effort is very much worthwhile. It is simple, the taste is supremely different, lifting pasta to its highest plane.

Last time I had it away from home was in San Marzano, not far from Pompeii, the area of small, green farms where most of Italy's plum tomatoes are grown commercially. This pasta was noodles, *tagliatelle,* made by the lady

POMPEII, the Via di Mercurio—Campania

of the house that morning before lunch. They hung drying, like strips of beaten gold, on a wooden rack in the kitchen. The sauce was made of tomatoes and basil from the garden, simmered in olive oil and seasoned with freshly milled black pepper. It was superb.

I had gone to San Marzano to look at the plum-tomato gardens (and to see Pompeii) and now sat in the kitchen sipping a glass of Lacrima Christi (tears of Christ), a fine white wine grown on slopes not far from old Pompeii. The pasta technique was the same as my mother-in-law had taught me. I watched, fascinated with this woman's skill, far above what I ever could accomplish.

THE TECHNIQUE OF MAKING PASTA FRESCA

She sifted 4 cups of semolina flour onto a large slab of marble in the center of the kitchen table; using two fingers, she made a well in the center, its bottom about halfway down into the mound of flour. Into this went 4 lightly beaten eggs, 1½ teaspoons of salt, 2 teaspoons of olive oil and 2 of warm water, the liquid added gradually to make the dough soft enough to handle. Flexing her fingers into it, she first used just her right hand until the flour, eggs and oil were well mixed into a ball. Then she removed the dough, wiped the marble clean, floured it lightly, and placed the dough ball back and began kneading with vigor, slapping it and pressing it down with the heel of her palms until it was smooth. I timed this operation. It took exactly ten minutes.

"Now I let it rest," she said, placing a large bowl over the well-kneaded pasta ball. "I don't know why," she said, as we went into the garden to pick the plum tomatoes and the basil, "but by the time we get back into the house, that dough will be ready to roll. Covering it makes it much easier."

Using a broom handle, cut to a 3-foot length (I use a tapered pastry roller), she then rolled out the pasta, after first dividing the large ball into four pieces. This was done only after that all-important slab of marble had been cleaned again and lightly floured. This expert lady was a large, well-formed woman with lots of strength, and she rolled that pasta dough out into much thinner sheets than I could have.

Next she took a sharp knife and cut the sheets into strips ¾ of an inch wide. About one pound of these she placed on a clean white cloth to dry for lunch, the rest she hung on the wooden rack for *pasta secca*—to dry long enough so that it didn't need refrigeration or have to be used immediately. The noodles on the cloth dried in exactly one hour, then went into a huge 12-quart pot of boiling water.

That was the method, which I have yet to see improved, and here are the ingredients again. They make 1½ pounds or so.

PASTA FRESCA ALL'UOVO

4 cups semolina flour
4 fresh eggs, lightly beaten
1½ teaspoons salt
2 teaspoons olive oil
2 teaspoons warm water

There are good reasons for using semolina flour. It makes tastier pasta that also holds up better in the cooking. But if you can't get it in a specialty shop or an Italian grocery store, don't fret. Common, run-of-the-mill, "all-purpose" flour will do nicely. I remember during World War II, when I was with the Fifth Army in Italy, in Florence, I took a bag of flour that our mess sergeant used for making bread and pastry and presented it to an Italian friend. She promptly converted it into delicious fresh *linguine* and made a sauce from a Belgian hare that she had been saving for just such an occasion.

There is one caution, though, if you use ordinary white flour. Your fresh pasta will cook very quickly. Keep your eye on it, and test to the tooth often, otherwise it will emerge from the water too soft and without flavor.

Do not use "self-raising" flours and avoid the new miracle flours, the so-called "instantized" flours. There is no such thing as instant pasta.

The thing to remember in kneading the pasta is, if the flour doesn't mix or hold together as you knead, add more liquid, slowly; or, if the dough is too soft, then add more flour—but either way, easy does it. Add small amounts of liquid as you mix the dough, or correspondingly, if it becomes too soft, add small amounts of flour to bring it back into form.

From this very dough made by the wife of that tomato-grower at San Marzano can come a variety of fresh pastas. I make from this same recipe *manicotti, fettuccine, lasagne, cannelloni,* and *tagliatelle.*

After the dough is rolled and before drying it, it must be cut. Rather than cutting long strips from the spread-out sheets, there is a quicker and more effective way of doing this: The original well-kneaded ball of dough has been divided into three or four pieces and each one rolled into a sheet as thin as you can make it, paper-thin. Now roll up or fold each sheet into a long roll. Then cut the roll crosswise, making strips any width you wish, depending upon what you are going to use them for. The strips may then be very gently unfolded and cut into special lengths if that is required. Or lightly toss the cut noodles to unfold them.

To Cut Manicotti: Cut the sheets of dough into 3-inch squares. Dry on cloth or floured board, covered with a cloth, for one hour. (See Index for fillings.)

To Cut Fettuccine: Cut rolled sheets of dough into ¼-inch strips. Unfold and dry for one hour, covered.

To Cut Lasagne: Cut dough into strips 2 inches wide, 4 to 6 inches long, depending on how broad you want this noodle. Dry for one hour, covered.

To Cut Cannelloni: The dough for this should not be any thicker than ⅛ inch, even thinner if possible; cut into 4- or 4½-inch squares. Dry for one hour, covered. Then cook 5 squares at a time, popped into 5 quarts of boiling water, for 4 minutes. Remove with a slotted spoon, and drain well on absorbent cloth. (See Index for fillings.)

To Cut Tagliatelle: These were the noodles, ¾ inch wide, prepared by the wife of the tomato-grower. They may be cut from rolled sheets of dough. *Tagliarini* are the smallest version of this noodle, cut ⅛ inch wide.

If you want to experiment, and this adds to the pleasure of making your own pasta, make the noodles wider, smaller, longer, shorter. But whatever you do dream up, the Italians have probably been there before you.

PASTA FRESCA FOR RAVIOLI AND TORTELLINI

This dough is handled a little differently. The ingredients below make about 1 pound of dough.

> 3½ cups semolina flour (see page 42)
> 1 teaspoon salt
> 2 eggs, lightly beaten
> 1 tablespoon olive (or salad) oil
> and/or
> 2 tablespoons warm water

Sift the flour onto the board or marble slab, sprinkle in the salt, make a center well, and add the eggs and oil gently so that they remain in the well. Now gradually mix well, kneading into a soft smooth dough, slowly adding drops of warm water to soften it if necessary. Knead from 5 to 10 minutes, long enough to have a smooth elastic dough; cover with pan or bowl for a half hour.

To Shape Ravioli: (See Index for fillings.) Reflour the board. Cut the dough into two sections, roll out each section to no more than ⅛ inch thick, and cut into 3-inch strips as long as the sheets. Place teaspoons of the filling 2½ inches apart on this long strip. Cover with a similar 3-inch-wide strip of dough, pressing the dough firmly around each spoonful of filling. Using a pastry wheel or a *ravioli* cutter, cut into 2- or 3-inch squares, depending upon how large you want the *ravioli*. They should dry, covered with a cloth, for at least 1½ hours before cooking.

I've discovered a gadget on sale in some Italian food stores that makes *ravioli* shaping easy. One brand is called "Ravioli-Chef, Raviolamp 12," or "Raviolamp 36, Brevettato." They are small metal trays, with depressions for the fillings and with squares with fluted edges marking the shape of the *ravioli*. The trays come complete with a small rolling pin. The dough is laid over the tray, the fillings are pressed into the depressions, then another sheet of dough is laid over, and all is rolled firmly with the rolling pin. The fluted edges on the tray neatly cut apart the *ravioli* into individual pieces.

To Shape Tortellini: This is done somewhat differently from *ravioli.* The dough is cut into 2-inch circles (with a glass or cooky cutter), the filling is placed atop, and each one is folded to form a half circle. Press the edges of each half circle firmly together, then bend it, seam side out, to form a ring, and press together firmly the overlapping points of the original half circle. *Tortellini* are a Bolognese specialty, and local legend has it that they resemble the navel of Venus, copied by a lusty innkeeper who sneaked a look. The legend is a good clue to the correct shape, for proper *tortellini* should look like large, well-formed navels.

A word of caution regarding *ravioli,* or any of the pastas that are to be filled. After you have rolled the rough and cut it into strips, place the filling in them immediately before the dough has dried. Dried dough is difficult to press into form. Spoon the filling in position and form the dough over and around it, according to what you are making. Place the filled pasta on a clean white cloth, cover with another cloth, and then let them dry for a half hour.

PASTA VERDE

This recipe makes a little more than 1 pound of green noodles.

> ¾ pound cleaned fresh spinach
> 4 cups semolina flour (see page 42)
> 2 eggs, lightly beaten
> 1 teaspoon salt

Cook spinach without water, well covered, until tender. Drain well, pressing out *all* the water. Then force through a sieve or purée in a food mill.

Sift the flour onto a board or marble slab, make the center well, and add the beaten eggs, the salt, and finally the spinach. Now knead until the dough is well mixed. Knead for 15 minutes, until it is smooth, adding water if it is too dry or flour if too soft. Separate the smooth ball of dough into three sections. Then, using preferably a tapered, 2-foot pastry rolling pin, flatten each piece, rolling it and pressing it into extremely thin sheets, ⅛ inch or thinner, if possible. To make cutting easier, these sheets can now be gently folded into long rolls, which then can be cut straight across into ⅓- or ¼-inch strips. The noodles should then be unfolded into the individual lengths, and dried on a clean white cloth for 1 hour before cooking.

All of the foregoing *paste fresche* are made with eggs, thus they are noodles. The following is a recipe for fresh pasta without eggs, in the manner of the commercial dry pasta, except that this one will not be hard and dry and it will be tastier.

PASTA FRESCA

3 cups semolina flour (see page 42)
1 teaspoon salt
2 tablespoons olive oil
1 cup warm water

Sift flour onto board, make center well, and add salt, olive oil, and small amount of water. Slowly mix, bringing flour from around edges, kneading together. Add more water if needed; continue kneading until dough is formed into a smooth ball. Cover dough with a bowl and let it rest for 10 minutes. Now reknead until dough is smooth and very elastic. Re-cover with bowl for 15 minutes, then divide dough ball into 3 pieces, and roll into ⅛-inch sheets. Cut strips into desired widths, or press through the small pasta machine (described on page 56) that has dies for making fresh spaghetti or other forms. Dry for 1 hour before cooking.

Do not worry when you are making homemade pasta if it seems too soft, or too hard, to handle; a little more water or more flour will take care of it.

Caution: Fresh pasta cooks much more quickly than dry, so be especially careful; test it often or it will be too soft.

From my pokings and peerings among the pots and pans in many restaurant kitchens in several Italian cities, I have discovered that most professional chefs handle pasta about the same way. Not long ago I made a survey of ten restaurant kitchens in Rome, watching pasta being cooked and served. Almost to a man, the chefs went about it this way:

The pasta was boiling merrily in a large, deep pot. The waiter would come, the chef would take a long fork and dip out the pasta, shaking it and holding it over the pot until most of the water had dripped off. Then he dropped it into a warm, rimmed soup bowl. Next he spooned from another pot the correct sauce and placed it on top of the pasta, without mixing. Then the waiter hurried off so that the dish would be hot when placed before the customer. There was a variation on this theme, with the chef sometimes using a huge warm bowl on the back of the stove to place the pasta in. He added butter and tossed the pasta in the bowl before giving it to the waiter. In three kitchens the chefs did this, then grated cheese over it, tossing cheese, butter and pasta together, then forked out the correct amounts into the warm bowls held by the waiters. The sauce always went on last, just a large spoonful in the center atop the pasta.

When I asked about the technique of forking the pasta directly out of the boiling water, one chef said: "This way the pasta stays hot longer, it is very lightly covered with moisture which keeps the strands separate. Each strand of pasta keeps its own personality and doesn't become dry. That is the danger; dry pasta is sticky pasta. Draining it in a sieve or colander also bunches it, can make it dry and sticky. Rinsing does the same thing. Most of this hot water comes off before I fork the pasta into the plate or mixing bowl, yet each strand is coated enough so that it is protected against the next strand, won't stick to it. Also that slight amount of water on each piece helps in the mixing when the diner puts pasta and sauce together."

This chef, at one of the great restaurants of Italy, did not mix together pasta and sauce, coating each strand as many of us believe is necessary. I asked why.

"Here in Rome," he said, "we seldom mix the pasta and sauce. Too much sauce destroys the flavor of the pasta, makes it heavy. Let each one mix to his own desire and demand."

Much of this is against long-stated so-called rules of pasta cookery, but it is the expert's way and I have found through trial and error and much ruined pasta that it is the best way. For home direction there are just a few steps to follow for cooking either fresh or dry pasta.

How to Cook P*A*STA

At least *seven quarts* of water should be used for one pound of pasta. It should be in a very deep pot, so the pasta has space to swim without the strands or pieces being forced against one another. *Two tablespoons* of salt should be added—after the water is sharply boiling, and at the instant *just before* the pasta goes in. I have discovered that if the water and salt boil together for long, the pasta will have a disagreeable odor, oddly like that of carbolic acid.

Let me repeat that, because I am not going to say it very often again: *For 1 pound of pasta, use 7 quarts of water and 2 tablespoons of salt.* This is the rule unless the recipe specifies otherwise, and I am not going to list water and salt every single time pasta is cooked in this book because my publisher tells me this redundant information would add at least 25 pages to the book. Look this up in the Index if you forget on what page you read it.

Note another technique to prevent pasta from sticking, a familiar one which the chefs also use—especially for fresh homemade pastas or for the large ones that are most inclined to stick—add a tablespoon of olive oil to the boiling water.

Now to keep the water at this boiling rate and temperature, having added the salt, turn up the heat, then gently add the pasta (without breaking!), and push it down until it is all submerged. As stated before, use a wooden fork to stir, separating the strands or the pieces as they cook. Continue this. Gently does it.

Now the timing. There are several schools of thought on this: some books have time charts for each type; others say a flat number of minutes. The professionals use only one test: the tooth. One pasta chef who has been standing over his pots for forty years told me that he keeps a small bowl on the back of the stove with a dollop of sauce in it. Every few seconds, after the first three minutes, he forks out a strand or a piece of pasta and dips it into the sauce and tastes it. He cautioned that the various types take different times, saying that *capelli d'angelo* (angel's hair) are so fine that he cooks them exactly two seconds. "The big ones you don't have to watch too carefully before the first three minutes, but the smaller they are, the more caution. Spaghettini and *vermicelli* I often test twelve times while they are cooking. *Rigatoni* perhaps only four times."

So it isn't just "place in boiling water and cook" for a certain number of minutes as directions on many a package of pasta state. It is test and test—to the tooth, *al dente,* for that is what this means. When ready, again according to my chef friends, the pasta should be biteable and have no flavor of flour—then it is done, *al dente.*

I like my pasta just a bit softer than *al dente*—a shade—still firm and chewy, however, but not *quite* so underdone as some Romans like it.

My testing method might not work for most. I use a medium wineglass of Chianti for spaghetti, a half for *vermicelli*, a glass and a half for *perciatelli*. I time my pasta by drinking the glass of wine. But this has taken much wine and much practice. I never bolt it. But on several occasions when I was cooking big *ziti* and *rigatoni* I was reeling a bit before I pronounced the pasta properly cooked. So my recommendation, at least in the beginning, is to follow the example of the pros—test it against the tooth. It is the safest, most effective way.

I differ slightly from the professionals in the handling of pasta, but the theory and result remain the same. I, too, think that rimmed soup bowls or heat-holding ramekins are the best serving dishes, always hot, always individually served.

I keep a large ceramic bowl on the back of the stove, with fresh unsalted butter in it. As it warms, the butter melts, ready for mixing. (Another method: if you like to mix butter with pasta—it adds much flavor—before saucing and serving, shave it into the cooked pasta, don't throw it in in a lump. The shaving permits the pasta to absorb it more quickly.)

But usually, I fork the pasta from the boiling pot into the warm bowl with the butter (one half a quarter-pound stick for a pound of pasta), letting the water drain off into its cooking pot before each forkful goes into the bowl. When it is all in the warm mixing bowl. I mill two turnings of pepper into it, toss it gently with wooden fork and spoon, being careful not to bruise it. Then, using a cylinder grater, I grind in Asiago or Parmesan cheese and toss again (three pieces of cheese each about the size of a walnut for a pound of pasta). Now the pasta is placed in the individual bowls, and a heaping spoonful of sauce goes over it (use a large kitchen spoon, or the one with which you are stirring the sauce), and it is brought to table piping hot. (Sometimes pasta and sauce *are* first tossed together; the recipe will say.)

A quarter of a pound of pasta is *more* than enough for each serving. At the elbow of each guest I place a small cylinder type of cheese grater, should he want more cheese. The test of good pasta is that each guest will eat all he has been given and will have the look that he wants more—which he shouldn't get, for properly another course follows.

Back to cooking techniques: These must be tempered with common sense. The fork-from-pot method can be used with the stranded pastas, *linguine, vermicelli,* spaghetti, the flat noodles, *fettuccine, tagliatelle,* etc. But with the shells, or *rigatoni, tufoli, ziti, lasagne,* broken or already cut to cooking length, I suggest removing them with a slotted spoon, or big flat, perforated skimmer, or go to the colander if you must; then into the warm bowl on the back of the stove—without rinsing—or, for baked pastas, directly to the casserole for the covering of sauce before the dish enters the oven.

It is my belief that the stranded pastas, those without holes or a bore, absorb or soak up sauce only from the outside, and thus can best be mixed to the taste of the diner by himself. But pasta with crevices, holes and flutes, benefits from being well mixed with the sauce before serving, offering a taste delight that only this type can: sauce on the outside, the inside, in the grooves and fluted surfaces.

Also, the dishes that depend upon cream and vegetables should be mixed well before serving, always adding a spoonful of the peas, or mushrooms, or whatever the main ingredient is, on top, just before bringing to the table.

51

VENICE—*Veneto Euganea*

PASTA Cheeses for Grating

A chapter on the methods of pasta cookery cannot be complete without a word on cheese. Good, aged cheese is as important as a fine grade of pasta: There are three, in my opinion, which should be mentioned first that properly are to be grated and mixed with pasta: Asiago, Parmesan, and Pecorino Romano. Asiago is a Grana type of cheese, originated in the province of Vicenza. Properly aged (it should be a golden color, hard, and at least three years old before it is used with pasta), Asiago is nuttier and has more flavor than either Parmesan or Romano. But it is also more difficult to obtain. The best I have had is produced by the Frigo family, which has been working with Asiago for six generations, an Asiago superior even to that made in Italy—it is made by the Frigos here in the United States, in Wisconsin. It is most easy to get from: Frigo Food Products Company, 109 South Main Street, Torrington, Connecticut 06790. Once you've used golden, aged Asiago with pasta, you are hooked. You will use no other. But if you can't find it, aged Parmesan is the first choice. This should be at least two years old. It is a popular cheese and more easily obtainable.

Let me say it again, for it makes all the difference: As in wine, age is important in pasta cheese. And it should be Italian, or at least made by Italians, for no one else has mastered the art of making Asiago, Parmesan, and Romano. There are American and South American substitutes. But they are just that, substitutes. The good stores are honest about pasta cheeses; quite often their reputations depend upon it, especially if they have many discerning customers. An aged Parmesan isn't white, but faintly yellow—and very hard. It should taste slightly sweet, slightly nutty, and it should not be salty. The best of the Parmesans is Parmigiano Reggiano (Grana), made the same way as it was in the 10th century. This is a finely textured, golden cheese that is always properly aged. Other very dependable brands are Polenghi, Galbani and Locatelli.

Romano is white, somewhat salty in flavor, and sharp; proper Parmesan is none of these. Some dishes call for one or the other, but I have found that even if a recipe does call for straight Romano, flavor is always enhanced by using half Parmesan. Cheeses under two years of age are not yet grown up enough to do anything good for your pasta. Young cheeses are all right for oven pasta dishes that are long-baking and have other flavor-adding ingredients. (Also, for baked pastas and for stuffed ones, other types of cheeses are often required. These are specified in the relevant recipes.)

The important thing to remember is that the cheese should always be freshly grated; never buy it already grated; it quickly loses its snap, picks up an almost sawdusty flavor, and does nothing for your dish.

Near PESARO, on the Adriatic—The Marches

And while we are on the subject of cheese, it is never (in Italy) added to pasta with seafood. Why, I've never been able to determine, but the rule is just. I tried *linguine* (this is nearly always teamed with seafood; why, again I couldn't find out) and white clam sauce in Taranto, and with the waiter glaring, grated some cheese over it. It didn't add anything and detracted from the seafood flavor, which is delicate and shouldn't be tampered with.

The subject of Italian grating cheeses cannot be brushed off with my saying that only three are worth consideration. Asiago, Parmesan, and Romano are my favorites, thus I mentioned them first. But there are several more which should be grated over pasta and sampled, so that you can come to your own conclusion. Ricotta siciliano is a soft, spicy, aged cheese, especially good over very thin pasta such as vermicelli. Caciocavallo is a grating cheese with a powerful personality, perhaps too powerful. Pepato comes impregnated with whole black peppercorns and is excellent grated over simple pasta dishes that need some such special authority. Ragusano, if you can get it, comes close to rivaling Parmesan; it is Sicilian, made from cow's milk, spicy, but also rich and nutty. Pecorino di Tavola, somewhat sharp, is very good with the old favorite, baked macaroni and cheese. Incanestrato, impressed with a braided basket design, is bitey, "different" and excellent. All are authentically Italian and deserve a trial mating with your pasta.

Equipment

Tools and cooking utensils are also important. Chefs have taught me that the enameled cast-iron pots from France and Belgium are not only handsome, heavy and serviceable, but perfect for pasta because they are good conductors and hold the heat so long. They are also excellent should you want to store leftover pasta and sauce in the refrigerator, for they have snug-fitting covers that prevent the food from picking up odors. I have them in various sizes, but the 10-quart pot receives the most use for boiling pasta, giving it enough water and plenty of room to swim.

Again going to the chef's system. I use copper pans for my sauces. They are the best conductors of heat, spreading it evenly. And a gas stove (chefs use nothing else) is preferable, for no matter what those who use electric ranges tell you, gas is the only reliable heat, the only heat that can be properly controlled at all times.

For removing the pasta from the pot there are "spaghetti forks" for sale in many markets, double forks on one handle, designed to lift stranded pasta easily from boiling water and to hold it firmly while the water is shaken off. A slotted spoon and a large skimmer are excellent for performing the job with other types, *ravioli,* etc. A wooden spoon should be used for mixing sauces, and *only* a wooden fork for stirring the pasta while it cooks.

Other tools: a 20-inch-square pastry board or marble slab; a 2-foot tapered rolling pin; a glass container marked for measuring in both ounces and cups; the usual nest of measuring spoons from ¼ teaspoon to a table-spoon; and a wire whisk for mixing and blending.

Mouli makes small cylindrical cheese graters that can handle a lump of freshly cut cheese easily and take all the labor from the job. This firm also manufactures a parsley mincer which is effective for that so-often chopped item and will mince other herbs, and onions, too. For garlic *that is to remain in the sauce,* a garlic press is indispensable. You should also have carbon-steel knives (no chef ever uses a stainless-steel knife)—a paring knife, a filletting knife, and a big chef's knife for chopping and mincing.

If you are going to try homemade pasta (and I hope you do, no other is so good), there are machines available in several sizes and prices with dies and cutting blades that will neatly shape your spaghetti or cut your noodles after you have properly prepared the dough. There are also *ravioli* cutters, and special *ravioli* form-trays, as described earlier, and various other cutters for pasta. Italian specialty shops have all of the items mentioned here ex-cept the pots and pans. A little thought regarding the proper tools to do the job will pay dividends in efficiency, cut down time and labor—and produce better pasta.

56

If you have difficulty finding the various pastas suggested in this book, or imported ingredients, cooking equipment, or the tools and gadgets to shape and cut homemade pastas, America's foremost Italian *drogheria* and *salumeria* (grocery and delicatessen), which has solved all these problems for me, is Manganaro's, famous since 1893 for Italian delicacies. These people will be happy to send you a free catalog of their foods and kitchen items. They mail to any place in the United States promptly. Address: Manganaro Foods, 488 Ninth Avenue, New York City, New York 10018.

Chapter IV

Basic Sauces
& Some Special Sauces

Doing a cookbook on pasta develops into a devious enterprise. At first glance, if you like to cook, it seems an interesting project, its one obvious hazard the fact that you may put on weight if you test every recipe (though I have not put on weight, but tested). But when you get into the organization, then the actual doing, the cooking, and the testing, suddenly comes an overwhelming realization: a book on pasta is virtually a book on Italian cookery, for without an interesting sauce, one with subtle, different flavor, pasta is simply a bland dish of spaghetti or what have you (the butter-and-pasta devotees will argue with this). The meats, fish, fowl or other elements that form the base of the sauce, and that are often served *after* the pasta, require dexterous know-how in preparation. Therein lies the deviousness: in the pages of a pasta cookbook is information on many forms of cooking. Thus, when you cook hare for a *fettuccine* sauce, the inspiration first comes with the proper preparation of the hare.

This holds true for everything from a pig's foot to a mussel. Master the art of making a proper pasta sauce, and you are a long way toward mastering the art of Italian cooking—acknowledged by experts as being among the best in the world. After all, the Italians brought the fork to France and fathered modern cookery during the Renaissance.

I am of the school that firmly believes that sauces should carry delicate flavor and that no one ingredient in them should dominate or overwhelm. (As I previously stated, I also am very much "anti" tomato paste in anything.) Thus I am wary of any recipe that lists "a cup of olive oil" or one that blithely suggests "a bunch of garlic" or "twelve garlic cloves." Largely, these are untested recipes and if one follows them they prove to be an assault on the stomach. I remember when a national magazine brought out its beautifully illustrated cookbook, and I eagerly tried the white clam sauce for linguine. This book was of the "cup" school. The clams were drowned in olive oil and garlic, with the result that when you ate the pasta with "clam" sauce, all you tasted was olive oil and garlic; the subtle flavor of the clams didn't have a chance. (See page 337 for a *good* white clam sauce.)

So, go carefully. Recipes are usually written to serve four or six people, which should involve an absolute maximum of one or one and a half pounds of pasta. Rarely should any such recipe need more than one clove of garlic; be suspicious if it calls for more than two. Olive oil should be used sparingly too. Two tablespoons are quite a lot for a pound of pasta; three tablespoons plenty, and four, time to be wary. And use good oil. A sauce is only as good as its ingredients.

Virgin olive oil, the first pressing, is the best and, especially for Italian food, Italian olive oil is the first choice. The oil should not be too heavy or have too penetrating an olive flavor. It should be light gold-green and have little odor. Through trial and error I have found that *Francesconi* is my first choice, *Berio* second, *Bertolli* third; next *Sasso*, *Pastene,* and *Madre Sicilia.* There is no need to buy blindly in olive oils. All reputable stores (especially

Italian) have some of these listed above. In my opinion, if you try to economize in buying olive oil, you are taking a chance.

The same rule of thumb goes for canned tomatoes. First try for the imported Italian brands, especially those from the noted tomato-growing area of San Marzano, the peeled plum tomatoes with basil leaf. They have less yellow pulp and seeds and more flavor than the American brands, or than any other, for that matter. Brands I have found excellent: Scalfani, Pope, Progresso, Luigi Vitelli.

In America many have the misconception that all Italian pasta sauces are made with tomato. Nothing could be further from the truth. There are many excellent sauces that have tomato as a base, and they are among my favorites, but the range of flavors, colors, and ingredients of pasta sauces is restricted only by the imagination. The Italians can whip up a delicious sauce with just butter and cauliflower, or a touch of olive oil and a few clams, and there are few tastier sauces than that made only with puréed fillets of anchovies.

However, in order not to frighten you off, let's start with something familiar, a simple tomato sauce that can be a basic sauce for any pasta and will be so called. This is a sauce often used to cover the meat for the main course while it cooks, the meat giving the sauce much added flavor, the sauce helping fix this flavor and also moistening the meat—each giving strength to the other.

To Prepare Fresh Tomatoes: You will be doing this often. It depends on the recipe whether they are seeded and diced or put through a food mill. They must always be peeled. To do this, plunge them briefly into boiling water and they will be easy to peel. To seed plum tomatoes, cut out the small core at the stem end with a pointed knife, and deseed the tomato by holding it in one hand and squeezing (the seeds, or most of them, pop out). Other varieties usually have to be cut in half before the seeds can be squeezed out. When a recipe calls for the fresh tomatoes to be put through a sieve or food mill, this will dispose of the seeds. (If you wonder why you are sometimes told to deseed tomatoes even though the *sauce* is later put through a sieve, this is because the seeds may give a bitter taste to the sauce as it cooks. This isn't necessarily true, but with certain types of tomato it is.)

PAESTUM, the Temple of Neptune—Campania

POMMAROLA
(Basic Tomato Sauce)

Always in a tomato sauce I prefer ripe, fresh tomatoes, but they are seasonal, so often it is necessary to use the canned.

> 3 pounds very ripe plum tomatoes, peeled, seeded, and diced or, 9 cups (two 2-pound, 3-ounce cans) *pomidori pelati italiani con basilico* (Italian peeled plum tomatoes with basil leaf)
> 1 garlic clove
> 2 tablespoons good olive oil
> 1 teaspoon salt
> A liberal amount of milled black pepper (preferably the black Indian Tellicherry peppercorn, the world's best)
> 1 tablespoon dried sweet basil

For this I prefer to peel, seed, and dice the tomatoes, but you can also grind them in a food mill or push them through a sieve, which will remove the seeds. If canned tomatoes are used, just put through the food mill, depulping and deseeding; save the whole basil leaf.

Peel garlic, cut into 3 pieces, and put in deep frypan with the olive oil. Simmer over a low flame until the garlic is brown (don't burn). Press the pieces of garlic flat in the pan and swish them around in the oil; then remove and discard them.

Now, in a swift, definite movement (don't pour in slowly or the oil will flare and geyser over the stove), dump the bowl of tomato into the pan. Add the salt and pepper and the dried basil (and the leaf from the canned tomatoes). Keeping your flame low, stir the sauce frequently with a wooden spoon, until it is well blended and bubbling. Keep the flame low for 10 minutes, then raise slightly, enough so the sauce is cooking well, but not bubbling so much that it is throwing tomato all over the stove. Continue to cook and stir in the uncovered pan until the water has evaporated and the sauce thickens. The right test here is to taste it. If it has body and flavor and isn't watery, then it is ready. Time is usually 30 minutes. The recipe makes 7 cups. This is a sauce that you can use for any pasta. It is light, tasty, and has a fresh flavor.

Note: Seven cups is, obviously, quite a lot of sauce. Two cups is what I usually allow to serve six people. The point is that, for certain simple sauces such as this one, it is no more trouble to make a big batch than a small one, *and,* again important, tomato sauces freeze very well. So why not use enough ingredients so that you will have sauce for the freezer that you can just pull out some other time when you need a quick dish of spaghetti?

For a number of the sauces in this chapter, the quantities given are large. They are the ones that I consider freeze particularly well, and several have multiple uses, so it is really simpler to make the one large batch rather than to go through the whole thing several times in small batches. Freeze the sauce in pint (2-cup) containers.

Now, to start you off in style on the theory of the dual use of a sauce —for the main dish of a meal as well as the first-course pasta—I am inserting here an unusual recipe that properly belongs in the chapter on meat. The basic tomato sauce, after being used as an ingredient of this recipe, becomes quite transformed and does for the spaghettini on which it is first served something that the original version could not have done. It is, in fact, an entirely new sauce and has meanwhile contributed mightily to the beef roll that is to follow—an excellent illustration of the importance of sauce to Italian cookery.

The beef roll is the creation of an old family friend, Catherine Spadaccino, a kitchen wizard. I've sat and watched this masterpiece develop several times in her kitchen in Danbury, Connecticut. Hers is one of the most impressive ground-meat dishes in the Italian repertoire, cleverly teaming beef, eggs, excellent cheese, and tangy sausage. And sauce. It is an unusual company dish and interesting to prepare. Don't get discouraged as you read. This is a project, but it is not a difficult dish. Just follow directions in steps.

CATHERINE SPADACCINO'S FOGGIA BEEF ROLL

5 pounds top-round steak, ground
2 cups rolled dry bread crumbs
4 leaves of fresh basil, chopped
1 tablespoon chopped fresh Italian parsley
7 fresh eggs, beaten
1 cup coarsely grated Romano cheese
1½ teaspoons salt
1 teaspoon freshly milled black pepper
1 tablespoon olive oil
4 four-inch-long Italian sweet sausages
4 hard-cooked eggs
4 slices of provolone cheese
4 cups Basic Tomato Sauce (page 63)
1 teaspoon sugar
¼ teaspoon ground cinnamon
½ teaspoon dried orégano
1 pound spaghettini
Butter
Parmesan cheese

Blend together beef, bread crumbs, basil, parsley, beaten eggs, ½ cup of the Romano, salt, and pepper. Spread the tablespoon of olive oil onto the board or table where you will make the roll. Reserve 1 cup of the meat mixture for patching the roll later, which it may need. Place the rest of the meat mixture on the oiled board. Flatten out (rolling pin helps) into a large round medallion ½ inch thick.

Broil the sausages. Place them whole on the flat meat; place hard-cooked eggs between, and surround with the slices of provolone. Sprinkle the remaining cup of grated Romano over everything; mill on more black pepper, sprinkle on more salt. Now carefully roll the meat until you have a firm, tubular roll. If there are holes or open places, patch them with the cup of ground meat that you saved. Now slide the roll into an oiled open pan or casserole; bake it in a 400° F. oven until it is firm and brown, about 45 minutes.

Meanwhile, heat basic tomato sauce, thicken with 2 tablespoons of drippings from meat pan, stir and simmer. Lower oven heat to 300° F. Cover the roll with the tomato sauce; lightly sprinkle with sugar, cinnamon, and orégano. Bake meat roll and sauce together for 30 minutes, spooning sauce occasionally over meat as it simmers. Then remove meat to a hot platter and let set, to become firm and slightly cooled for easier slicing. Serves 6 to 8.

Shortly before the meat is done, cook the spaghettini. When the pasta is *al dente,* remove with the fork-from-pot method, place in warm bowl with butter and grated cheese, and toss. (The correct way to do all this is explained in How to Cook Pasta on pages 49-51.) Serve with a spoonful of sauce over each individual serving.

Here is a particular secret of pasta: with this dish of spaghettini topped with the piquant sauce, you get the full flavor of the tomato, the meat, and the subtle seasonings, and together they herald the triumph to come—the meat roll which arrives at the table whole, is carved before the guests, and displays when it is sliced the colorful pattern of hard-cooked eggs, sausages, and melted cheese centering each slice. The remaining sauce is brought in a bowl for guests to spoon over the sliced meat. It is the sauce that makes a success of the whole meal, not merely of one or the other course.

The uninitiated may imagine that, once they have learned to make and cook pasta, all that a pasta cookbook can then tell them is how to make pasta sauces. This is too simple a view, as the preceding recipe for the Foggia Beef Roll has shown. Nevertheless, it is true that you will encounter an uncommon number of sauces in this book, so this separate chapter of sauces may seem redundant. However, it contains the basic ones that need to be isolated because they are repeatedly called for later. And the remainder, though some are specifically mentioned again only a few times, have been chosen to make here a group that will give you a foretaste of the immense variety of pasta sauces to come. They include a few classics that are so famous that one would tend to call them, also, "basic" sauces, and a few unusual ones to whet your appetite to read on.

FILETTO DI POMODORO
(*Neapolitan Light Tomato Sauce*)

*This is a favorite sauce with the "like-it-light" people in the Naples region.
Simple and savory, it is also versatile, can be cooked quickly, and goes well
with any form of pasta. Many Italian restaurants, and the few good ones
in this country, consider this a summer-Sunday sauce. That day they make it
fresh; they make the pasta fresh, too (usually a noodle), toss it with butter
and cheese, and spoon* filetto di pomodoro *over the individual dishes or bowls
of pasta. Enough to make you say "Ever on Sunday!" If I were restricted to
one sauce, this, or the white-truffle-and-butter (page 320), would be the one
I would choose. The reason: simplicity and flavor. One of the virtues of
Italian cookery is this simplicity, and it is that very asset, in my opinion, that
lifts it above any other.*

4 heaping tablespoons of minced prosciutto fat (and
only prosciutto fat)
2 tablespoons olive oil (the best you can buy)
1 tablespoon butter
3 large white onions, chopped
4 large fresh basil leaves, minced or, 1 tablespoon dried
sweet basil
10 very large ripe plum tomatoes, peeled and diced or,
9 cups (two 2-pound 3-ounce cans) Italian plum
tomatoes, put through a food mill
Freshly milled black pepper
½ teaspoon salt

Sauté the finely minced prosciutto fat in the oil and butter until it is crisp,
but not overly brown. Add the onions and basil. Simmer for 6 minutes. Add
the tomatoes to the pan and stir everything well with a wooden spoon;
simmer for 20 minutes, stirring frequently. Mill in a generous amount of
pepper, add the salt, and stir well. Raise heat, stir, and cook off any excess
water from tomatoes. Makes 7 cups.

MARINARA SAUCE

I first had marinara sauce cooked on a boat anchored off Taranto in southern Italy. Cooked by fishermen who daily still tow their nets into the sea. Cooked over a charcoal brazier on deck, this tomato sauce was ready in twenty minutes. Fishermen never have the sauce plain; they use it as a quick and piquant base in which to cook the ocean harvest. That day we stirred in a handful (a large fisherman's hand) of tender baby squid. They also drop in small fish, shrimp, clams, mussels, snails—most anything that comes from the sea. I am not certain that marinara is connected with or derived from the sea or marine; but I am certain that the fisherman's way improves it. As you'll see, marinara, the light, quick sauce, is an inspiration, even without help from the sea.

> 2 tablespoons olive oil
> 2 small white onions, chopped
> 2 small carrots, chopped
> 1 garlic clove, minced
> Liberal amount of milled black pepper
> 18 medium-sized very ripe plum tomatoes, peeled, seeded, and diced or, 9 cups (two 2-pound 3-ounce cans) Italian plum tomatoes
> 1 teaspoon salt
> 3 tablespoons butter
> ¼ teaspoon dried hot red pepper

One of the virtues of a marinara sauce is that it is so quick and easy to prepare, and light. Sauté in the oil the onions, carrots, and garlic until onions are soft. Mill in the black pepper, and add the tomatoes. Stir the sauce well, add the salt, and cook, uncovered, for 20 minutes. Now push the sauce through a food mill. It will emerge velvety. Melt butter in a pan and add the strained sauce. Stirring often, cook for 15 minutes. For extra personality, at this stage you can stir in the hot red pepper. Makes 7 cups.

BEEF SAUCE

    2 garlic cloves, minced
    2 tablespoons olive oil
    2 tablespoons butter
    1 pound beef chuck, ground twice
    1½ teaspoons salt
    Liberal amount of milled black pepper
    2 cups beef stock or bouillon
    1 tablespoon chopped parsley

Sauté garlic in oil and butter until soft. Stir in beef, breaking it up with a wooden spoon; add the salt and pepper, and cook for 15 minutes. Stir in beef stock and simmer, uncovered, for 10 minutes. Add parsley, stir, and serve. Makes about 3 cups.

BOLOGNA, the Neptune Fountain—Emilia-Romagna

BOLOGNESE SAUCE

I discovered this sauce after a wild-boar hunting trip in the Apennines, when I went to Bologna to taste civilization again. I had it, just a spoonful over some light, marvelous tortellini, and sat in the restaurant until I finally wheedled the chef, who was also the owner, into giving me the recipe. I was eventually lucky enough to be invited into his kitchen to watch him prepare it. It is one of the most famous of pasta sauces and has many variations, but I believe this is the classic one.

> 3 tablespoons chopped bacon
> 3 tablespoons butter
> 4 tablespoons chopped prosciutto
> 2 small white onions, chopped
> 2 small carrots, chopped
> 2 celery ribs, chopped
> ½ pound beef chuck, chopped
> ½ pound veal, chopped
> ¼ pound lean pork, chopped
> 1 cup Chicken Broth (page 84)
> 1 cup dry white wine
> 3 large ripe tomatoes, peeled and diced or, 2 cups (one 1-pound can) Italian plum tomatoes
> 1 teaspoon salt
> Liberal amount of milled black pepper
> 1 clove
> ⅓ teaspoon grated nutmeg
> 2 cups hot water
> ½ pound mushrooms, sliced
> 3 raw chicken livers, chopped
> ¾ cup heavy cream

Cook bacon in butter until soft; add prosciutto and simmer for 2 minutes. Add onions, carrots, celery; cook until soft. Stir in the beef, veal and pork; simmer until half done, the beef pink. Then stir in the broth and wine, raise heat slightly, and cook until sauce thickens, stirring constantly. Blend in

71

the tomatoes (if canned, first put through strainer or food mill). Add salt, pepper, clove, nutmeg, stir in well, and taste for correct amounts. Blend in hot water, cover pan, and simmer over low heat for 1 hour, raising cover and stirring frequently. Now blend in the mushrooms and the chicken livers. Raise heat slightly and cook, uncovered, for 5 minutes. Just before using the sauce, blend in the heavy cream, stirring the mixture well. Makes about 5 cups.

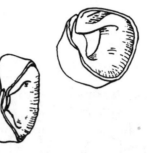

HAM SAUCE

½ pound sliced raw ham, diced (preferably prosciut-
tino or prosciutto)
3 tablespoons butter
1 tablespoon olive oil
1 cup Chicken Broth (page 84)
½ teaspoon salt
Liberal amount of milled black pepper
2 tablespoons freshly chopped parsley
2 cups heavy cream

Sauté ham in butter and oil until crisp. Stir in broth, salt and pepper and cook, uncovered, for 15 minutes. Add parsley, stirring well. Cook for 10 minutes, until sauce begins to thicken, then stir in heavy cream. Makes about 3 cups.

BÉCHAMEL SAUCE

6 tablespoons butter
4 tablespoons flour
1 teaspoon salt
Milled pepper
2½ cups milk, warmed
Pinch of grated nutmeg

In a double boiler melt the butter; add the flour as butter melts and stir smooth as you sprinkle in the salt and mill in the pepper. When mixture is golden and velvety, *slowly* stir in the warm milk, stirring constantly, and stir for 15 minutes, until sauce is thickened and of smooth consistency. Taste for flavor: add more salt or pepper if needed and stir in the pinch of nutmeg. Makes about 2½ cups.

MORNAY SAUCE

6 tablespoons butter
1½ tablespoons sifted flour
2 cups milk, warm
1 teaspoon salt
Milled black pepper
2 egg yolks
6 tablespoons grated Parmesan or Romano cheese

Melt butter in a pan; stir in flour to make a smooth paste. Slowly add the warm milk. Simmer and stir for 5 to 10 minutes, until sauce thickens. Keep the flame low and your spoon busy or sauce will burn. Season to taste with salt and pepper. Beat egg yolks; remove sauce from stove and stir in the egg yolks and cheese. Stir well and quickly. Makes about 2½ cups.

MUSHROOM AND CHEESE SAUCE

5 tablespoons chopped shallots
8 tablespoons butter
1 pound fresh mushrooms, chopped
7 tablespoons flour
2½ cups milk, warmed
2 cups heavy cream, warmed
1 cup grated Gruyère cheese
1 cup grated Parmesan cheese
1½ teaspoons salt
Much milled black pepper

Sauté the shallots in the butter in a deep saucepan until soft. Add mushrooms and simmer for 10 minutes, stirring often. Blend in the flour, the milk, and the cream, stirring constantly until sauce is smooth and thickened. Add the cheeses, season with salt and pepper, and stir well until all ingredients are perfectly blended. Makes about 4½ cups.

SALSA ALLA MERETRICE
(*Harlot's Sauce*)

This is a sauce reputed to have been created by the prostitutes of Naples, possibly because it can be prepared quickly and between assignments. It was first served to me in the private dining room of that splendid Roman hotel of my friend, Alberto Wirth, The Victoria, with his remark, "Unfortunately without the presence of a representative of its originators."

2 garlic cloves, minced
2 tablespoons olive oil
8 anchovies, cut into pieces
4½ cups (one 2-pound 3-ounce can) Italian plum
   tomatoes, pushed through food mill
8 stuffed green olives, sliced
8 pitted black olives, sliced
1 teaspoon capers
1 teaspoon dried sweet basil
¼ teaspoon (or a pinch of) dried red pepper

Sauté garlic in the oil until soft; add the anchovies. When anchovies have broken apart, add the tomatoes; simmer for 10 minutes. Blend in olives, capers, basil, and red pepper. Simmer in uncovered pan for 20 minutes, or until sauce has thickened. Serve on *vermicelli*, among other pastas. See page 130 and page 304. Makes about 4 cups.

SALSA D'OLIO, AGLIO E ALICI
(*Olive Oil, Garlic and Anchovy Sauce*)

Although this sauce appears in several other places in somewhat different versions, the principle of blending the hot-oil sauce with the pasta is the same for each of them—and it is tricky. If the sizzling oil is mixed with the cooked pasta too fast, it will make the pasta gummy. Here is the way my friend, Anthony Colunio, head chef at Moretti's Restaurant in Elmira, New York (one of the good restaurants), does it. He feels it is important to use good anchovies and, among others, recommends Roadel flat fillets from Portugal for the base of the sauce, and then the especially fine Coletta Italian anchovies (in glass jars), for his technique of dressing the individual dishes of pasta with whole anchovy fillets.

¾ cup fine olive oil, in all
4 garlic cloves, halved
2 cans (2 ounces each) anchovy fillets
4 tablespoons butter
Freshly milled black pepper

Heat ½ cup of the oil in a saucepan; brown garlic in this, being careful not to burn it. Discard garlic. Stir in one 2-ounce can of anchovies (the Portuguese), and break them up with a wooden spoon as they cook. Simmer over low heat until anchovies become a sauce. Drain the second 2-ounce can of anchovies (the finer ones, the Coletta), cut one third of them into small pieces, and set these and the whole fillets aside. Just before serving the pasta, add the cut-up anchovies to the hot sauce. Place the drained pasta in a warm bowl in which butter has been melted, toss pasta well, coating each strand. (This prevents the hot oil in the sauce from cooking the pasta further and making it gummy.) Mill in pepper. Now add the hot anchovy sauce, a spoonful at a time, tossing carefully after each spoonful. (This spoon-by-spoon technique also prevents the pasta from gumming.)

Meanwhile, you have heated the remaining 4 tablespoons of olive oil in a small saucepan. Now, using a fork, or your fingers as Chef Colunio does, quickly run the remaining whole Coletta anchovy fillets through the hot oil. Arrange two over each individual dish of pasta, and serve immediately. This sauce is sufficient for 1½ pounds of pasta to serve 8.

Note: You will see oil remaining in the bowl in which you mixed the pasta. Leave it there. The pasta has enough after the mixing; more would make it too oily.

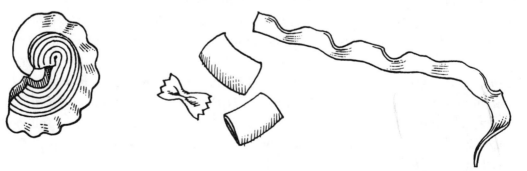

SALSA D'ARAGOSTA ROSSA
(Red Lobster Sauce)

> 1 live lobster (1 pound)
> 3 tablespoons olive oil
> 1 bottle (8 ounces) clam juice
> 1 whole white onion, peeled
> 1 celery rib
> 4 cups Marinara Sauce (page 69)

Rinse the lobster well in cold water. A half inch down on the underside of the head, pierce it with a rigid, sharp, pointed knife. When the lobster is motionless, split it from that point down to the tail. Remove the solid dark green string in the tail. Separate claws and tail from the body. Heat the oil in a frypan and place the pieces of lobster, still in the shell and under sides down, in the oil. Cook over medium heat until shell gets red, or for about 10 minutes, turning often. Pour in clam juice, add onion and celery, cover pan, and simmer for 10 minutes.

Prepare the marinara sauce in a large saucepan. Remove onion and celery from the lobster pan and discard them. Add lobster and its liquid to the marinara sauce. Stir well, and simmer, uncovered, for 20 minutes, lifting the lobster pieces from the pan frequently to drain the liquid in the shells into the sauce. When the sauce has thickened, stir, then remove from heat. Remove lobster meat from shells, discard shells, and put lobster back into the sauce.

This sauce is served on *linguine,* among other pastas. See pages 152 and 343. Spoon liberal amounts of sauce over each portion and center a piece of lobster meat atop the pasta in each dish. Makes about 4½ cups.

SALSA CON LE VONGOLE IN BIANCO
(*White Clam Sauce*)

Americans knows this sauce perhaps as well as any except the tomato-paste-ridden "meat-sauce" of our misguided restaurants. White clam sauce, too, is usually abused, being made with far too much garlic and oil. A correct version is given in the "Mina Quartet," the contribution of a talented sister-in-law to Chapter XI; see page 337. It may be used for vermicelli, as there, or for linguine or spaghettini. Another sauce, with fresh clams, is given in the seafood chapter; see page 146.

FETTUCCINE CON PARMIGIANO E BURRO
(*Fettuccine with Parmesan and Butter*)

Freshly grated cheese and butter, with the addition of milled black pepper, are the classic and incomparable "sauce" for a variety of pastas but best of all for fettuccine. The recipe is given on page 324, in the chapter called Particular Pastas where I have included a special section on this most particular of pastas and several variations on the butter-and-cheese theme.

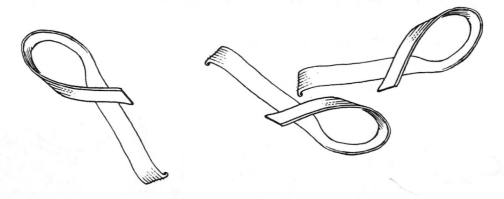

SALSA VERDE
(Green Sauce)

¾ pound sweet butter
1 tablespoon olive oil
½ garlic clove, minced
2 small white onions, minced
2 cups finely chopped Italian parsley (use only Italian
   parsley)

Combine butter and oil in pan over low heat. When butter is melted, stir in garlic and onions and sauté until onions are soft. Stir in parsley quickly. Pour over cooked drained pasta, toss until well mixed, and serve immediately. Makes enough for 1½ pounds of pasta to serve 8 people as a first course.

VAL DI FASSA—Trentino-Alto Adige

PESTO ALLA GENOVESE

Pesto is found most often in Genoa, and there it is made the hard way, by making a paste of the ingredients in a mortar with a pestle, thus the name. I tried it that way the first time I tested it; the next time I used the electric blender. In this case, I think the new way is best, the blender doing a much better job of combining the ingredients into a paste than the hand and eye and muscle.

2 cups fresh basil leaves
1 cup fresh Italian parsley
½ cup grated Parmesan cheese
½ cup grated Romano cheese
1 tablespoon *pignoli* (pine nuts)
12 blanched almonds
12 blanched walnut halves
1 garlic clove
3 tablespoons butter
½ cup olive oil

The almonds and walnuts are blanched in boiling water to help in removing their skins. Next, blending is the objective: place all the ingredients in the blender and whir into a smooth paste; place the paste in a large warm bowl.

Cook pasta, such as *trenette* or *fettuccine, al dente.* Using the fork-from-pot system, fork the pasta directly into the bowl with the *pesto;* toss well. Add 4 tablespoons of hot water from the pasta pot, and toss again. Serve the beautifully green-speckled pasta immediately in hot soup bowls. Serves 4 to 6.

Note: You will probably find that you will have more *pesto* here than you need to serve only four persons. Save the extra. Place it in a covered bowl and refrigerate; it will keep well for a week. You can make another dish of pasta to use it up. Or try stirring a tablespoon of *pesto* into a hot bowl of soup for lunch. It makes the soup sing; in fact I like it as well in soup as I do on pasta.

The genuine *pesto,* of course, is made only with fresh basil leaves, but when they aren't available, I have found that you can produce a green pasta with excellent flavor by substituting fresh spinach leaves which always seem to be in the markets.

PESTO CON SPINACI
(Pesto with Spinach)

> 3 cups fresh spinach leaves
> 1½ cups fresh parsley sprigs
> ½ cup grated Parmesan cheese
> ½ cup grated Romano cheese
> 2 tablespoons *pignoli* (pine nuts)
> 12 blanched almonds
> 12 blanched walnut halves
> 2 garlic cloves
> 4 tablespoons butter
> ½ cup olive oil

Proceed as for regular *pesto.* For this quantity you will need to add about 6 tablespoons of hot water from the pasta pot when you toss the green paste with the pasta. Serves 6 to 8.

Note: In Genoa, you may be served *pesto* made with the grating cheese called sardo, which is shipped in from the nearby island of Sardinia. It is exported to the United States, too, and is quite inexpensive.

Chapter V

Soups: *PASTA in Brodo*

$\mathcal{G}$ood food like good music brings back memories that make life worthwhile. It takes a soup, for example, to make me remember Pisa, and Lord Byron, probably the world's most dashing poet. It was several years ago when I entered Pisa early one winter, with a cold rain blanking out the landscape, the usually dignified and impressive cathedral square dark and deserted, the only living object a cat so wet that it looked as if it hadn't yet grown hair, the entire city with its ancient buildings seeming a place from another time from which all life had fled.

I hurried into a small resturant not far from number 11 Lungerno Mediceo, a dank, gray 16th-century palace. Byron had lived here, while he wrote *Don Juan,* and probably had gotten inspiration at times in a tiny restaurant much like the one I entered.

I got more than inspiration. I got warm; a bowl of soup not only brought me quickly to life, but gave that dark old city new dimension. My *pasta in brodo* was *occhi di trota* (trout's eyes), small tubes of pasta, many upended in the rich broth, the openings like staring eyes; nuggets of beef, flecks of fresh parsley, and slivers of carrots made it a soup to remember. I can almost hear the sound of trumpets and envision the medieval pageantry that once was Pisa when I think back on its sight and its smell, the savory, steaming stuff sending its scent throughout the little *trattoria* as the waiter brought it to my table. I walked out into the rain a new man, and the city now became romantic, not old and dismal.

Soup does have this way of renewing the spirit. Even Napoleon is supposed to have said, "Soup makes the soldier." There is no doubt that it makes the meal.

Note: If you cannot find the various pastas such as *anellini* (little rings) or *semi di melone* (melon seeds) and many of the others in your neighborhood, then use the easy-to-come-by varieties such as *pastina, tubettini, ditalini.* I indicate here the pastas originally used in the recipes that were given to me or that I gathered in Italy. The unusual shapes do add appeal to the soup—the little cockscombs, the small sausages, the tiny nuts and rice. But if you can't get to an Italian store to get them, then most any of the small soup pastas can be substituted.

BRODO DI POLLO
(*Chicken Broth*)

The *brodo,* the broth for your pasta, can be prepared in several ways. Personally I prefer chicken broth, using a fat, yellow-skinned stewing chicken, two carrots, an onion, two celery sticks (with tops), a half handful of fresh parsley, freshly milled black pepper, three teaspoons of salt. Simmer the chicken and vegetables, completely covered with cold water, in a covered ten-quart pot until tender. Then remove the chicken (for other meals), leave the cover off the pot, and boil the stock until it is reduced by at least half. I then strain it, pour it into proper containers, and freeze it. Thus I always have the makings for *pasta in brodo,* a great wintertime dish, an unusual first course any time.

I have discovered that chicken wings can be purchased about any time at a reasonable price. I often substitute these for the stewing chicken. The broth isn't quite so rich, but it is excellent.

BRODO DI MANZO
(Beef Broth)

Beef is handled much the same with a couple of innovations. I use shin, shank, stewing beef, chuck clod. Remove the beef when tender, but not overcooked and stringy, and reduce broth by boiling rapidly. Stock is reduced to evaporate some of the water, giving the soup more body and much more flavor. When the beef is cooled, I cut it into small nuggets, about the size of a five-cent piece, and place them in the broth. Both go into a bowl, then into the refrigerator overnight. By morning a thick coat of fat has formed on top. This is removed, the broth is rewarmed and strained. Then, with the meat equally divided, it is placed in containers and popped into the freezer.

Contrary to some beliefs, in my opinion freezing does not detract from the flavor; in fact, it concentrates and enhances it.

If making homemade broth seems too time-consuming, canned College Inn chicken broth and beef broth are both excellent.

When you are ready for *pasta in brodo,* the next steps are simple. But don't start off the wrong way, as many do, by cooking your pasta in the broth

85

at the beginning. This clouds it and is only done with certain particularly fragile pastas. Much of the appeal of *pasta in brodo* is the appearance of the rich, clear broth floating the golden pasta. Cooking the pasta in the broth destroys much of this.

Cook your pasta, just as you do for any other dish, in a large quantity of briskly boiling water, but this time without salt, as the broth will be sufficiently seasoned. Remove the pasta when it is *firmer* than *al dente,* definitely on the chewy side. Drain it, then add it to the warm soup and simmer for five minutes. I like to add thinly sliced fresh vegetables, carrots, onions, sometimes a tablespoon of fresh peas, for the five minutes of simmering, then bring the *pasta in brodo* to table with a spoon of fresh minced parsley floating on it, and I often grate Parmesan on it just before serving.

ACINI DI PEPE CON BRODO DI BUE E SPINACI
("Peppercorns" with Beef Broth and Spinach)

> 3 tablespoons *acini de pepe*
> 2 quarts Beef Broth (page 85)
> ½ cup cooked, chopped spinach, well drained
> 2 egg yolks, beaten
> ⅓ cup grated Parmesan cheese

Cook *acini di pepe al dente;* drain. Add to beef broth which is simmering gently, stir in well, and blend in the spinach. Simmer for 10 minutes. Bring to a boil and remove from fire; stir in beaten egg yolks, blend well. Serve in hot soup bowls with Parmesan lightly sprinkled atop. Serves 4 to 6.

SALAMINI IN BRODO
("Tiny Sausages" in Broth)

> 2 quarts clear Beef Broth (page 85)
> ¾ cup *salamini*
> ⅓ cup grated Parmesan cheese
> 1 tablespoon chopped Italian parsley

Bring the broth to a simmer. Cook the *salamini al dente;* drain. Add to broth. Serve in hot soup bowls, sprinkled with cheese and parsley. Serves 4 to 6.

BRODO CON PASTA GRATTUGIATA
(Broth with Grated Pasta)

> ½ recipe Pasta Fresca all'Uovo (page 42)
> 3 quarts Chicken Broth (page 84)
> 2 tablespoons chopped Italian parsley
> ½ cup of grated Parmesan cheese

Prepare the dough; let it rest in kneaded ball for 10 minutes; then grate it into pieces, using the flat type of grater. Reflour your pastry board; dry the pieces of grated pasta on it for 40 minutes. Bring the chicken broth to a boil; reduce heat and add the pasta gratings; simmer for 10 minutes. Stir in the parsley; simmer for another 5 minutes. Serve in hot soup bowls with Parmesan sprinkled atop. Serves 8.

PALERMO, detail of the Cathedral—Sicily

CHICCHI DI RISO IN BRODO
(Pasta "Grains of Rice" in Broth)

2 quarts clear Beef Broth (page 85)
2 carrots, diced
2 teaspoons dehydrated white onion
3 tablespoons *chicchi di riso*
1 tablespoon chopped Italian parsley

Bring the broth to a simmer, stir in the carrots and the dehydrated onion, and simmer, covered, for 20 minutes. Cook the *chicchi di riso* less than *al dente*, drain, and stir into the beef broth. Simmer for 4 minutes, uncovered. Serve in hot soup bowls with parsley sprinkled over. Serves 4 to 6.

ANELLINI CON ZUPPA DI BUE E LEGUME
("Little Rings" with Beef Vegetable Soup)

⅓ cup *anellini*
1 small white onion, chopped
2 small carrots, chopped
3 tablespoons cooked lima beans
¼ pound beef chuck, ground
2 quarts Beef Broth (page 85)
½ teaspoon salt

Cook *anellini* in plenty of boiling water less than *al dente;* drain. Add vegetables (except beans) and raw beef to simmering beef broth; cook until carrots are tender. Stir in the drained pasta and lima beans and sprinkle in the salt; simmer for 5 minutes. Serve in hot soup bowls. Serves 4 to 6.

SPAGHETTINI E UOVA IN BRODO ALLA MARIA
(Spaghettini and Eggs in Broth alla Maria)

½ cup 1½-inch pieces of spaghettini
2 quarts Chicken Broth (page 84)
3 eggs, beaten
⅓ cup grated Romano cheese

Cook spaghettini *al dente;* drain. When chicken broth is boiling, stir in spaghettini. Remove from fire and blend in the beaten eggs, stirring rapidly until the eggs float in shreds. Ladle into warm soup bowls. Sprinkle Romano atop each serving. Serves 4 to 6.

ZUPPA DI BUE CON SPAGHETTINI
(Spaghettini with Beef Soup)

1 recipe Beef Sauce (page 70)
2 egg yolks
2 cups heavy cream
2 quarts Beef Broth (page 85)
½ cup 1½-inch pieces of spaghettini

Prepare beef sauce. Place eggs in a very large bowl and beat with whisk, slowly adding the cream and the beef broth, blending well. Stir this into the beef sauce which should be simmering. Cook the spaghettini *al dente,* drain, and stir into the beef soup, mixing everything well. Simmer for 4 minutes. Serve in hot soup bowls. Serves 8.

ZUPPA DI CAPELVENERE E FUNGHI
("Maidenhair Fern" and Mushroom Soup)

2 quarts Chicken Broth (page 84)
⅓ cup chopped carrots
⅓ cup chopped celery
2 tablespoons chopped shallots
1 teaspoon salt
8 small mushrooms, sliced
¼ pound *capelvenere*

Bring the broth to a simmer, add the carrots, celery, shallots and salt, and simmer for 10 minutes. Stir in the mushrooms and *capelvenere,* stirring mixture well with a wooden fork. Cook for about 15 minutes. These fine noodles cook quickly, and the vegetables should be on the crunchy side, not overdone. Serves 4 to 6.

ZUPPA DI SCAROLA E VERMICELLI ALLA MARIA
(Maria's Escarole and Vermicelli Soup)

½ cup 1½-inch pieces of *vermicelli*
1 head of young escarole, cut into bite-sized pieces
2 tablespoons chopped carrot
2 quarts Chicken Broth (page 84)
½ teaspoon salt
Milled black pepper

Cook *vermicelli* less than *al dente;* drain. Simmer escarole and carrot in chicken broth seasoned with the salt for 20 minutes. Add the pasta and simmer for another 3 minutes. Mill in black pepper, stir well. Ladle into hot soup bowls. Serves 6.

ZUPPA DI SCAROLA CON FUNGHINI E PISELLI
(*Escarole Soup with "Little Mushrooms" and Peas*)

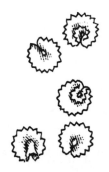

2½ cups dried whole peas
2 quarts water
2 white onions, chopped
4 tablespoons chopped prosciutto fat
2 tablespoons olive oil
1½ tablespoons rice flour
1½ teaspoons salt
Liberal amount of milled black pepper
1 head of escarole, chopped or shredded
½ cup *funghini*

Cover the peas with water and bring to a boil. Remove from fire, let soak for 45 minutes, and drain. Put the drained peas in a large pot and add the 2 quarts of water; cover pot and simmer for 1 hour. Sauté onions and prosciutto fat in the oil until onions are soft and fat is golden brown; blend in the rice flour and stir. Add mixture to the pot of peas; sprinkle in salt and mill in pepper to taste. Stir in escarole and simmer, uncovered, for 20 minutes. Cook the *funghini al dente*; drain. Stir into soup pot, simmer for 5 minutes, and serve. Serves 4 to 6.

ZUPPA DI BROCCOLI ALLA ROMANO
(*Broccoli Soup Roman Style*)

2 white onions, minced
1 garlic clove, minced
4 thick slices of prosciutto, diced
1 tablespoon olive oil
Liberal amount of milled black pepper
1 bunch of broccoli

¼ pound salt pork, diced
2 tablespoons butter
3 cup Chicken Broth (page 84)
½ cup 1½-inch pieces of spaghettini
¼ cup grated Romano cheese

In a large pot, sauté onions, garlic and prosciutto in the oil until soft. Mill in pepper and stir in water to cover. Simmer with the pot covered for 20 minutes. Use just the tips of the broccoli; wash them, barely cover with water, and cook *al dente*. Sauté the diced salt pork in the butter until crisp. Stir in the drained broccoli and simmer for 5 minutes. Add to the onions, garlic and prosciutto mixture, blending well. Stir in the chicken broth. Do not cook further; broccoli tips should be firm and intact. Cook spaghettini *al dente* in plenty of boiling salted water; drain. Gently stir into the soup. Serve in hot soup bowls with Romano sprinkled atop. Serves 4 to 6.

ZUPPA DEL VILLAGGIO CON CAPELLINI
(*Soup of the Village with Fine Vermicelli*)

1 pound leeks, sliced thin
4 tablespoons butter
1 teaspoon salt
3 quarts Chicken Broth (page 84)
3 small potatoes, diced
½ small cabbage, parboiled for 15 minutes and chopped
¼ pound *capellini*
¼ pound Asiago cheese, grated

In a large pot, sauté the leeks in the butter, add salt, and simmer until soft. Stir in chicken broth, potatoes and cabbage. Simmer, uncovered, for 1 hour, or until potatoes are soft but not mushy. Add the *capellini* directly to the broth; cook for 2 minutes. Serve in hot soup bowls with Asiago sprinkled atop. Serves 6 to 8.

VALTOURNANCHE—*Valle d'Aosta*

MINESTRA DI FORATINI FINI E CAVOLFIORE
(*Soup of "Tiny Pierced" Pasta and Cauliflower*)

> 1 medium cauliflower
> 3 shallots, chopped
> 1 cup chopped lean pork
> 3 tablespoons olive oil
> 1 large ripe tomato, peeled and diced
> 2½ quarts Chicken Broth (page 84), warm
> 1 teaspoon salt
> Milled black pepper
> ¼ pound *foratini fini*
> ⅓ cup grated Parmesan cheese

Wash cauliflower, cut off leaves, then break into flowerets. Soak the flowerets in a bowl of salted water for 15 minutes; drain. Sauté shallots and pork in the oil until shallots are soft and pork almost crisp. Blend in tomato and 1 cup of the chicken broth; add salt and pepper, and break up the tomato with a wooden spoon as it cooks. Simmer for 15 minutes, uncovered. Stir in cauliflowerets and remaining broth and simmer for 25 minutes, uncovered, stirring gently often. Cook *foratini fini* less than *al dente;* watch carefully as they cook quickly. Drain, add to cauliflower and broth, and simmer for 5 minutes. Serve in hot soup bowls with Parmesan sprinked atop each serving. Serves 6.

ZUPPA DI PERLINE MICROSCOPICI E CAVOLO ROSSO
(*Soup of "Tiny Pearls" and Red Cabbage*)

> ¼ pound lean pork, finely minced
> ¼ pound Canadian bacon, minced
> 1 white onion, chopped
> 3 tablespoons butter

6 very ripe plum tomatoes, peeled and diced
1 teaspoon salt
Milled black pepper
1 small firm red cabbage, chopped
3 quarts Chicken Broth (page 84)
4 tablespoons *perline microscopici*
¼ cup grated Asiago cheese

Sauté pork, bacon and onion in butter until onion is soft; stir in tomatoes and salt and mill in pepper. Simmer for 20 minutes, stirring and breaking up tomatoes with a wooden spoon as they cook. Add the red cabbage; simmer for 15 minutes. Blend the whole mixture with simmering chicken broth, cover, and cook for 45 minutes. Stir in the *perline microscopici* and simmer, uncovered, for another 10 minutes. Serve in hot soup bowls with Asiago sprinkled atop. Serves 8.

SEMI DI MELA CON PURÉ DI CAROTE
(*"Apple Seeds" with Puréed Carrot Soup*)

¼ pound butter
1 pound carrots, chopped
4 onions, chopped
1 teaspoon salt
1 teaspoon sugar
2 quarts Chicken Broth (page 84)
2 tablespoons chopped parsley
½ cup *semi di mela*
½ teaspoon minced chervil

Melt two-thirds of the butter in a large pot; stir in carrots, onions, salt and sugar; simmer until carrots are soft, about 20 minutes. Add 1 quart of warm chicken broth, stir in the parsley, and bring to a boil. Reduce heat and simmer, uncovered, for 30 minutes. Put the contents through a sieve, return to the pot, and add the rest of the broth. Simmer, uncovered, for another 15 minutes. Cook the *semi di mela al dente;* drain. Add to the broth and simmer for 3 minutes. Take from the fire; stir in the remaining butter and the chervil. Serve in hot soup bowls. Serves 4 to 6.

NOCCIOLE CON PURÉ DI POMIDORO
(Pasta "Nuts" with Puréed Tomato Soup)

> ¼ pound butter
> 3 white onions, chopped
> 1 garlic clove, minced
> 1 *bouquet garni* of parsley, thyme and bay leaf
> 2 pounds ripe tomatoes, peeled, diced and drained
> 1 teaspoon salt
> 1 teaspoon white pepper
> 2 quarts Beef Broth (page 85)
> ½ cup *nocciole*

Melt butter in a large pot; stir in the onions and garlic and simmer until onions are soft. Add the *bouquet garni,* the tomatoes, the salt and white pepper. Simmer for 25 minutes, stirring often and breaking up the tomatoes with a wooden spoon. Add 1 quart of beef broth; simmer for 30 minutes. Remove and discard the *bouquet garni.* Put the contents of the pot through a sieve. Return the puréed mixture to the pot and simmer for 10 minutes, adding the remaining broth as the soup cooks. Cook the *nocciole al dente,* drain, and stir into the soup. Simmer for 4 minutes. Serve in hot soup bowls, dotted with butter. Serves 4 to 6.

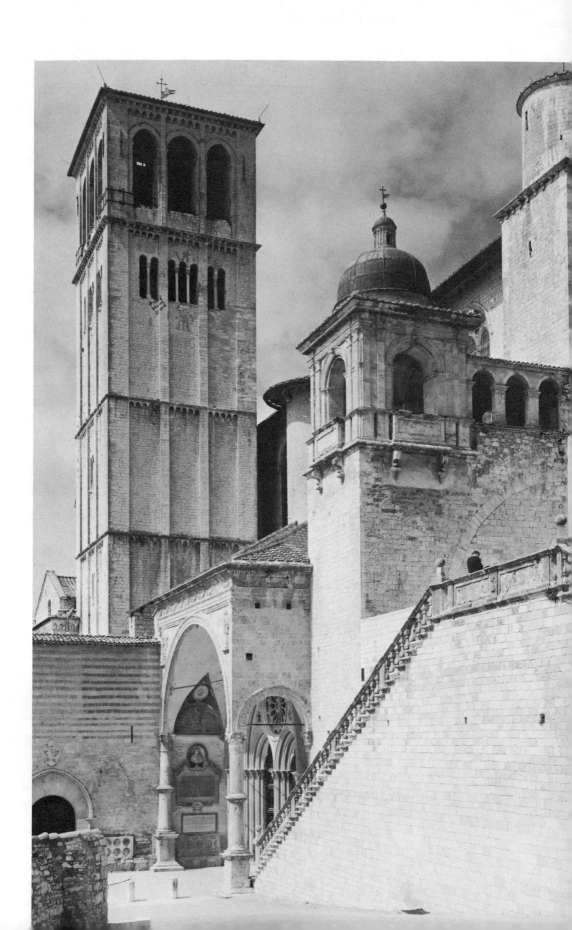

CAPPELLI DI PAGLIACCIO CON ZUPPA DI RAPE
(*"Clown's Hats" with Turnip Soup*)

> 2 small white turnips, peeled and diced
> ½-pound chunk of lean smoked bacon, chopped
> 2 tablespoons butter
> 2 tablespoons olive oil
> 2 quarts Beef Broth (page 85)
> 1 tablespoon chopped Italian parsley
> ⅛ teaspoon dried rosemary
> 1 teaspoon salt
> ⅓ cup *cappelli di pagliaccio*
> Milled black pepper
> ⅓ cup grated Parmesan cheese

Sauté turnips and bacon in butter and oil, until bacon is soft and beginning to crisp. Bring broth to boil and stir in turnips and bacon. Add parsley, rosemary and salt; simmer, uncovered, for 35 minutes. Cook the clown's hats less than *al dente,* drain, and stir into soup pot. Mill in black pepper, stir well, and simmer for 5 minutes. Serve in hot soup bowls with grated Parmesan sprinkled atop each serving. Serves 4 to 6.

ZUPPA DI CAPELLINI E ZUCCHINI
(*Fine Vermicelli and Zucchini Soup*)

> 1 medium zucchini, diced
> 2 tablespoons butter
> 2 tablespoons olive oil
> 1 teaspoon salt
> Liberal amount of milled black pepper
> 2 quarts Chicken Broth (page 84)
> 2 eggs, beaten

¼ cup grated Asiago cheese
1 tablespoon chopped Italian parsley
2 fresh basil leaves, chopped
¼ pound *capellini*

Sauté zucchini in butter and oil for 10 minutes; sprinkle with salt and pepper. Add the broth, stir well, and simmer, covered, for 25 minutes. Place eggs in bowl and beat with a whisk, blending in cheese, parsley and basil. Cook *capellini al dente;* watch carefully as it is very fine and cooks rapidly. Drain, stir into egg mixture, and add all to soup pot. Remove from fire, blend well with wooden fork. Serve in hot soup bowls. Serves 4 to 6.

ZUPPA DI CRESTE DI GALLI E PISELLI
("Cockscomb" Soup with Peas)

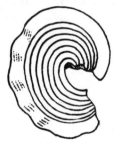

3 tablespoons olive oil
2 small onions, chopped
1 garlic clove, minced
¼ pound bacon, diced
½ pound fresh peas, shelled
1 teaspoon salt
3 quarts Chicken Broth (page 84)
½ cup *creste di galli*

In a large pot, heat the oil and in it sauté the onions and garlic. Stir in the diced bacon and cook until soft. Add the peas, salt and 5 cups of the broth. Simmer, covered, until peas are tender, about 15 minutes. Remove cover and stir in remaining broth. Cook the *creste di galli* in boiling water until *al dente;* drain. Add to the pea soup, stir, and simmer for 5 minutes. Serve in hot soup bowls. Serves 6.

ZUPPA DI MUGHETTO CON PESTO
(*"Lily-of-the-Valley" Soup with Pesto*)

⅓ recipe Pesto alla Genovese (page 80)
3 tablespoons olive oil
¼ pound shell beans, shelled
¼ pound spinach, washed and chopped
¼ pound beets, washed and diced
2 white onions, chopped
1 leek, chopped
3 medium potatoes, peeled and diced
1 small cabbage, shredded
1½ teaspoons salt
Liberal amount of milled black pepper
4 quarts water
½ cup *mughetto*

Prepare the *pesto* and put aside. Heat the olive oil in a 6-quart pot and slowly add all of the vegetables, stirring them into the oil. Cook for 15 minutes, stirring often. Add the salt and pepper, and the water; cover the pot and simmer for 1½ hours. Remove the cover and stir in the *mughetto*, which has been cooked *al dente* and drained; add the *pesto*, stirring it in well. Simmer for 5 minutes. Serve in hot soup bowls. Serves 4 to 6.

ZUPPA DI DITALINI E FAGIOLI FRESCHI
(*"Little Thimbles" and Fresh Lima Bean Soup*)

4 tablespoons olive oil
3 tablespoons butter
2 white onions, chopped
1 celery rib, chopped
2 cups (one 1-pound can) Italian plum tomatoes

1½ pounds fresh lima beans, shelled
2 quarts Chicken Broth (page 84)
¼ teaspoon dried sweet basil
1 heart of romaine lettuce, shredded
1 teaspoon salt
Liberal amount of milled black pepper
⅓ cup *ditalini*
⅓ cup grated Romano cheese
⅓ cup grated Parmesan cheese

In the olive oil and butter sauté onions and celery until onions are soft. Stir in tomatoes and simmer for 15 minutes, breaking them up with a wooden spoon as they cook. Blend in lima beans and broth and simmer, covered, for 45 minutes or less, until lima beans are tender. Add basil and the shredded lettuce; sprinkle in salt and pepper. Cook *ditalini al dente,* drain, and stir into the soup. Simmer for 5 minutes, uncovered. Mix the two cheeses and pass at table with soup which has been served in hot bowls. Serves 4 to 6.

ZUPPA DI CECI ALLA TOSCANA
(Chick-Pea Soup Tuscan Style)

1 pound *ceci* (chick-peas)
1 teaspoon salt
2 sprigs or branches of rosemary, wrapped and tied in cheesecloth
1 garlic clove, minced
4 anchovy fillets, drained
2 tablespoons olive oil
2 tomatoes, peeled and diced
2 quarts Chicken Broth (page 84)
½ cup *conchigliette* (tiny shells)

Soak the *ceci* in water for 3 hours. Drain and cover with fresh cold water. Add the salt and the rosemary. Cover and cook for 40 minutes, or until *ceci* are tender. Discard the rosemary and put *ceci* and liquid through a food mill. Sauté the garlic and anchovies in the oil until smooth and well blended. Stir in the tomatoes and add the hot chicken broth. Simmer for 25 minutes, uncovered. Blend in the puréed *ceci*. Cook *conchigliette al dente* separately; drain. Stir into the soup; simmer for 5 minutes. Serve in hot soup bowls. Serves 4 to 6.

FLORENCE, the Ponte Vecchio—Tuscany

LUMACHINE E CECI
("Small Snails" and Chick-Peas)

    1 pound *ceci* (chick-peas)
    2 teaspoons salt
    4 tablespoons olive oil
    1 garlic clove, minced
    ¼ teaspoon crushed red pepper
    2 slices of bacon, diced
    6 very ripe tomatoes, peeled and diced
    ½ teaspoon dried tarragon
    ½ cup *lumachine*

Soak the *ceci* in water for 3 hours; drain. Place in a pot with 4 quarts water and 1 teaspoon of the salt. Cover and simmer until tender, about 40 minutes, stirring often, and carefully, with a wooden spoon.

    Make a sauce, what Italians call a *soffritto*, by sautéing in the oil the garlic, red pepper, bacon, tomatoes, remaining teaspoon of salt and the tarragon. Simmer the sauce, breaking up the tomatoes with a wooden spoon as they cook. When sauce is smooth, in about 15 minutes, remove from fire and stir it into the soup pot. Leave the cover off the pot and let the mixture simmer gently while you cook the *lumachine* less than *al dente*. Drain the "little snails" well and stir them into the chick-peas. Simmer for another 5 minutes. Serve in hot soup bowls. Serves 4 to 6.

ZUPPA DI SEMI DI MELONE
("Melon Seeds" Soup)

    2 small white onions, chopped
    1 garlic clove, minced
    1 large celery rib, chopped
    2 tablespoons olive oil
    3 quarts Beef Broth (page 85), simmering

1 cup cooked *ceci* (chick-peas)
1 cup shredded cabbage
4 large tomatoes, peeled and diced
⅓ cup *semi di melone*
⅓ cup grated Parmesan cheese

Sauté onions, garlic and celery in the oil, and add to the simmering beef broth. Add *ceci*, cabbage and tomatoes. Cover the pot and cook for 25 minutes. Cook *semi di melone* separately *al dente*, drain, and add to soup pot. Simmer for 5 minutes. Serve in hot soup bowls with Parmesan sprinkled atop. Serves 6.

TRIFOGLI CON COTECHINI E LENTICCHIE
(*"Cloverleaves" with Sausage and Lentils*)

½ pound dried lentils, soaked in water 5 hours
1 small *cotechini* sausage
2 teaspoons salt
2 tablespoons olive oil
2 small white onions, chopped
1 tablespoon flour
Milled black pepper
2 cups Chicken Broth (page 84), warm
½ cup *trifogli*

Drain the lentils and place in a large pot with the whole sausage. Cover with water, add 1 teaspoon of the salt, cover, and simmer for 1½ hours, or until lentils are tender. Heat the olive oil in a saucepan and sauté the onions in it until soft. Stir in the flour, remaining salt and the pepper. Slowly add the broth, stirring the mixture into a smooth sauce. Add this to the lentils and stir in well. Cook the *trifogli al dente*, drain, and stir into the lentil pot. Remove the skin from the sausage and cut sausage into rounds; then quarter the rounds. Serve lentil soup in hot soup bowls with 4 pieces of sausage in each bowl. Serves 4 to 6.

ZUPPA ALLA PAESANA
(Soup Country Style)

    1 pound dried lentils, soaked in water for 5 hours
    8 anchovies, drained, soaked in cold water, then drained
       again
    1 tablespoon olive oil
    1 tablespoon butter
    2 celery ribs, chopped
    1 garlic clove, minced
    1 tablespoon chopped parsley
    2 pounds tomatoes, peeled and diced
    2 quarts water
    ½ cup *chiocciole* ("snail shells")
    ⅓ cup grated Parmesan cheese

Drain the lentils and cook in a 4-quart pot, covered, for 1 hour, or until tender. Mash the anchovies in a mortar. Sauté them in oil and butter with the celery, garlic and parsley, until celery is soft. Stir in the tomatoes, add the water, bring to boil, and simmer, uncovered, for 25 minutes. Drain lentils, saving the liquid they were cooked in. Stir the lentils and 4 tablespoons of this liquid into the anchovy sauce; simmer for 5 minutes. Cook the *chiocciole* in the remaining lentil liquid until *al dente*. Remove with a slotted spoon or skimmer, without draining, directly into the lentil-and-anchovy pan; stir well; simmer for 5 minutes. Serve in hot soup bowls with Parmesan sprinkled atop. Serves 6.

107

ZUPPA DI TUBETTI E LENTICCHIE
(*"Little Tubes" and Lentil Soup*)

½ pound dried lentils
3 quarts water
1 leftover ham bone
1 teaspoon salt
Milled black pepper
2 small white onions, chopped
2 celery ribs with leaves, chopped
3 tablespoons olive oil
⅓ cup *tubetti*

Soak the lentils in water for 5 hours; drain. Place lentils in a large pot with the water, the ham bone, salt and pepper; simmer for 1½ hours. Brown onions and celery in 2 tablespoons of the oil; stir into soup pot. Simmer for 20 minutes, uncovered. Cook *tubetti* in plenty of salted water *al dente;* drain and add to soup, stirring in well. Blend in the remaining oil and mill in more black pepper. Remove ham bone; dice its meat and return this to the soup. Serve in hot soup bowls. Serves 4 to 6.

VERMICELLI CON CIAVATTONI E COTICHE
(*Vermicelli with White Beans and Pork Rinds*)

½ pound dried white beans
2 quarts water
1 teaspoon salt
½ pound pork rinds, cut into strips
8 ripe tomatoes, peeled and diced
Milled black pepper
3 tablespoons chopped pork or ham fat

2 tablespoons olive oil
1 garlic clove
½ cup white wine
⅓ cup 1½-inch pieces of *vermicelli*

Soak the beans in water for 3 hours; drain. Place in a large pot with the water, salt, pork rinds, half of the tomatoes, and some pepper. Simmer, covered, for 1½ hours. In a frypan, sauté the chopped pork fat in oil. Add the garlic and cook until pork and garlic are soft. Mill in some pepper and blend in remaining tomatoes and the wine, breaking up tomatoes with a wooden spoon as they cook. Simmer for 20 minutes, then stir the pork mixture into the bean pot, blending well. Cook slowly, uncovered, for 15 minutes, stirring often and taking care not to break up the beans. Cook *vermicelli al dente;* drain, stir into bean pot, and simmer for 3 minutes. Serve in hot soup bowls. Serves 4 to 6.

MINESTRA DI MARUZZELLE
(*Soup of "Small Seashells"*)

1 garlic clove, minced
4 anchovies, mashed
2 tablespoons chopped Italian parsley
4 tablespoons olive oil
2½ cups (one 1-pound 4-ounce can) fava beans, undrained
1 teaspoon dried tarragon
4 tomatoes, peeled and diced
3 quarts water
½ teaspoon salt
⅓ cup *maruzzelle*
⅓ cup grated Parmesan cheese

Sauté the garlic, anchovies and parsley in the oil until garlic is soft and anchovies dissolve. Pour in the fava beans, tarragon and tomatoes; simmer for 15 minutes, breaking up the tomatoes with a wooden spoon as they cook. Add the water and salt and simmer, uncovered, for 20 minutes. Cook the *maruzzelle* less than *al dente,* drain, and stir into the bean pot. Simmer, uncovered, for 5 minutes. Serve in hot soup bowls with Parmesan lightly sprinkled atop each serving. Serves 4 to 6.

MINESTRA DI VERDURA E PROSCIUTTO
(*Vegetable and Ham Soup*)

½ pound lima beans, shelled
2 celery ribs, chopped
1 head of escarole, chopped
¼ pound spinach, chopped
6 small beets, diced
1½ teaspoons salt
Milled black pepper
2 tablespoons olive oil
2 white onions, chopped
1 carrot, chopped
3 tablespoons minced ham fat
½-pound slice of ham
1 pig's foot
¼ teaspoon dried marjoram
½ cup *cannolicchi* (small pasta tubes)
⅓ cup grated Parmesan cheese

In a large pot place the lima beans, celery, escarole, spinach, beets, salt, and pepper. Add enough water to cover the vegetables; cover the pot. Bring to a boil, then reduce heat, and simmer for 10 minutes. In another very large pot, heat the oil and sauté onions and carrot in it until onions are soft. Stir in the minced ham fat, add the ham and pig's foot, mill in pepper, and add the marjoram. Simmer for 15 minutes. Then add the water from the vegetable pot and all the vegetables from that pot. Simmer all together, covered, until pig's foot is tender to the fork, about 40 minutes. Remove the pig's foot and ham slice, dice both, and return them to soup pot. Cook the *cannolicchi* less than *al dente,* drain, and stir into soup pot. Simmer for 5 minutes, uncovered. Serve in hot soup bowls with Parmesan sprinkled atop. Serves 6.

MINESTRONE ALLA CONTADINA
(*Countrywoman's Minestrone*)

½ cup dried kidney beans
½ cup dried lentils
1 large white onion, chopped
½ pound salt pork, diced
2 tablespoons olive oil
2 cups (one 1-pound can) Italian plum tomatoes
Milled black pepper
1 teaspoon salt
1 small firm cabbage, chopped
2 carrots, cut into small bite-sized pieces
2 leeks, cut into ½-inch pieces
4 quarts Beef Broth (page 85)
2 tablespoons fresh peas
1 medium zucchini, cut into small bite-sized chunks
3 small potatoes, diced
½ cup *ditali* ("thimbles")
½ cup grated Asiago cheese

Soak kidney beans and lentils in water for 5 hours; drain. Sauté onion and salt pork in the oil until onion is soft and salt pork nearly crisp. Add tomatoes and break up with a wooden spoon; mill in black pepper and add the salt. Place beans, lentils, cabbage, carrots and leeks in a large pot with the beef broth. Simmer until vegetables are half done and beans and lentils are still firm, about 25 minutes. Stir in peas, zucchini, potatoes and tomato-onion-salt-pork mixture. Mill in more black pepper and simmer until beans, lentils and vegetables are tender. Cook *ditali al dente,* drain well, and stir into the bean pot. Simmer for 5 minutes. Serve in hot soup bowls with Asiago grated atop each serving. Serves 6 to 8.

Note: If more liquid is needed, add small amounts of hot water, stirring it in well.

MINESTRONE GIOVANNINO

½ cup dried chick-peas
½ cup dried kidney beans
3 quarts Beef Broth (page 85)
2 small white onions, chopped
1 garlic clove, minced
3 tablespoons olive oil
2 cups (one 1-pound can) Italian plum tomatoes
½ cup chopped cabbage
½ cup chopped carrot
½ cup chopped celery
⅓ cup *ditalini* ("little thimbles")
Milled black pepper
¼ teaspoon crushed dried red pepper
⅓ cup grated Parmesan cheese

Soak chick-peas and beans in water for 5 hours. Drain, and place in a large pot with the beef broth. Simmer for 40 minutes, or until beans are almost cooked, but still slightly on hard side. Sauté onions and garlic in oil, then stir in tomatoes, breaking them up with a wooden spoon. Cook cabbage, carrot and celery until half done; drain. Cook *ditalini* in boiling water until much less than *al dente,* firm and chewy. Blend tomato mixture, cooked vegetables and *ditalini* into the beans and broth. Mill in black pepper, stir in red pepper, and simmer for 15 minutes, uncovered, stirring often. Serve in hot soup bowls, with a sprinkle of freshly grated Parmesan over each serving. Serves 6 to 8.

Near CAMPITELLO, the Dolomites—Trentino-Alto Adige

RAVIOLINI IN BRODO

    1 recipe for Pasta Fresca for Ravioli (page 44)
    ½ cup ricotta cheese, drained
    ½ cup grated Parmesan cheese
    2 egg yolks
    1 tablespoon chopped Italian parsley
    4 quarts Chicken Broth (page 84)

Prepare dough and roll into sheets as for *ravioli*. Mix the cheeses, egg yolks and parsley, blending well. Place teaspoons of the cheese filling 1 inch apart on one sheet of the dough; cover with the other sheet of dough, pressing it around each mound of filling. Using a pastry cutter, cut 1-inch squares, rather than the usual 2-inch, since these are to be used in soup. Press the edges of each square again to make sure they are sealed. Dry for 25 minutes. Bring half of the chicken broth to a simmer. Drop 6 *raviolini* at a time into the broth and cook for 6 minutes. Remove them with a slotted spoon onto paper towels to drain. Continue until all are cooked. In another pot bring remaining broth to a boil. Ladle it into individual soup bowls and float 6 *raviolini* in each bowl. Serves 4 to 6.

ZUPPA DI PESCE CON STIVALETTI
(Fish Soup with "Little Boots")

    2 pounds cod fillets
    2 pounds whiting
    2 pounds porgies, rockfish, or any inexpensive fish
    3 tablespoons butter
    3 tablespoons olive oil
    4 celery ribs, chopped
    4 onions, chopped
    2 leeks, diced

> 2 carrots, chopped
> 4 ripe tomatoes, peeled and diced
> 1½ teaspoons salt
> Milled black pepper
> ½ teaspoon dried rosemary
> ½ cup *stivaletti*

Have the fish cleaned and scaled. In an 8-quart pot heat the butter and oil; sauté celery, onions, leeks and carrots in it until soft. Stir in tomatoes and season with salt and pepper and rosemary. Simmer for 15 minutes. Fill pot with hot water, bring to boil, reduce heat, cover, and simmer for 20 minutes. Add the whole fish and the fillets. Simmer, uncovered, for 30 minutes. Remove the cod fillets while still firm to use for second course. Strain remainder through sieve, forcing fish, vegetables and stock through. Now bring this strained soup to a boil; stir in the *stivaletti* and cook, uncovered, *al dente*. Serve in large soup bowls. The hot cod fillets follow, as entrée, drenched with melted butter and accompanied by boiled potatoes and a green salad. Serves 6.

ZUPPA DI GAMBERI CON AVENA
(Shrimp Soup with Pasta "Oats")

> 2 tablespoons olive oil
> 2 tablespoons butter
> 2 carrots, chopped
> 2 celery ribs, chopped
> 2 basil leaves, chopped
> 1 tablespoon chopped parsley
> 2 white onions, chopped
> 1½ teaspoons salt
> Liberal amount of milled black pepper
> 2 dozen fresh shrimps in their shells

    2 quarts Chicken Broth (page 84)
    ½ cup dry white wine
    ½ cup marsala wine
    ⅓ cup *avena*

In a large pot heat the oil and butter and sauté the carrots, celery, basil, parsley and onions in it. Sprinkle in the salt and some pepper and simmer for 10 minutes. Add the shrimps in their shells and the chicken broth; simmer, covered, for 20 minutes. Uncover and add the white wine and marsala, stirring in well. Remove shrimps, peel, cut each one into 3 pieces, and return to pot. Cook the *avena al dente;* stir into the soup. Simmer 3 minutes. Serve in hot soup bowls. Serves 4 to 6.

ZUPPA DI GAMBE DI RANOCCHI
(Frogs' Legs Soup)

    4 tablespoons olive oil
    2 garlic cloves, minced
    1 tablespoon chopped parsley
    1 carrot, chopped
    1 celery rib, chopped
    2 small white onions, chopped
    3 fresh basil leaves, minced
    24 frogs (or substitute fresh or frozen seafood, such as shrimps, crabs, etc.)
    8 very ripe tomatoes, peeled and diced
    2 quarts water
    2 tablespoons dried mushrooms
    ¼ pound *capelli d'angelo* ("angel's hair")

Heat the oil in a large pot and sauté the garlic, parsley, carrot, celery, onions, and basil in it until onions are soft. Remove hind legs from the cleaned and washed frogs and set aside. Place the rest of the frogs in the pan with the sautéed vegetables and brown; turn often so frogs do not stick to the pan.

Add the tomatoes and increase heat until the mixture comes to a boil. Stir well, reduce heat, and add the water. Simmer until the meat begins to separate from the bones. Put everything through a sieve, pressing through, so that only bones remain in the sieve. Return the soup to the pot; simmer frogs' hind legs in this until tender, about 10 minutes. Take meat from bones, dice, and return to the soup. Stir in the mushrooms and simmer, uncovered, for 10 minutes. Bring soup to a boil and remove from fire. Stir in the *capelli d'angelo*. This pasta is so fine that it cooks in seconds, so it is not necessary to replace the pot on the stove; stir everything well and serve in hot soup bowls. Serves 4 to 6.

ZUPPA DI SALSICCIE E CRAVATTE
(*Sausage Soup with "Bow Ties"*)

> ½ pound dried white pea beans
> 3 quarts Chicken Broth (page 84)
> 3 tablespoons olive oil
> Four 4-inch "hot" Italian sausages
> 3 potatoes, diced
> 1 carrot, chopped
> 1 small white onion, chopped
> 1 celery rib, chopped
> 4 ripe tomatoes, peeled and diced
> 1½ teaspoons salt
> Milled black pepper
> ½ cup *cravatte*

Soak the beans in water for 3 hours; drain. Cover with 2 quarts of the broth and simmer for 1½ hours, or until beans are almost tender but still firm. Heat the oil in a large saucepan; add the sausages, pricked with a fork, and brown. Stir in the potatoes, carrot, onion, celery and tomatoes; sprinkle with salt and mill in black pepper. Simmer for 15 minutes, then stir in the remaining broth and simmer, uncovered, for 20 minutes. Add this to the bean pot, stirring in well. Cook the *cravatte al dente,* drain, and stir into the bean pot. Simmer, uncovered, for 5 minutes. Serve in hot soup bowls with the sausage in slices, 4 slices to each bowl of soup. Serves 4 to 6.

PASTINA ALLA TOSCANA

1 pound beef round
5 medium chicken livers
2 small white onions, minced
2 tablespoons olive oil
2 tablespoons butter
1 tablespoon minced Italian parsley
2 fresh basil leaves, minced
4 very ripe tomatoes, peeled and diced
1½ teaspoons salt
Milled black pepper
3 quarts Chicken Broth (page 84), warm
¼ pound fresh spinach, chopped
¼ pound escarole, chopped
3 tablespoons *pastina* (small pasta for soup)

Cut the beef into pieces half the size of your thumbnail; chop the chicken livers. Sauté the beef and livers with the onions in the oil and butter for 15 minutes. Stir in the minced herbs and the tomatoes, breaking up the tomatoes with a wooden spoon as they simmer. Sprinkle on the salt and the pepper. Simmer for 30 minutes, uncovered, stirring often. Now add the warm chicken broth and stir in the chopped spinach and escarole. Simmer for 20 minutes. Stir in the *pastina* and simmer for another 5 minutes. Serve in hot soup bowls. Serves 6.

PULCINI ZUPPA ALL'ANTONIO
("Little Chickens" Soup Antonio)

This recipe comes from a barber in Milan who is also an artist in the kitchen.

> 1 veal sweetbread
> 3 tablespoons butter
> 1 carrot, chopped
> ½ teaspoon salt
> Milled black pepper
> 2 artichoke hearts, diced
> ½ cup *pulcini*
> 2 quarts Chicken Broth (page 84)
> 1 tablespoon chopped Italian parsley

Parboil the sweetbread; cool, remove skin and membranes, and dice. In the butter, melted, sauté the sweetbread and carrot, sprinkling with salt and pepper, until the pieces are brown. Stir in the diced artichoke hearts and simmer for 5 minutes. Cook the *pulcini al dente;* drain. Bring the chicken broth to a simmer, stir in the sweetbread-and-artichoke mixture and the pasta; simmer for 5 minutes. Serve in hot soup bowls with parsley sprinkled atop each serving. Serves 4 to 6.

Near L'AQUILA, wheat harvest—Abruzzi

VERMICELLI ALLA SALVATORE

This was prepared for me one cold winter's evening by a chef in Venice; the rain was falling over the canals like mist; the landscape was dreary, the gondoliers wet and sullen. After the soup, the dark day didn't bother me a bit. Venice was as she is supposed to be: full of water and excellent restaurants.

> 3 veal sweetbreads
> 4 chicken livers
> 5 tablespoons butter
> 2 eggs
> Juice of ½ lemon
> 1 teaspoon salt
> Liberal amount of milled black pepper
> 1 tablespoon chopped Italian parsley
> ⅛ teaspoon dried sweet basil
> 2 quarts Chicken Broth (page 84)
> ⅓ cup 1½-inch pieces of *vermicelli*
> ⅓ cup grated Parmesan cheese

Parboil the sweetbreads; remove the skin and membranes and dice the sweetbreads. Chop the chicken livers. Sauté the sweetbreads and livers in butter for 8 minutes. In a large bowl, beat the eggs with a whisk; blend in lemon, salt, pepper, parsley and basil. Slowly stir in all of the broth. Pour into a large pot, and stir in the sweetbreads and livers. Simmer for 20 minutes, stirring often. Cook *vermicelli* less than *al dente*; drain, add to the soup pot, and simmer for 3 minutes. Pass the Parmesan. Serves 4 to 6.

ZUPPA DI POMODORO CON POLPETTINE DI VITELLO
(Tomato Soup with Veal Meatballs)

3 tablespoons butter
2 tablespoons minced ham fat
1 carrot, minced
1 white onion, minced
1 celery rib, minced
1 tablespoon minced Italian parsley
2 pounds plum tomatoes, peeled and diced
3 quarts Chicken Broth (page 84)
2 slices of bread without crusts
1 cup milk
½ pound veal, ground twice
1 shallot, minced
2 egg yolks, beaten
1 teaspoon salt
Pinch of grated nutmeg
4 tablespoons flour
⅓ cup 1½-inch pieces of *vermicelli*

Heat 2 tablespoons of the butter in a large pot, stir in ham fat, and cook until soft. Then add the carrot, onion, celery, and parsley; simmer for 10 minutes. Stir in the tomatoes, blend in half the broth, cover the pot, and simmer for 1 hour.

Meanwhile, prepare meatballs. Soak the bread in the milk; press out the liquid, then mix bread with the veal in a bowl. Heat the remaining butter and sauté the shallot in it until tender. Add shallot and butter, the beaten egg yolks, and the salt and nutmeg to the bread and veal. Blend everything well. Form into meatballs the size of marbles.

Bring the remaining broth to a simmer. Roll the meatballs in the flour, and drop them into the broth. Cook for 10 minutes. Strain the vegetable mixture and return it to its soup pot. Then stir meatballs and their broth into the pot. Cook the *vermicelli al dente* in plenty of boiling water; drain well. Stir into the soup and simmer, uncovered, for 3 minutes. Serve in hot soup bowls with 6 meatballs in each bowl. Serves 4 to 6.

ZUPPA DI CIMA ALLA GENOVESE CON LINGUINE FINE
(*Genoese Veal Soup with Fine Noodles*)

This is a famous soup from Genoa that first requires that you prepare cima, *a stuffed breast of veal.*

> ½ pound lean pork, ground
> ¼ pound prosciutto, minced
> 4 slices of bread, soaked in milk, then squeezed dry
> 1 tablespoon grated Parmesan cheese
> 1 tablespoon minced pistachios
> 2½ teaspoons salt
> Liberal amount of milled black pepper
> Pinch of grated nutmeg
> 5 eggs, in all
> One 3-pound breast of veal, boned
> 1 large carrot, chopped
> 1 large onion, chopped
> 1 bay leaf
> 1 tablespoon minced fresh marjoram
> ¼ pound *linguine fine*, broken into 2-inch pieces

In a large bowl place the pork, prosciutto, bread, Parmesan, pistachios, 1½ teaspoons of the salt, some pepper, the nutmeg, and 3 of the eggs. Mix all together well to make a filling. Spread the breast of veal flat; spoon the filling over the veal. Fold the meat over, sewing it together to seal in the filling com-

123

pletely. Then tie with string. Place the roll in a 6-quart pot and cover with water. Stir in the carrot, onion, bay leaf and remaining teaspoon of salt. Cover the pot and simmer for 1½ hours, or until breast is tender. Remove to a platter and place a heavy weight atop to press the meat into its flat Genoese shape.

Add the marjoram to the liquid remaining in the pot in which the veal cooked. Simmer this broth, uncovered, for 20 minutes. Add the *linguine fine* directly to the pot; cook *al dente*. Beat the 2 remaining eggs and stir them into the broth; bring it to a boil. Remove from the heat and ladle soup quickly into hot soup bowls. Serve the *cima*, sliced thin, as the entrée, accompanied by a vegetable. Serves 4 to 6.

ZUPPA DI POLLO CON STELLINI
(Chicken Soup with "Little Stars")

1 fat, yellow-skinned stewing chicken
½ cup diced okra
2 cups (one 1-pound can) Italian plum tomatoes
1 onion, chopped
2 celery ribs, chopped
Salt and pepper
⅓ cup *stellini*

Cover chicken with water, and simmer for 3 hours; take from pot and dice meat. Return chicken meat to pot; stir in vegetables. Season and simmer for 25 minutes. Cook *stellini al dente*; drain, blend with soup. Serves 4 to 6.

PICCIONE BOLLITO CON ARANCINI
(Boiled Pigeon with "Little Oranges")

  2 pigeons (or substitute a fat stewing chicken)
  8 quarts water
  2 large carrots
  2 large celery ribs with leaves
  1 large onion
  6 peppercorns, cracked
  1 tablespoon salt
  ⅓ cup *arancini*
  1 tablespoon chopped Italian parsley

Put the pigeons in the water with all of the ingredients except the pasta and parsley. Simmer, covered, for 4 hours, or until birds are tender. Remove pigeons, cool, and dice meat from the breasts. Cook remaining stock in the uncovered pot until it is reduced by half. Strain; put vegetables through sieve; return vegetable purée and diced pigeon to the strained stock, and simmer for 10 minutes. Cook *arancini* in boiling salted water until *al dente,* drain, and add to soup pot; simmer for 5 minutes. Serve in hot soup bowls topped with chopped parsley. Serves 4 to 6.

Chapter VI

ATRANI—Campania

Seafood with PASTA

Pasta and seafood is to me a dawn sea. It is the little Sicilian fishing port of Licata, a small boat chugging through the darkness as I went netting sardines with three fishermen several years ago. It is little boats with bobbing lanterns that send spots of shimmering light; it is dawn coming over the island in staggering waves of light that fall upon the dark sea, making it clear blue and the hauled-in nets of fish a flashing sheet of silver.

But even more than that, it is perhaps the best breakfast, certainly the most unusual, that I have ever had—on a beach, as the sun became warm, and the fish and the pasta cooked.

As we anchored, one fisherman filled an old black pot with seawater and put it over a brazier. Driftwood was gathered, the fire built, the pot boiled merrily. Another fisherman, using a small instrument like a buttonhook, inserted it in the mouth of each sardine and pulled innards and bones out. When four dozen were ready, they went into another pot, with olive oil, on the brazier over the driftwood fire.

The pasta, a pound of *linguine,* was ready in eight minutes; so were the fish that literally had jumped from the sea into the pot. We sat on the shore and ate that famous dish of Sicily, *pasta alle sarde,* the *linguine* mixed with a bit of the oil that the fish had cooked in, fresh fennel leaves rubbed through the hands over it, some *pignoli* nuts added, black pepper grated over, and then each person received six crisp, golden sardines on top of his pasta. As I touched a fish, its delicate white meat spilled onto the *linguine,* I twirled it with several strands, and washed it down with one of the best white wines I have tasted, the cold, crisp Sicilian Corvo.

That was my introduction to that creative combination—pasta and seafood. Today, probably because of those early circumstances, it still remains my favorite. Surrounded as she is by the sea, Italy makes quite a thing of pasta and myriad creatures from the ocean, and the farther south you go, it seems to me, the more unusual and superb the combinations become. Everything from a sardine to a squid lends its personality.

LINGUINE ALLEGRE
(*Lively Linguine with Anchovies*)

Here is a recipe from a waiter in Rome's famed L'Escargot. He had seen the chef do it so often that he could rattle it off from memory—which he did. I wrote it down as he appeared between courses. I was there on a Friday and everyone in the place was eating this dish.

4 cups Basic Tomato Sauce (page 63)
3 tablespoons butter
3 tablespoons olive oil
6 anchovies, finely minced
3 basil leaves, minced
2 tablespoons minced Italian parsley
1 garlic clove, minced
1 celery rib, minced
½ tablespoon capers, minced
6 large black olives, pitted and minced
1 sweet red pepper, minced
1 pound *linguine*

Prepare the tomato sauce and while it gently simmers, heat butter and oil. Sauté the anchovies, basil, parsley, garlic, celery, capers, olives and red pepper in the oil until soft and browned. Blend the mixture into the tomato sauce and simmer, uncovered, for 40 minutes, stirring often with a wooden spoon. Cook *linguine al dente* using only 1 tablespoon salt since anchovies are salty; drain. Toss *linguine* gently with half of the sauce, using wooden forks. Serve in hot soup bowls and spoon remaining sauce on top. Serves 4 to 6.

VERMICELLI ALLA MERETRICE
(*Harlot's Pasta*)

This is similar to the previous anchovy recipe but a little quicker to make because you do not first have to make the basic tomato sauce. The recipe for Salsa alla Meretrice, which is used on other pastas too, is on page 74. For this dish, cook 1 pound of vermicelli al dente; watch carefully, as they are fine and cook quickly—6 minutes could do it. Drain the vermicelli. Serve in hot soup bowls, with a lavish spooning of sauce over each serving. Do not toss, as this is a fragile pasta and too much forking can make it sticky. Serves 4 to 6.

Pastas with anchovies, or other seafood, that are not, strictly speaking, seafood dishes, are . . .

Maria Limoncelli's "Sparrows' Tongues" (or spaghetti) with Anchovies, page 295.
Linguine with Eggs and Anchovies, page 300.
Bucatini with Anchovies and Mushrooms, page 273.
Baked Stuffed Tomatoes Sicilian Style (with sardines), page 311.
"Tiny Tubes" and Salmon Pie, page 314.

FETTUCCE E PESCE
(*Wide Fettuccine with Fish*)

2 tablespoons olive oil
3 small white onions, chopped
1 garlic clove, minced
1 small red pepper, chopped
1 small green pepper, chopped
1 can (2 ounces) anchovies, chopped

Liberal amount of milled black pepper
2 cups Basic Tomato Sauce (page 63)
½ teaspoon dried tarragon
2 medium cod or haddock fillets, cut into bite-size pieces
1 pound *fettucce*

Heat the oil in a heavy cooking pot. Add onions, garlic, peppers, and anchovies with oil; mill in black pepper. Sauté until vegetables are soft. Stir in the tomato sauce, then add the tarragon and the pieces of fish. Simmer, uncovered, until fish is tender but not falling apart. Cook the *fettucce al dente,* drain, and toss gently with half of the fish sauce, using forks. Serve in hot bowls with the remaining sauce atop each serving. Serves 4 to 6.

LINGUE DI PASSERI CON BACCALÀ
(*"Sparrows' Tongues" with Dried Cod*)

It is the rare Italian market here or abroad that doesn't have dried, heavily salted cod the length of your arm, stacked just inside the entrance like cordwood. Cod treated like this lasts indefinitely and was the old-world way of preserving heavy catches for future meals. In their usual imaginative way the Italians created a number of dishes from the fish. Baccalà teamed sometimes with pasta, sometimes with polenta, is a tart and tasty dish usually served during the Christmas holiday season.

3 pounds dried cod
⅓ cup flour
1 tablespoon olive oil
3 tablespoons butter
2 garlic cloves
Liberal amount of milled black pepper
3 mint leaves, chopped
3 basil leaves, chopped

½ teaspoon capers
4 pitted large black olives, sliced
3 cups Marinara Sauce (page 69)
1 pound *lingue di passeri*

Soak the cod in cold water for 24 hours, changing water at least 6 times. Just before beginning the recipe, wash the cod once more in cold water. Cut it into 1-inch pieces, remove skin, drain, and roll in flour. Heat oil and butter in a heavy skillet. Add fish and garlic and brown, removing garlic when it turns golden and turning fish so it will brown on both sides. Mill in black pepper; stir in mint and basil leaves, capers, olives and marinara sauce. Simmer for 20 minutes uncovered. Cook *lingue di passeri al dente*, omitting salt from water since cod is salty; drain. Toss with half of the cod and marinara sauce and serve in hot bowls. Spoon remaining sauce and cod on top. Serves 6.

TAGLIARINI CON BACCALÀ
(*Baked Noodles with Dried Cod*)

1 medium-sized dried cod
3 tablespoons olive oil
Liberal amount of milled black pepper
1½ cups heavy cream
1 pound *tagliarini*
3 tablespoons butter

Soak the cod for 24 hours, rinsing and changing the water 6 times. Drain cod, cut into pieces, and boil for 20 minutes. Drain, and remove skin and bones. With mortar and pestle (or a blender) mash cod into a paste, slowly stirring in olive oil and milling in black pepper. Continue to mash and stir until mixture is a smooth creamy paste. (Use olive oil sparingly.) When cod is smooth, whip the heavy cream until it is stiff and blend the fish paste into it. Cook *tagliarini al dente*; no salt is needed; drain. Toss with the cod and whipped cream, blending well. Place in a buttered casserole or baking dish and dot with the butter. Bake in preheated 400° F. oven for 20 minutes, until bubbling and brown. Serves 4 to 6.

FETTUCCE RICCIE COLLE ANGUILLE
(*"Curly Ribbons" with Eel*)

4 small eels
1 garlic clove
2 tablespoons olive oil
3 tablespoons butter
1 white onion, chopped
3 strips of lemon peel
Pinch of dried orégano
Pinch of dried rosemary
1 teaspoon salt
Milled black pepper
6 very ripe tomatoes, peeled and diced
1 cup white wine
1 pound *fettucce riccie*

Have your fishman clean the eels and remove the skins. Cut them into 1-inch pieces and wash well in cold water. Drain on paper towels. Sauté garlic in oil and butter, mashing it and swishing it around in pan until brown; remove and discard garlic. Add eel pieces and brown. Stir in onion, lemon strips, orégano and rosemary, salt and pepper, and tomatoes. Simmer for 20 minutes, breaking up tomatoes with a wooden spoon as they cook. Stir in wine; cook until sauce is thickened and most of the moisture evaporated. Discard lemon strips. Cook *fettucce riccie al dente;* drain. Toss with half of the eels and sauce. Serve in hot bowls and spoon the remaining eel and sauce over the top. Serves 4 to 6.

BAVETTINE CON INVOLTINI DI PASSERINO
(Bavettine with Rolled Flounder)

3 tablespoons lemon juice
6 small flounder fillets
1 teaspoon salt
Milled black pepper
3 tablespoons butter
½ cup clam juice
1 small white onion, minced
¾ cup white Chianti wine
1 tablespoon chopped parsley
2 cups (one 1-pound can) Italian plum tomatoes,
   pushed through food mill
1 pound *bavettine* (very narrow *linguine*)

Sprinkle lemon juice over the fillets; season with salt and pepper; roll and tie fillets so rolls will not open when cooking. Melt butter in a saucepan and add fish rolls. When brown, stir in the clam juice, onion, wine, parsley and tomatoes. Cover the pan and simmer for 20 minutes, turning rolls once carefully to avoid breaking. Remove fish rolls to warm platter; continue to cook sauce, uncovered, until it is thickened and smooth. Cook *bavettine al dente*; drain. Place 2 ounces of *bavettine* in each of 6 warm soup bowls. Untie fish rolls and place one atop each serving of pasta. Put two large spoonfuls of sauce over each serving. Serves 6.

TAGLIATELLE CON SGOMBRO ALLA GENOVESE
(Noodles with Mackerel Genoese Style)

2 tablespoons olive oil
2 tablespoons butter
2 shallots, chopped
3 tablespoons white wine

3 mushrooms, sliced
½ teaspoon salt
Liberal amount of milled black pepper
3 anchovies, diced
½ recipe Basic Tomato Sauce (page 63)
2 fresh mackerel fillets, cut into 2-inch pieces
1 pound *tagliatelle*

Heat oil and butter in a saucepan, stir in the shallots, and simmer until soft. Stir in the wine and mushrooms, the salt, pepper and anchovies. Simmer, uncovered, until anchovies have melted into a sauce. Stir in the tomato sauce, blending well, and simmer, uncovered, for 15 minutes. Place mackerel pieces in another saucepan, pour the tomato sauce over them, and simmer, uncovered, for 15 minutes, until fish is tender. Cook *tagliatelle al dente*, with only 1 tablespoon of salt in the water; drain. Serve in hot soup bowls with the fish-tomato sauce liberally spooned atop. Serves 4 to 6.

SPAGHETTI CON TRIGLIE ED UOVA
(*Spaghetti with Red Mullet and Eggs*)

2 red mullets, filleted
½ teaspoon salt
1½ cups white wine
1 recipe Béchamel Sauce (page 73)
3 hard-cooked eggs, chopped
3 tablespoons chopped parsley
½ tablespoon chopped fresh mint
1 pound spaghetti

Place the fish fillets in a saucepan, sprinkle lightly with salt, and cover with the wine. Simmer for 10 minutes, breaking up the fish as it simmers with a wooden spoon and making sure any bones are removed. Prepare the Béchamel sauce; bring to a simmer. Drain fish and add it to the sauce. Stir in the hard-cooked eggs, parsley and mint. Simmer, uncovered, for 15 minutes. Cook spaghetti *al dente,* drain, and add directly to the sauce in the saucepan. Toss well and serve immediately in hot soup bowls. Serves 4 to 6.

FETTUCCINE CON PESCI PERSICI ALLA FIORENTINA

(Baked Fettuccine with Perch Florentine)

1 recipe Béchamel Sauce (page 73)
12 small fillets of ocean perch
1 teaspoon salt
Milled black pepper
2 cups white wine
3 pounds spinach
1 pound *fettuccine*
4 tablespoons grated Ragusano cheese

Prepare Béchamel sauce and keep it warm. Wash and dry fillets and place them in a saucepan; sprinkle with salt and pepper and cover with wine. Simmer for 15 minutes or less, being careful to keep the fish intact. Cook the spinach in a small amount of salted water, drain well, and chop. Arrange a layer of the spinach in a baking dish. Cook *fettuccine al dente;* drain. Arrange a layer of the noodles atop the spinach. Add a layer of fish, then repeat the layers of spinach, noodles and fish. Pour the warm Béchamel sauce over all; sprinkle liberally with grated Ragusano. Bake in a preheated 400° F. oven for 20 minutes, or until top is bubbly and brown. Serve 2 fillets per person atop a mound of noodles and spinach. Serves 6.

ZITI TAGLIATI CON SALSA DI SARDE
("Short Bridegrooms" with Sardine Sauce)

2 tablespoons butter
2 tablespoons olive oil
2 small white onions, minced
2 fresh basil leaves, minced
4 very ripe tomatoes, peeled and diced
1 pound fresh sardines, cleaned and cut into 2-inch pieces
½ teaspoon salt
Liberal amount of milled black pepper
½ cup clam juice
6 large black olives, sliced
1 tablespoon *pignoli* (pine nuts)
1 pound *ziti tagliati*

Heat butter and oil in a saucepan and add onions, basil and tomatoes. Simmer until onions are soft. Add the sardine pieces, breaking up tomatoes and sardines with a wooden spoon as they cook. Sprinkle in salt and pepper and add the clam juice, a tablespoon at a time, stirring it in well. Simmer, uncovered, until the sauce is smooth and not watery. This should take about 25 minutes. Stir in the olives and the pine nuts; simmer for 10 minutes, uncovered. Cook the *ziti tagliati al dente*, drain, and place in a large hot bowl. Pour in half of the sardine sauce; toss well but gently with wooden forks. Serve in hot soup bowls with the remaining sauce spooned atop. Serves 6.

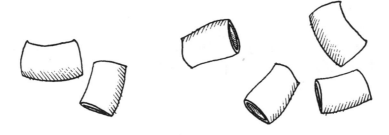

SPAGHETTINI CON FINOCCHI E PICCOLE ARINGHE
(*Spaghettini with Fennel and Smelts*)

> 1 pound fennel
> 3 tablespoons butter
> 2 tablespoons olive oil
> 2 white onions, minced
> 1 pound smelts, cleaned and boned
> 1 tablespoon pine nuts
> 1 tablespoon chopped raisins
> 1 teaspoon salt
> Milled black pepper
> 2 cups water
> 1 pound spaghettini
> ⅓ cup bread crumbs, toasted

Wash and trim the fennel, but do not remove the leaves. Cook it in boiling water for 25 minutes. Drain and mince. Heat the butter and oil and sauté the onions in it until soft. Add the smelts and brown them quickly on both sides. Stir in the minced fennel, pine nuts, raisins, salt, pepper and water. Simmer, uncovered, for 15 minutes, stirring frequently, being careful to keep the fish intact. Cook spaghettini *al dente,* drain, and place in a warm bowl. With wooden forks toss pasta with half of the fennel and fish sauce. Add half of the bread crumbs and toss gently again. Serve in hot soup bowls with remainder of bread crumbs, sauce, and whole smelts spooned atop. Serves 4 to 6.

Note: In Milan, the above sauce is given piquancy by adding 3 chopped drained anchovies and a chopped peeled ripe tomato.

TRIANGOLI CON SOGLIOLA
(*"Triangles" with Sole*)

       2 sole fillets
       2 tablespoons butter
       3 cups Marinara Sauce (page 69)
       1 pound *triangoli*

Cook sole in the butter until about half done. Since this fish has most fragile connective tissues, *undercook*. Remove from the pan and make certain there are no bones in the fish. Carefully break it into small pieces with a wooden spoon and stir it into the hot marinara sauce. Remove from the heat immediately. Cook the *triangoli al dente,* drain, and place in a warm bowl. Pour in the fish and tomato sauce, toss, and serve in warm bowls. Serves 4 to 6.

FETTUCCELLE ALLA VENEZIANA
(*"Little Ribbons" Baked Venetian Style*)

       2 white onions, sliced
       1 cup white wine
       1½ teaspoons salt
       1½ pounds lemon sole fillets, cut into ½-inch cubes
       1 cup light cream
       1 pound *fettuccelle* (narrow *fettuccine*)
       ½ pound shrimps, cooked and shelled
       2 tablespoons grated Asiago cheese
       2 tablespoons grated Romano cheese
       1 tablespoon butter

Simmer onions in the wine with 1 teaspoon of the salt. Stir in 1 pound of the sole pieces; cook for 10 minutes. Place the remaining raw fish in a blender with 2 tablespoons of broth from fish and onion mixture. Mix to a smooth paste. Remove from blender and fold in the cream, stirring well into a smooth mixture. Simmer this over very low heat, just until mixture thickens, then add remaining ½ teaspoon salt and stir until sauce is smooth.

Cook *fettuccelle al dente;* drain. Butter a baking dish. Spread a layer of noodles in the bottom of the dish. Arrange a layer of fish cubes and shrimps atop, then a thin layer of fish paste. Repeat layers until all of noodles, fish, shrimps and fish paste have been used. Mix the the two cheeses and sprinkle the mixture on top; dot with butter. Place under the broiler until sauce bubbles and top browns. Serves 6.

LINGUE DI PASSERI CON DUE PESCI
("Sparrows' Tongues" with Two Fishes)

15 medium black olives, pitted
1 can (7 ounces) tuna
1 can (2 ounces) anchovy fillets, drained
3 cups Mushroom and Cheese Sauce (page 74)
1 pound *lingue di passeri*

Slice the olives. Drain tuna and break up with a fork. Blend olives, tuna, anchovies and mushroom and cheese sauce in a pan. Simmer for 15 minutes. Cook *lingue di passeri al dente;* drain well. Place sauce in a warm bowl and toss in pasta. Serve quickly in warm bowls. Serves 4 to 6.

SPAGHETTI CON TONNO ALLA MARIA LIMONCELLI
(Spaghetti with Tuna alla Maria Limoncelli)

1 medium can (9¼ ounces) white tuna in olive oil
3 tablespoons butter
½ teaspoon chopped chives
1 tablespoon chopped Italian parsley
1 cup heavy cream, hot
½ teaspoon salt
Liberal amount of milled black pepper
1 pound spaghetti

With a fork, break up the tuna in its oil. Melt butter, add tuna, chives and parsley; simmer for 5 minutes. Blend in the cup of cream, add the salt, and mill in black pepper; simmer for 5 minutes. Cook spaghetti *al dente*; drain. Mix with tuna sauce, tossing gently with wooden forks. Serves 4 to 6.

NAPLES—Campania

SPAGHETTINI CON TONNO ED ACCIUGHE
(*Spaghettini with Tuna and Anchovies*)

Most Italians when thinking of pasta with seafood immediately reach for a can of tuna and one of anchovies. They team them in many ways and can whip up a tasty dish in minutes. This is one I had on a Friday in Naples after returning late from the opera. It was ready in 20 minutes.

> 2 tablespoons butter
> 1 can (7 ounces) white tuna in oil
> Liberal amount of milled black pepper
> 1 can (2 ounces) anchovies, drained
> 1 teaspoon capers
> 1 pound spaghettini

Melt the butter in a saucepan and stir in the tuna with its oil, breaking it up into small pieces. Mill in pepper liberally, add anchovies and capers, and simmer for 15 minutes, stirring constantly. Cook spaghettini *al dente*, omitting salt from cooking water. Drain well and toss right in the saucepan with the tuna and anchovies, coating the strands of pasta well; toss gently with wooden forks. Serves 4 to 6.

VERMICELLI CON PISELLI E TONNO
(*Vermicelli with Peas and Tuna*)

> 2 white onions, minced
> 2 tablespoons butter
> 1 can (7 ounces) white tuna in olive oil
> 2 cups (one 1-pound can) tomatoes, pushed through food mill
> 1 teaspoon salt

Milled black pepper
½ pound fresh peas, shelled and half cooked
1 pound *vermicelli*

Sauté onions in the butter until soft. Stir in the tuna with its oil, breaking it into pieces; simmer for 10 minutes. Add the tomatoes, salt and pepper; simmer, uncovered, for 10 minutes. Blend in the peas, stir well, and simmer for 10 minutes more. Cook *vermicelli al dente;* drain. Serve in hot soup bowls with 2 spoonfuls of the sauce over each portion. Serves 4 to 6.

VERMICELLI AL CAVIALE
(*Vermicelli with Caviar*)

I am of the school that believes that the only way to eat the eggs of the Caspian sturgeon, the world's best caviar, is with a slender piece of toast and a spoon, or just with a spoon. I was somewhat shocked therefore when a friend in Rome who had just received a container of fresh caviar from Iran invited me to dinner, and served the caviar as first course—with pasta! Even though it is an ideal mating, I have it only once a year, for my wife still believes that the only thing that goes with caviar is a spoon.

1 pound *vermicelli*
¼ pound butter, soft
4 ounces Beluga caviar
Juice of ½ lemon

Cook *vermicelli al dente.* Have a large hot bowl at hand with the soft butter in it. Lift the pasta directly from its boiling pot into the bowl, draining it over its pot before forking it into the bowl. It must be hot, and it must be *al dente.* Have 4 or 6 *hot* soup bowls ready. Now mix the caviar into the pasta in its bowl, tossing well with wooden forks. Add the lemon juice and toss again. Serve immediately in the hot soup bowls. Serves 4 to 6.

LINGUINE FINE CON VONGOLE ALLA MARIA
(*Maria's Fine Linguine with Clams*)

18 cherrystone clams, in their shells
6 tablespoons olive oil
3 garlic cloves
4 tablespoons chopped Italian parsley
¼ teaspoon crushed red pepper
Much freshly milled black pepper
Pinch of dried sweet basil
1 pound *linguine fine*

Using a stiff brush, scrub the clams well, rinsing them carefully under cold running water. Heat the oil in a pan large enough to hold the 18 clams. Brown the garlic in it, then discard the garlic. Place the clams, parsley, red and black pepper, and basil in the pan. Cover and simmer for 10 minutes. Uncover, tip the clam shells to pour their juice into the pan, and simmer, uncovered for 5 minutes longer. Cook *linguine fine al dente,* drain, and place in a hot bowl. Remove the clams in their shells from the saucepan; pour the liquid from that pan over the *linguine* and toss well, but gently, with wooden forks. Serve in hot soup bowls with 3 clams in their shells atop each serving of pasta. Serves 6.

LINGUINE CON SALSA ROSSA E VONGOLE
(*Linguine with Red Clam Sauce*)

3 small white onions, chopped
1 garlic clove, minced
3 tablespoons olive oil
4 cups (one 2-pound can) Italian plum tomatoes
1 teaspoon salt
Milled black pepper
1 teaspoon crushed red pepper

   1 teaspoon dried orégano
   4 anchovies, chopped
   1 large can (10½ ounces) minced clams
   1 pound *linguine*

Sauté onions and garlic in oil until onions are soft. Put tomatoes through a food mill, and blend into onion-garlic mixture. Simmer for 10 minutes. Add salt, black and red pepper, orégano, and anchovies; cover and simmer for 20 minutes. Add the clams with their juice; stir well, mill in more black pepper, and simmer, uncovered, until sauce thickens. Cook *linguine al dente*, drain, and place in a warm bowl. Pour in half the red clam sauce; toss well, but gently, with wooden forks. Serve in hot rimmed soup bowls with the rest of the sauce spooned over. Serves 4 to 6.

For a recipe for White Clam Sauce, see page 337.

SPAGHETTI CON VONGOLE ED ACCIUGHE

(*Spaghetti with Clams and Anchovies*)

   2 white onions, chopped
   2 tablespoons olive oil
  30 shucked cherrystone clams and liquid
   6 anchovy fillets, drained
  10 ripe tomatoes, peeled and chopped
   2 small green peppers, chopped
   1 garlic clove, minced
   1 pound spaghetti

Sauté onions in the oil until soft. Add clam liquid and the anchovies; simmer for 8 minutes. Stir in tomatoes, green peppers, and garlic; cook for 30 minutes, until about half the moisture has evaporated. Add clams, cook 5 minutes. Cook spaghetti *al dente,* drain, and place in a warm bowl. Pour the clam sauce over the spaghetti and toss. Serve in hot bowls. Serves 4 to 6.

SPAGHETTI CON VONGOLE ED OSTRICHE
(*Spaghetti with Clams and Oysters*)

This dish was whipped up for me in Copenhagen by an SAS pilot who had spent much time in Rome. He had it ready before we finished our first drink.

> 2 garlic cloves
> 3 tablespoons olive oil
> ¼ teaspoon crushed red pepper
> 1 tablespoon minced fresh parsley
> 1 can (7½ ounces) clams, minced
> 1 can (11 ounces) oysters, minced
> 1 pound spaghetti

Sauté the garlic in the oil until brown. Discard garlic, and stir in red pepper, parsley, and the clams with their juice. Simmer, uncovered, for 5 minutes, stirring often. Add the oysters with one third of their juice; simmer for 5 minutes. Cook spaghetti *al dente*, drain, and place in a large hot bowl. Pour the clam-oyster sauce over pasta, toss well, and serve immediately. Serves 4 to 6.

CAPELLINI CON OSTRICHE
(*Baked Fine Vermicelli with Oysters*)

> 2 dozen fresh oysters, shucked, with their liquid
> ½ pound *capellini*
> 6 tablespoons butter, in all
> ½ cup dry bread crumbs
> ½ cup grated Parmesan cheese
> ¼ cup flour
> 2⅓ teaspoons salt, in all
> ⅜ teaspoon pepper, in all

1 tablespoon Worcestershire sauce
2 cups milk
⅓ cup Marsala wine
Dash of paprika

Drain oysters, reserving ½ cup of the liquid. Cook *capellini* less than *al dente;* watch closely as they cook quickly. Drain, and place in the bottom of a buttered casserole. Blend 4 tablespoons of the butter with the bread crumbs and cheese. Melt remaining butter, add flour, 2 teaspoons of the salt, ¼ teaspoon of the pepper, and the Worcestershire, slowly stir in reserved oyster liquid and the milk. Simmer until sauce is smooth (about 8 minutes), stirring often, then blend in the Marsala. Now arrange the oysters on the *capellini.* Sprinkle in ⅓ teaspoon of salt, ⅛ teaspoon of pepper, and the paprika. Pour the sauce over all, and spread the buttered bread crumbs and cheese on top. Bake, uncovered, at 400° F. for 30 minutes. Serves 4 to 6.

SPAGHETTI CON COZZE
(*Spaghetti with Mussels*)

3 quarts mussels
1 garlic clove
3 tablespoons olive oil
4 cups (one 2-pound can) Italian plum tomatoes
½ teaspoon dried marjoram
1 teaspoon salt
Milled black pepper
1 pound spaghetti

Scrub mussels well, rinsing several times under cold water. Place them in a large pot with 1 cup hot water, cover the pot, and steam until the mussels are opened. Lift out the mussels and set aside. Strain their liquid into a bowl. Reserve 12 mussels in their shells. Remove the rest from the shells and add to the strained liquid.

Sauté garlic in the oil until soft. Add tomatoes, breaking them up with a wooden spoon as they cook. Add marjoram, salt and pepper, and simmer, covered, for 20 minutes. Add the shelled mussels and the strained liquid and simmer for another 10 minutes, stirring often until sauce thickens. Cook spaghetti *al dente,* drain, and place in a warm bowl. Pour half of the mussel sauce over the spaghetti and toss. Serve in hot rimmed soup bowls, with another spoon of sauce over each serving and 2 open mussels in their shells atop. Serves 4 to 6.

VERMICELLI CON COZZE ED UOVA
(*Vermicelli with Mussels and Eggs*)

2 dozen mussels
1 tablespoon salt
2 tablespoons butter
2 tablespoons olive oil
2 small white onions, minced
1 tablespoon minced parsley
½ teaspoon salt
Liberal amount of milled black pepper
Juice of 1 lemon
3 eggs, beaten
1 pound *vermicelli*

Scrub the mussels well; cover with cold water, add the tablespoon of salt, and soak for 4 hours. This will open the mussels and get rid of most of the sandy residue that shellfish of this kind usually have. In a saucepan, heat butter and oil. Stir in onions, parsley, ½ teaspoon salt and some pepper, and simmer until onions are soft. Add the opened mussels in their shells; cover pan and simmer for 10 minutes. Stir in the lemon juice and the beaten eggs, blending everything well. Simmer, uncovered, for 5 minutes. Cook *vermicelli al dente;* drain. Serve in hot soup bowls with the mussels in their sauce spooned atop. Serves 4 to 6.

PALERMO—Sicily

LINGUINE CON ARAGOSTA ROSSA ALLA GIOVANNINO
(Linguine with Red Lobster Sauce)

1½ cups Red Lobster Sauce (page 77)
½ pound *linguine*
4 live lobsters (1 pound each)
Melted butter

Make the red lobster sauce. Cook *linguine al dente,* drain, and place in hot soup bowls. Spoon liberal amounts of sauce over each portion and place a piece of lobster from the sauce atop the *linguine* in each bowl. Follow with an entrée of boiled or broiled lobsters served with melted butter. Serves 4.

SPAGHETTINI CON CARNE DI GRANCHIO
(Spaghettini with Crabmeat)

½ cup chopped onions
1 celery rib, chopped
1 garlic clove, minced
1 teaspoon chopped parsley
¼ cup olive oil
1 cup drained canned Italian plum tomatoes
2 cups Basic Tomato Sauce (page 63)
1 cup water
Milled black pepper
1 teaspoon salt
½ teaspoon paprika
1 pound fresh or frozen crabmeat
¼ cup sherry
1 pound spaghettini

Sauté onions, celery, garlic and parsley in the oil until soft. Add tomatoes, tomato sauce, water and seasonings; simmer for 1 hour. Add crabmeat and wine, stir well, and cook over low heat for 10 minutes. Cook spaghettini *al dente,* drain, add to sauce, and toss. Serve in hot soup bowls. Serves 4 to 6.

LINGUINE ED ARAGOSTA BIANCA
(*Linguine and White Lobster*)

        ¼ pound butter
        1 tablespoon olive oil
        1 garlic clove, minced
        2 small white onions, chopped
        1 large carrot, chopped
        1 tablespoon chopped parsley
        Pinch of crushed red pepper
        2 live lobsters (1 pound each)
        1 tablespoon salt
        Milled black pepper
        1 pound *linguine*

Heat the butter and oil and in it sauté the garlic, onions, carrot, parsley and red pepper until onions are soft. Cook the lobsters in boiling water with 1 tablespoon of salt in a 10-quart pot. Remove immediately when they turn red. When cool, remove the meat from the shells and dice. Return the shells to the pot and boil the liquid, uncovered, for 40 minutes. Strain this broth and set aside. Add the lobster meat to the vegetables and butter, stir in 1 cup of the strained lobster broth, and add pepper. Simmer for 20 minutes, uncovered.

Cook *linguine al dente* in the strained lobster broth; drain. Place in a large hot bowl; pour half of the diced lobster and vegetable sauce over and toss gently. Serve in hot soup bowls with the remaining lobster and vegetable sauce spooned atop. Serves 4 to 6.

SPAGHETTINI CON SALSA BESCIAMELLA E GAMBERI
(Spaghettini with Béchamel Sauce and Shrimps)

1 recipe Béchamel Sauce (page 73)
4 ounces dried mushrooms
2 dozen shrimps, shelled and chopped
1 pound spaghettini

Prepare the Béchamel sauce and bring to a simmer. Soak the mushrooms in cold water for about 15 minutes; drain. Add the shrimps and mushrooms to the sauce and simmer for 15 minutes, uncovered. Cook spaghettini *al dente*, drain, and place in a hot bowl. Pour half of the sauce mixture over the spaghettini and toss well with wooden forks. Serve in hot soup bowls with the remaining sauce spooned atop. Serves 4 to 6.

LINGUINE FINE ALLA MARINARA
(Fine Linguine with Fresh Tomato Sauce and Shrimp)

3 white onions, chopped
2 garlic cloves, minced
3 tablespoons olive oil
8 large ripe tomatoes
3 teaspoons salt
1 teaspoon sugar
1 cup white wine
1 pound raw shrimps, shelled
2 tablespoons chopped parsley
1 pound *linguine fine*

Cook onions and garlic in oil until soft. Peel tomatoes, cut into pieces, and add to onions and garlic together with salt and sugar. Simmer for 25 minutes. Bring wine to a boil; drop in the shrimps and simmer for 3 minutes. Add wine and shrimps to the tomato sauce. Stir in parsley and cook for 5 minutes. Cook *linguine al dente,* drain, and place in a warm bowl. Pour half of the sauce over and toss lightly. Serve in individual bowls with some of remaining sauce and several shrimps atop each serving. Serves 4 to 6.

RICCIOLINI CON GAMBERI E PETTINI
(*"Little Curls" with Shrimps and Scallops*)

2 garlic cloves
2 tablespoons butter
2 tablespoons olive oil
½ pound shrimps, shelled and cleaned
½ pound bay scallops
1 tablespoon chopped parsley
3 fresh basil leaves, chopped
1 teaspoon salt
Milled black pepper
4 cups (one 2-pound can) Italian plum tomatoes, pushed through food mill
1 pound *ricciolini*

Sauté garlic in butter and oil until brown; discard garlic and add shrimps and scallops, parsley, basil, salt and pepper. Simmer for 5 minutes. Add the tomatoes and stir in well; simmer, uncovered, until sauce thickens and shrimps and scallops are tender but not overdone. Cook *ricciolini al dente;* drain. Place in a hot bowl and toss well with half of the sauce; spoon remainder atop individual portions, and put equal shares of shrimps and of scallops atop each serving. Serves 4 to 6.

SPAGHETTINI E CROSTACEI ALLO SPIEDINO
(Spaghettini and Skewered Shellfish)

This is a dish designed to give color and dash to a serving of pasta.

>6 lobster tails
>½ pound shrimps
>½ pound scallops
>¾ cup Marsala wine
>2 tablespoons olive oil
>½ teaspoon ground ginger
>½ teaspoon salt
>1 garlic clove, minced
>¼ cup soy sauce
>1 pound spaghettini
>2 tablespoons butter

Boil lobster tails and shrimps until tender; take from shells. Put lobster, shrimps and raw scallops in a bowl. Make a mixture of the wine, oil, ginger, salt and garlic. Pour it over the seafood, tossing well to make sure seafood is then well covered. Let the mixture marinate for 1 hour. Cut each lobster tail into 3 pieces. Divide the seafood into 6 portions and thread the pieces on 6 individual skewers. Brush with soy sauce and broil, turning skewers until seafood is browned on all sides and scallops are tender. Cook spaghettini *al dente,* drain, and toss with the butter. Serve pasta in hot individual bowls, with one skewer of seafood atop each serving. Serves 6.

LINGUINE TUTTO MARE
(*Linguine All Sea*)

> 8 tablespoons olive oil
> 2 garlic cloves
> 4 cups (one 2-pound can) Italian plum tomatoes
> 1 tablespoon chopped Italian parsley
> Pinch of dried rosemary
> ½ teaspoon capers
> 1 teaspoon salt
> Milled black pepper
> 6 littleneck clams, scrubbed
> 6 mussels, scrubbed
> 12 shrimps, shelled and deveined
> 6 *calamari* (small squid), cleaned and diced
> 1 pound *linguine*

Heat 6 tablespoons of the olive oil in a saucepan, add garlic, and sauté until light brown. Remove garlic and discard. Add the tomatoes, breaking them up with a wooden spoon as they simmer, the parsley, rosemary, capers, salt and pepper. Simmer, uncovered, for 40 minutes. Place the remaining oil in another large pan; add the clams and mussels and cook over very low heat until shells open. Take meat from shells and add clams, mussels and all their juices to the tomato sauce. Stir in the shrimps and the *calamari* and simmer, uncovered, for 15 minutes. Cook *linguine al dente* and drain. Toss with half of the seafood sauce and spoon the remainder over individual portions before they are served. Serves 6.

CONCHIGLIE (SCUNGILLI) ALLA MARINARA
(Linguine and Conch with Tomato Sauce)

> 1 small can (10 ounces) *conchiglie* (conch)
> 2 tablespoons olive oil
> 1 garlic clove
> 2 cups (one 1-pound can) Italian plum tomatoes
> 1 teaspoon dried sweet basil
> ¼ teaspoon crushed red pepper
> 1 pound *linguine*

Rinse the *conchiglie* three times, once in hot water, twice in cold, then drain and dice it. Heat the oil, add the garlic and diced conch, and sauté for 5 minutes. Remove and discard garlic. When conch bits are browned, stir in the tomatoes, breaking them up with a wooden spoon as they cook. When the sauce is smooth, stir in basil and red pepper. Simmer for 15 minutes, until conch is tender and sauce is no longer watery. Cook *linguine al dente*; drain. Serve the pasta in hot soup bowls with the *conchiglie* sauce over each serving. Serves 4 to 6.

LINGUINE E CALAMARETTI AL BURRO
(Linguine with Tiny Squid and Butter)

This is a dish I have often had in restaurants along the Adriatic coast. Calamaretti are tiny inkfish, a species of squid. About the size of a five-cent piece, they are nut-sweet and delicious.

> 1 tablespoon olive oil
> ¼ pound butter
> 2 dozen whole *calamaretti* (tiny squid)
> ½ teaspoon salt
> Milled black pepper
> 1 pound *linguine*

Heat the oil and butter in a saucepan. Add the *calamaretti,* sprinkle with the salt, and liberally mill pepper over them. Sauté, uncovered, for 15 minutes until the tiny squid are tender. Cook *linguine al dente,* drain, and place in a hot bowl. Pour squid with their liquid over the pasta; toss well but gently with wooden forks. Serve immediately in hot soup bowls. Serves 4 to 6.

Note: This is often varied with an addition of shrimps or *scampi,* sometimes with a dozen tiny whole fish, too.

SPAGHETTINI COI CALAMARI
(*Spaghettini with Baby Squid*)

This Italian dish is usually served before baked eel with bay leaf, on Christmas Eve. The small calamari *are used, and there is quite a difference between squid and octopus in the Italian culinary repertoire. The octopi, always larger and tougher, actually need a beating before they are cooked to make them tender.* Calamari *are naturally tender and sweet flavored.*

> 12 fresh *calamari* (baby squid)
> 3 tablespoons olive oil
> 1 garlic clove, cut into 3 pieces
> 4 cups (one 2-pound can) Italian plum tomatoes
> ¼ teaspoon crushed red pepper
> 1 pound spaghettini

Clean the *calamari,* removing the bones, which lift out like pieces of plastic. Split down the center, wash away the gelatinous matter, and rinse well. Then cut into pieces straight across, as you would slice a loaf of bread. Heat the oil and sauté the squid and garlic in it until the squid pieces curl into circles. Add the tomatoes, breaking them up with a wooden spoon as they simmer. Stir in red pepper; simmer, uncovered, for 15 minutes, until sauce thickens and pieces of *calamari* become fork-tender. Cook spaghettini *al dente;* drain well; serve in hot soup bowls with *calamari* sauce spooned liberally over each portion. Serves 4 to 6.

Chapter VII

CHÂTEAU DE FENIS—Valle d'Aosta

Meats with PASTA

When I think of pasta with meat, I remember an evening several years ago when I called to invite a friend for supper. "Come over and have a dish of pasta and a glass or two of wine," I said.

"Pasta," he said.

Not wanting to get involved, I said, "Yes, you know, spaghetti?"

"And meatballs?"

I told him yes, meatballs, too, if he wanted, and he said he loved that dish. Whenever he thought of spaghetti, he thought of spaghetti and meatballs. "Like liver and bacon," he said, "Elizabeth Tayor and Richard Burton. They go together."

In America they do, so much so that they are a cliché. But in Italy, except possibly in some poorer homes and in Americanized restaurants, spaghetti and meatballs is an almost unknown combination. I have never seen it on a good restaurant menu, never had it in an Italian home, and never served it myself.

For this supper I had an inspiration. The meal took a little longer than I had originally planned. I had been thinking of a simple dish of *fettuccine* with cheese and cream, to be followed with broiled chicken and salad of hearts of Bibb lettuce with lemon and oil. But sometimes it is satisfying to make a point with a meal.

We had our dish of spaghetti first, two ounces each, topped with a light tomato sauce. My friend ate his quickly, then as he sat waiting, he said, "Is that it?"

"Yes, the first course."

Next I brought a meatball the size of a cantaloupe, my mother-in-law's, Maria Limoncelli's, recipe. With it I served fresh string beans and the Bibb lettuce and passed a boat of sauce for the meat, the same that had topped the pasta. As I sliced the big ball at the table, its aroma sailing around the room, my friend said, 'That spaghetti certainly has stoked up my appetite. I'm going to do honor to your midget meatball."

He did indeed, and the giant ball was a subject of conversation for some time after that. He never referred to "spaghetti and meatballs" again without chuckling. That was a small victory, made sweet by the fact, as further dinners proved (twice in restaurants, when my friend ordered a small dish of pasta to start and followed with a meat course), that I had made a convert. Pasta had a new devotee.

The recipe follows:

SPAGHETTINI E POLPETTONE
(*Spaghettini and Meatball*)

    2 white onions, chopped
    4 tablespoons olive oil
    3 pounds beef chuck, freshly ground

3 whole eggs, beaten
2 cups bread crumbs
2 tablespoons chopped fresh parsley
1 cup freshly grated Asiago cheese
1 tablespoon minced raisins
2 teaspoons salt
Liberal amount of milled black pepper
1 recipe Basic Tomato Sauce (page 63)
1½ pounds spaghettini

Cook the onions in 1 tablespoon of the oil until they are soft and yellow but not brown or burned. Place another spoon of oil on a pastry board, put all of the meat on it, and work it with the hands until the meat is soft and malleable. Then add the beaten eggs, bread crumbs, parsley and half of the cheese, working them all in well. Now add the cooked onions, the raisins, and salt, and mill in pepper liberally. Knead everything into the meat, forming it into a large solid ball and patting it into shape.

Pour the remaining 2 tablespoons of oil into a large pot, one that can go into the oven. On top of the stove over a low fire, brown the big ball of meat, turning it as it becomes crisp so that all areas of the surface are brown and firm. Heat the tomato sauce and pour over the meatball. Cover the pot and bake in a 350° F. oven until the meat is cooked through; every 10 minutes spoon more sauce liberally over it, basting it as it cooks. Time should be about 1 hour.

Place meatball on a warm serving platter. Cook the spaghettini *al dente*, drain, and serve in individual hot soup bowls. Spoon some of the sauce that simmered with the meat over each serving. Serve remaining cheese at table with the pasta. Follow with the whole meatball on its platter and carve at the table. Serve remaining sauce in a sauceboat with the meat. Serves 6.

SPAGHETTI ALLA BOLOGNESE

A classic dish. This should be done for company at least every other month, to keep your hand in for making the sauce and taste buds in trim. In my opinion, it is the best of all meat sauces and has been the means of con-verting many a gourmet who pooh-poohs pasta as an insignificant food. The last convert I made was a French chef, a duck-shooting companion who placed Italian cookery on the same plane with American—which can be pretty low. He ate so much of the pasta in this sauce, demanding second helpings, that the entrée of fillet of beef was left for another day.

    3 cups Bolognese Sauce (page 71)
    2 tablespoons butter
    ¼ pound Romano cheese, grated
    ¼ pound Parmesan cheese, grated
    1 pound spaghetti

Prepare the Bolognese sauce and simmer, uncovered. Mix the butter and half of the cheese and place in a large hot bowl. Cook spaghetti *al dente*, drain, and place in the bowl. Toss well but gently with butter and cheese, making certain each strand is coated. Serve in hot soup bowls with Bolognese sauce liberally spooned atop each serving. Pass remaining cheese at table. Serves 6.

BUCATINI CON SALSA DI MANZO
(*Bucatini with Beef Sauce*)

I have had this simple and classic dish in several homes in Rome and was lucky enough to get the recipe from one of my hostesses.

    ½ recipe Beef Sauce (page 70)
    1 pound *bucatini* (small macaroni)

4 tablespoons butter, melted
½ cup grated Asiago cheese
Milled black pepper

Prepare the beef sauce. Cook the *bucatini al dente,* drain, and place in a hot bowl with the melted butter. Toss well with wooden forks. Mix the grated Asiago with liberal amounts of milled black pepper. Add to the pasta and toss again, gently. Serve in hot soup bowls with a large spoonful of the beef sauce atop each serving. Serves 4 to 6.

FETTUCCELLE CON BISTECCA ALLA PIZZAIOLA
("Little Ribbons" with Steak and Pizzaiola Sauce)

4 tablespoons olive oil
2 garlic cloves
4 cups (one 2-pound can) Italian plum tomatoes, pushed through food mill
1 teaspoon salt
Liberal amount of milled black pepper
1 tablespoon chopped Italian parsley
¼ teaspoon dried orégano
1 pound prime sirloin steak
1 pound *fettuccelle* (narrow *fettuccine*)

Heat 2 tablespoons of the oil; sauté garlic until brown; discard garlic. Stir in tomatoes, salt, pepper, parsley and orégano; simmer, uncovered, stirring often, for 20 minutes, or until sauce has thickened Slice the steak into thin bite-sized pieces. In another saucepan heat the remaining olive oil and add the steak pieces. Sauté for 5 minutes, turning once. Pieces of steak should be pink and tender. When tomato sauce is sufficiently thickened, stir in the steak slices. Remove sauce from fire. Cook *fettuccelle al dente;* drain. Serve immediately in hot soup bowls with the sauce and steak slices generously spooned atop each portion. Serves 6.

LINGUINE CON BISTECCA TRITATA ALLA GIOVANNINO
(*Linguine and Chopped Beef alla Giovannino*)

> 2½ pounds beef sirloin, chopped
> ½ pound ripe Gorgonzola cheese
> 1 teaspoon salt
> 5 tablespoons butter, in all
> ½ pound *linguine*

Make 5 meat patties 2½ inches thick. In the center of each bury a 1½-inch cube of Gorgonzola cheese, centering it and molding the meat well around it so the cheese is completely covered. Sprinkle lightly with salt. Cook the patties in a frypan with 2 tablespoons of the butter, in the French style, sautéing, turning often, until they are browned outside but the meat inside is pink and the cheese melted. This takes about 20 minutes. Remove 4 of the patties to a warm plate; crumble the one remaining in pan, stirring the meat well into the browned butter in the pan, adding another 2 tablespoons of butter as you stir.

Cook *linguine* in rapidly boiling salted water until *al dente,* drain, and toss with remaining tablespoon of butter. Then toss with half of the meat mixture, spooning what is remaining over individual servings. Follow with the sirloin-cheese patties, with fresh broccoli and a romaine salad. Serves 4.

BAVETTINE ALLA CARNACINA GIOVANNINO
(*Giovannino's Bavettine with Meat*)

Since I like to cook on a chafing dish right in the dining room where I can talk with my guests, I dreamed up this recipe one night when I had an extra fillet of beef and a few slices of prosciutto in the refrigerator. This is one of the pleasures of pasta—it blends happily with almost everything and gives free rein to the imagination.

> 1 beef fillet (¾ pound), uncooked
> 4 thin slices of prosciutto
> 5 tablespoons butter
> 4 shallots, chopped
> 1 garlic clove, minced
> 6 medium mushrooms, thinly sliced
> 1 pound *bavettine* (very narrow *linguine*)
> 1 cup dry white wine
> ⅓ cup grated Asiago cheese
> 2 tablespoons chopped Italian parsley

Between drinks and conversation, chop the beef and the prosciutto on a board until very fine. Melt the butter in a copper chafing dish over high flame. Sauté the shallots and garlic in the butter until they are soft. Stir in the mushrooms and the chopped beef and prosciutto. Cook for just under 10 minutes, stirring constantly. Cook *bavettine* only until chewy, just over half done; drain. Lower the flame under the chafing dish, stir in the wine, and blend well with the meat sauce. Add the underdone pasta, toss gently but well, and sprinkle in the cheese. Cook 3 minutes. Put out the flame, toss again, and sprinkle in the parsley. Serve immediately from the chafing dish. Serves 4 to 6.

LINGUE DI PASSERI ALLA MACELLAIO
("Sparrows' Tongues" Butcher's Style)

> 4 tablespoons chopped prosciutto fat (only the fat)
> 1 garlic clove, peeled and cut into quarters
> 2 tablespoons olive oil
> ½ pound beef chuck, ground

½ teaspoon salt
Liberal amount of milled black pepper
2 cups (one 1-pound can) Italian plum tomatoes
1 pound *lingue di passeri*
2 tablespoons butter

Cook prosciutto fat and garlic in the oil in a frypan until crisp. Add the ground beef and salt and pepper, mixing well together. Cook until beef is done but not overdone, on the pink side. Put the tomatoes through food mill; stir the purée into the meat mixture, blending well. Mill in more black pepper, stir, and cook until most of the water has evaporated from the tomatoes. Cook *lingue di passeri al dente;* drain. Toss in the butter, then two spoonfuls of the meat combination. Serve in individual hot bowls, with another spoonful of meat sauce on top of each portion. Serves 4 to 6.

MOSTACCIOLI CON MANZO E MELANZANE
("Small Moustaches" with Beef and Eggplant)

Here is an old-fashioned Italian "Sunday special" right out of Campobasso.

8 tablespoons olive oil, in all
4 slices of prosciutto, minced
2 white onions, chopped
2-pound piece of top round of beef
1 cup white wine
2½ pounds tomatoes, peeled and diced
1¼ teaspoons salt, in all
Milled black pepper
2 tablespoons butter
5 mushrooms, sliced
3 chicken livers, chopped
1 pound *mostaccioli*
1 eggplant (1½ pounds), cut in small strips
¼ cup grated Parmesan cheese

Heat 2 tablespoons of the oil in a large deep saucepan; stir in the prosciutto and onions and sauté until soft. Add the beef round and brown over high flame; lower heat, add the wine and cook, uncovered, stirring and turning the meat until the wine has evaporated. Stir in the tomatoes and season with 1 teaspoon salt and some pepper. Cover the pan and simmer, stirring often and frequently basting the meat, for 2 hours, or until meat is tender.

In another large saucepan, sauté in the butter the mushrooms and livers for 5 minutes; sprinkle with ¼ teaspoon salt, stir, and keep warm. Pour the sauce from the beef pot through a sieve; dice the beef; add beef and sauce to livers and mushrooms; blend well. Cook the *mostaccioli al dente*, drain, and place in a hot bowl. Sauté the eggplant strips in remaining olive oil until tender and lightly browned. Sprinkle Parmesan on the pasta; toss. Add half of the sauce and toss again well but gently. Serve in hot soup bowls, with strips of eggplant atop each serving. Pass extra sauce and grated cheese at table. Serves 6.

FUSILLI CON FEGATO DI MANZO
("Twists" with Beef Liver)

In Rome beef liver may be used instead of calf's liver. Some believe that it has more flavor. I agree—if the liver is prepared their way; it must be sliced thin and cooked quickly.

5 tablespoons butter
1 tablespoon olive oil
10 mushrooms, chopped fine
1 white onion, minced
1 carrot, minced
1 celery rib, minced
½ cup Marsala wine
1 cup Beef Broth (page 85)
1 pound beef liver, cut into slices ¼ inch thick

1 teaspoon salt
Liberal amount of milled black pepper
1 pound *fusilli*
¾ cup grated Asiago cheese

Melt 4 tablespoons of the butter, add the oil, and in it sauté mushrooms, onion, carrot and celery until onion is soft. Add wine and simmer until it has evaporated. Stir in beef broth and simmer. Dice liver, season with salt and pepper, and put in another saucepan with 1 tablespoon of butter. Cook for 1 minute, turn the pieces, and cook for another minute. Liver should be pink. Add to the vegetable sauce and blend well. Remove from heat. Cook *fusilli al dente;* drain. Place in a large hot bowl, pour the liver sauce over pasta, and toss well. Serve immediately in hot rimmed soup bowls. Pass cheese at table. Serves 6.

SPAGHETTINI CON DADINI DI VITELLO
(*Spaghettini with Little Veal Cubes*)

2 tablespoons olive oil
2 tablespoons butter
2 white onions, chopped
1 pound veal steak, cubed
1½ tablespoons flour
1 teaspoon salt
Milled black pepper
Pinch of dried orégano
1 cup Chicken Broth (page 84)
Juice of ½ lemon
¼ cup grated Parmesan cheese
1 pound spaghettini

Heat oil and butter and sauté onions in it until soft. Roll the veal cubes in flour and season with salt, pepper and orégano; brown in the oil and butter.

Stir in the chicken broth and simmer, uncovered, for 10 minutes. Remove from fire and stir in the lemon juice. Place the mixture in a baking dish, sprinkle with a little of the cheese, and cover. Cook in a preheated 400° F. oven for 20 minutes, or until sauce is thickened and veal fork-tender. Cook spaghettini *al dente,* drain, and place in a hot bowl. Toss with the remaining cheese, then with half of the veal mixture. Spoon the rest of the veal sauce atop individual portions served in hot soup bowls. Serves 4 to 6.

MACCHERONI ALLA BOLOGNESE

This recipe comes from a housewife in the Po Valley and is a specialty of her family, handed down from her grandmother. In that region they use macaroni a bit larger than medium, called "horse's teeth." Anything from ziti to elbow macaroni will do.

5 tablespoons butter
1 tablespoon olive oil
2 small white onions, chopped
2 small carrots, chopped
1 celery rib, chopped
½ pound veal rump, ground twice
2 ounces dried beef, minced
Pinch of flour
Milled black pepper
2 cups Beef Broth (page 85)
2 chicken livers, chopped
1 pound macaroni
¼ cup grated Parmesan cheese
1 white truffle, thinly sliced
½ cup heavy cream, warmed

Sauté in the butter and oil the onions, carrots and celery until soft. Stir in the veal and beef and sauté until veal is brown; add the flour, pepper and broth, blending well. Simmer, uncovered, stirring often, for 20 minutes. Add the chicken livers and simmer for 5 minutes, stirring in well. Cook macaroni *al dente* without salt, for dried beef is salty; drain, place in a large warm bowl, stir in the sauce and toss well. Add the cheese, half of the truffle and all of the cream; toss again. Serve immediately in hot bowls with the remaining truffle atop; pass more grated cheese at table. Serves 4 to 6.

SPAGHETTI CON ROGNONI DI VITELLO
(Spaghetti with Veal Kidneys)

> 2 garlic cloves, mashed
> ¼ pound butter
> 2 pounds veal kidneys, cleaned, cored, and sliced thin
> 2 tablespoons flour
> 1½ teaspoons salt
> Liberal amount of milled black pepper
> 6 anchovy fillets, drained and minced
> Juice of ½ lemon
> ½ teaspoon dried tarragon or chopped fresh tarragon
> 1 tablespoon chopped parsley
> 1 pound spaghetti

Sauté garlic in butter until brown; discard garlic. Dust kidneys lightly with flour, sprinkle with salt and pepper, and sauté in the butter for 30 seconds on each side. Stir in the anchovies; add the lemon juice, tarragon and parsley; blend. Simmer for 5 minutes, breaking up the anchovies. Cook spaghetti *al dente;* drain. Place in a large hot bowl, pour the kidney sauce over, and toss well. Serve immediately in hot rimmed soup bowls. Serves 6.

PIACENZA, *the Piazza Cavalli—Emilia-Romagna*

RIGATONI CON FEGATO DI VITELLO
(*Rigatoni with Calf's Liver*)

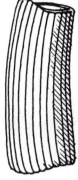

½ pound calf's liver
12 medium mushrooms, cleaned and peeled
2 tablespoons butter
1 tablespoon olive oil
1 teaspoon salt
Liberal amount of milled black pepper
½ cup white Chianti
1 pound *rigatoni* (grooved pasta tubes)
¼ cup grated Asiago cheese

Put liver and mushrooms through food chopper, or mince with a sharp knife. Sauté for 5 minutes in the butter and oil, stirring often; season with salt and pepper. Blend in wine and simmer for 8 minutes. Cook *rigatoni al dente*; drain. Place in a large hot bowl, pour the liver sauce over, and toss, mixing well. Serve immediately in hot bowls with Asiago sprinkled atop. Serves 6.

SPAGHETTINI CON ANIMELLE DI VITELLO E PISELLI
(*Spaghettini with Veal Sweetbreads and Peas*)

4 small veal sweetbreads
2 tablespoons butter
2 tablespoons olive oil
1 teaspoon salt
Liberal amount of milled black pepper
3 tablespoons fresh peas
1 pound spaghettini

Parboil sweetbreads in rapidly boiling water for 5 minutes; remove and plunge into cold water. When cool, remove the skins and membranes and cut into pieces the size of a fingernail. Sauté them in butter and oil, sprinkled with salt and pepper, for 15 minutes. Cook peas *al dente,* drain, and add to the sweetbreads; simmer for 10 minutes. Cook spaghettini *al dente,* drain, and place right in the saucepan with the sweetbreads and peas. Toss well and serve in hot bowls. Serves 4 to 6.

TAGLIATELLE CON TRIPPA ALLA ROMANA
(Noodles with Tripe Roman Style)

> 3 pounds fresh white veal honeycomb tripe
> 2 tablespoons chopped salt pork
> 3 tablespoons olive oil
> 1 lemon, cut into 1-inch slices
> 4 cups (one 2-pound can) Italian plum tomatoes, mashed
> ⅓ teaspoon dried orégano
> 2 bay leaves
> ½ teaspoon salt
> Liberal amount of milled black pepper
> ¼ teaspoon dried red pepper
> 3 tablespoons fresh peas, half cooked
> 1 pound *tagliatelle*

Wash tripe thoroughly in several waters; boil for about 3 hours in 4 quarts of salted water, covered, until tender, pouring off water twice during the boiling and replacing it with fresh hot water. When cooked, drain and cut into ½- by 2-inch pieces. Sauté salt pork in the oil, add lemon slices, tomatoes, orégano, bay leaves, salt, black pepper, red pepper and drained tripe. Simmer, uncovered, for 30 minutes, until sauce has thickened. Add the peas and simmer for 10 minutes longer. Remove and discard lemon slices and bay leaves. Cook *tagliatelle al dente;* drain. Serve in hot soup bowls with tripe sauce liberally spooned over each portion. Serves 4 to 6.

PERCIATELLI ALLA CARRETTIERE
("Pierced" Pasta Cart Driver's Style)

> 3 tablespoons olive oil
> 1 garlic clove, minced
> 2 white onions, chopped
> 1 small piece of green *peperoncino* (hot pepper), diced finely
> ¼ pound pig's jaw, mostly lean, diced
> ½ teaspoon salt
> 3 large very ripe tomatoes, peeled and diced
> 1 can (3½ ounces) tuna in olive oil, broken into pieces
> 4 mushrooms, sliced
> 4½ tablespoons grated Romano cheese
> 1 pound *perciatelli*

Sauté in oil the garlic, onions and green pepper; add the pig's jaw and sauté until soft. Sprinkle lightly with salt and stir in the tomatoes. Simmer, uncovered, for 25 minutes, until pork is tender and sauce thickened. Add the tuna, mushrooms and ½ tablespoon of the cheese; blend well; simmer for 10 minutes. Cook *perciatelli al dente,* drain, and place in a large hot bowl. Sprinkle in the cheese and half of the sauce; toss well with wooden forks. Serve immediately in hot soup bowls with generous spoonings of remaining sauce atop each portion. Pass more grated cheese at the table. Serves 6.

MAGLIETTE SPACCATE CON DUE CARNI
("Split Links" with Two Meats)

> ½ pound beef, chopped
> ½ pound lean pork, chopped
> 2 garlic cloves, minced
> 2 tablespoons olive oil

179

> 4 cups (one 2-pound can) Italian plum tomatoes,
>   pushed through a food mill
> 1 teaspoon salt
> Freshly milled black pepper
> 1 teaspoon sugar
> 1 teaspoon dried sweet basil
> 1 pound *magliette spaccate*
> 1 tablespoon soft butter
> ¼ cup grated ricotta siciliano cheese

Brown meats and garlic in the oil; stir in tomatoes, and add salt, pepper, sugar and basil. Simmer sauce for 1 hour, uncovered, stirring often with a wooden spoon. Cook *magliette spaccate al dente*, drain, and toss with butter and cheese. Pour in half of the sauce and toss again. Serve in hot bowls with generous spoonful of remaining sauce atop each serving. Pass more grated cheese at the table. Serves 4 to 6.

FARFALLONI ALLA FRANCESCO
("Big Butterflies" Francesco)

This is a memorable dish cooked by a chef named Francesco in a little res-taurant at San Remo. It overlooked a famous five-acre carnation garden that flowed like a red tide toward the sea, the perfume from the flowers so sweet and strong that I can never forget them—nor the dish.

> 6 tablespoons butter, in all
> 1 tablespoon olive oil
> 4 shallots, chopped
> 2 celery ribs, chopped
> 1 garlic clove, minced
> 6 mushrooms, sliced
> ¼ pound veal, ground twice
> ¼ pound pork, ground twice

    ¼ pound beef, ground twice
    3 pounds fresh tomatoes, peeled and diced
    1 bay leaf
    Pinch of dried orégano
    1 teaspoon salt
    Liberal amount of milled black pepper
    1 pound *farfalloni*
    1 tablespoon chopped Italian parsley
    ¼ pound Parmesan cheese, grated

Heat 4 tablespoons of the butter and the oil in a deep saucepan. Sauté shallots, celery, garlic, mushrooms and the meats until meats are browned. Stir in the tomatoes, bay leaf, orégano, salt and pepper. Simmer, uncovered, stirring often with a wooden spoon, for 35 minutes, or until sauce is thickened and smooth. Cook *farfalloni al dente;* drain. Place in a large hot bowl, add remaining butter, the parsley and half of the cheese; toss well. Serve in large, hot soup bowls with sauce liberally spooned atop each portion. Pass the remaining cheese at table. Serves 6.

PASTA E FAGIOLI ALLA PASQUALE
(*Pasquale's Pasta and Beans*)

    1 pound dried pea beans
    3-pound loin of pork
    2 teaspoons salt
    Milled black pepper
    1 garlic clove
    3 tablespoons olive oil
    2 cups (one 1-pound can) Italian plum tomatoes,
        pushed through a food mill
    2 cups *ditalini* ("little thimbles")

Soak beans in water for 5 hours; drain. Place pork in a large pot with 4 quarts water, cook for 1 hour, then pour off water. Add 4 quarts fresh water, 2 teaspoons salt, a liberal amount of pepper, the garlic and oil. Add the drained beans and puréed tomatoes. Simmer for 40 minutes, or until beans and pork are tender, stirring often, but carefully.

Cook *ditalini al dente,* drain, and add to the bean pot, stirring in well. Simmer, uncovered, for 10 minutes. Slice the pork. Serve beans and pasta in hot soup bowls, with pork slices on top and buttered hot Italian bread on the side. This is a main dish, not a first course. Serves 4 to 6.

LINGUE DI PASSERI CON SALSA D'UOVA
(*"Sparrows' Tongues" and Pork in Egg Sauce*)

> 2 eggs
> 3 tablespoons butter, in all
> 1 tablespoon olive oil
> ½ pound lean pork, ground
> ¼ pound lean salt pork, cubed
> Light pinch of cayenne pepper
> ¼ pound Parmesan cheese, grated
> Rind of ½ lemon, grated
> 1 pound *lingue di passeri*

Take eggs from refrigerator to remove chill. Heat 1 tablespoon of the butter and the oil in a saucepan. Make little fingers of the ground pork, about half the size of your little finger, and sauté with the diced salt pork, turning often until browned. In a large warm bowl beat together the eggs, cayenne pepper, cheese and lemon rind with a whisk until well blended and creamy. Stir in pork fingers and salt pork with their oil and butter. Cook *lingue di passeri al dente.* Fork directly from the boiling pot, draining water from each forkful back into the pot, into the bowl with the eggs and pork. Hot *pasta* should set eggs. Melt remaining butter, and pour hot over the pasta in the egg bowl. Toss all quickly and serve immediately in hot soup bowls. Serves 4 to 6.

182

ROME, *the Arch of Constantine*

BUCATINI ALL'AMATRICIANA

This is a famous dish in Rome, where nearly every good restaurant offers it with pride. It is said to have originated in the Abruzzi region, known for its lusty but simple dishes, although I never found it there. It should be made with the cheek of a young pig, using all of the lean and half of the fat. Often it is made with a small hot red pepper chopped in, but as I had it in Rome, a sweet pepper was substituted, and bacon was used rather than pork cheek.

2 small white onions, chopped
1 sweet red pepper, chopped
¼ pound salt pork, diced
3 tablespoons olive oil
8 slices of bacon, diced
4 cups (one 2-pound can) Italian plum tomatoes
 or, 2 pounds fresh tomatoes, peeled and diced
Liberal amount of milled black pepper
1 pound *bucatini* (thin macaroni)
2 tablespoons butter
½ cup grated Romano cheese

Sauté onions and pepper with salt pork in the oil until pork is nearly crisp but not too hard; stir, add bacon, and cook for 5 minutes. Blend in tomatoes, mill in pepper, and stir. Taste for seasoning. If salt is needed, add to taste, but salt pork and bacon should make it sufficiently salty. Stir well and simmer, uncovered, for 40 minutes. Cook *bucatini al dente*, drain. Place in a bowl with the butter, toss, add the cheese, mill in black pepper, and toss again. Serve pasta in individual hot bowls, with a liberal spooning of the sauce over each portion. Serves 4 to 6.

LINGUINE ALLA CARBONARA

Pasta alla carbonara is a favorite way of serving bacon and eggs in Rome. I had it in that city in a small trattoria, *in 1960, at a luncheon to which I carried the world's largest hangover. The dish, aided by a generous carafe of white Frascati from the nearby hills, brought back life. Since then, with or without hangover, it has been one of my favorite pasta dishes and I have done quite a lot of experimenting with it. There are perhaps a dozen ways to prepare it: the bacon undercooked; the pasta tossed in the frypan with the bacon or with ham; mixed in a bowl, with wine and onion; (and a friend's version, which appears on page 364); but the following I believe is the best— at least for my taste. The name is a difficult one to pin down. Carbonara refers both to a secret society that at one time tried to overthrow the Italian government and to the men who work with coal. To me, however, it is one of the most unusual of the pasta dishes, and I read nothing else into its name except flavor.*

    12 slices of bacon
    4 eggs, beaten
    1 cup grated Parmesan cheese
    3 tablespoons chopped Italian parsley
    Much milled black pepper
    1 pound *linguine*

Cut bacon into pieces the size of a fingernail; fry until crisp, pouring off the grease as it cooks. In a large bowl, combine the eggs, cheese and parsley; mill in plenty of black pepper. Beat with a whisk, or an electric beater, until the mixture is creamy and very well blended. Add a tablespoon of the crisp bacon; mix again. Place the bowl on the back of the stove so that it warms, but doesn't get too hot and cook the eggs. Cook the *linguine al dente.* This is my favorite pasta, both for ease in twirling on one's plate and for its ability to hold up to cooking without becoming too soft, too fast. *Do not drain.* Fork directly from the pasta cooking pot into the warm bowl with the egg sauce, shaking off the water before you add each forkful of pasta to the bowl. The pasta *must* be very hot, so that it slightly sets the eggs as you toss it. Toss well, but gently, with forks. Serve in very hot soup bowls, with a large spoonful of the crisp hot bacon pieces atop each serving. Serves 4 to 6.

PASTICCIO DI PASTA E PROSCIUTTO
(*Fresh Pasta and Ham Pie*)

Italians occasionally do get fancy with their national dish, as in the following that I had in Siena.

> 1 recipe Pasta Fresca for Ravioli (page 44)
> 5 tablespoons butter, softened
> 2 eggs, separated
> 6 slices of prosciutto, diced
> 1 cup yogurt
> 2 tablespoons bread crumbs

Prepare dough, cut into squares, and dry, according to recipe. Cook *al dente;* drain well. Place butter, egg yolks, prosciutto and yogurt in a large bowl and beat with a whisk until well blended and creamy; stir in the pasta squares. Beat the 2 eggs whites until stiff and stir them into the bowl, blending well. Butter a baking dish, dust it with the bread crumbs, and pour in the egg-ham-pasta mixture. Bake in a preheated 350° F. oven for 35 minutes. Serves 4 to 6.

TAGLIARINI FRESCHI ALLA GIUSEPPE
(*Homemade Noodles alla Joseph*)

> 1 pound *tagliarini,* fresh (page 42-43)
> ¼ pound butter
> ¼ pound lean bacon, diced
> 1 pound fresh ricotta cheese
> ¼ pound Parmesan cheese, grated

Prepare the *tagliarini* and dry. While they are drying, melt butter in a saucepan, add the bacon, and cook until brown but not crisp. Cook the fresh pasta *al dente;* watch carefully, as fresh pasta cooks quickly; drain. Into hot soup bowls spoon a layer of ricotta cheese; place the drained *tagliarini* atop, spoon the bacon-and-butter sauce over it, and sprinkle with Parmesan. Serve immediately. Serves 6.

MAFALDA ALLA MARIA LIMONCELLI
(*Maria's Broad Noodles with Bacon, Veal and Chicken Livers*)

> 10 slices of bacon, chopped
> 4 white onions, chopped
> ½ pound veal, chopped
> 2 tablespoons butter
> 1 very ripe large beefsteak tomato, peeled and coarsely chopped
> 1 teaspoon salt
> Liberal amount of milled black pepper
> 1¼ cups Chicken Broth (page 84)
> 6 chicken livers, chopped
> 1 pound *mafalda* (a broad noodle, rippled on both edges)

Fry the bacon in a large frypan; when soft, add the onions and cook until golden. Add the chopped veal and cook, stirring bacon, veal and onions together, until veal is lightly browned. Simmer over low flame; add the butter, tomato, and salt, and mill in pepper. Add the chicken broth, cover, and simmer for 45 minutes. Blend in chicken livers and simmer, uncovered, for another 15 minutes. Cook *mafalda al dente,* drain, and serve in hot bowls. Spoon sauce over the pasta. Serves 4 to 6.

MAGLIETTE RIGATE ALLA GIOVANNINO
(*"Grooved Links" Giovannino*)

12 slices of bacon
2 white onions, chopped
Tips of 2 celery ribs, with leaves
8 fresh basil leaves, chopped
   or 1 tablespoon dried sweet basil
4 cups (one 2-pound can) Italian plum tomatoes,
   pushed through a food mill
Liberal amount of milled black pepper
1 pound *magliette rigate*
2 tablespoons butter
½ cup grated Asiago cheese

Chop bacon and sauté in a large frypan until half done. Add onions and celery; simmer until vegetables are soft. Add the basil and the tomatoes, mill in black pepper, stir well, and simmer for 15 minutes. Then cook for another 15 minutes over high flame to reduce the sauce and thicken it. Prepare *magliette rigate al dente;* be careful not to break the pasta tubes; drain. Toss in a hot bowl with the butter and cheese; pour half the sauce over the pasta and toss gently again. Serve in hot soup bowls with the remaining sauce spooned over individual portions. Serves 4 to 6.

QUADRETTINI AFFOGATI ALL'SAN MARINO
(*Smothered "Small Squares"*)

> 1 package (10 ounces) frozen chopped broccoli
> ½ pound prosciutto, chopped
> 3 tablespoons butter
> ½ cup grated Parmesan cheese
> ½ pound *quadrettini*

Cook the broccoli in a small amount of salted water; drain well. Sauté prosciutto in the butter for 10 minutes; stir in the broccoli, then the cheese. Remove from fire. Cook *quadrettini al dente*. Drain well and place in the pan with the other ingredients; blend well. Butter ramekins; divide the *quadrettini* mixture according to the number to be served. Brown under broiler for 5 minutes. Serves 4 to 6.

SPAGHETTINI CON PROSCIUTTO
(*Spaghettini with Italian Ham*)

This is a simple but classic dish often served in Parma, the region from which comes the best of that black-pepper-cured raw ham, prosciutto.

> ¼ pound unsalted butter
> ½ pound prosciutto, cut into long julienne strips
> 1 pound spaghettini
> Milled black pepper

Melt butter in a saucepan, add the ham, and sauté until it begins to crisp. Cook spaghettini *al dente;* drain. Place in a hot bowl, pour in all of the butter and ham, mill in black pepper liberally, and toss well with wooden forks. Serve immediately in hot soup bowls. Serves 6.

GEMELLI GIOVANNINO
("Twins" Giovannino)

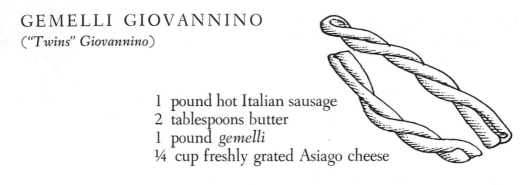

    1 pound hot Italian sausage
    2 tablespoons butter
    1 pound *gemelli*
    ¼ cup freshly grated Asiago cheese

Remove sausage casings and cook the loose meat in ½ tablespoon of the butter, over low fire, stirring and breaking up the meat as it browns. If it is especially fatty sausage, pour off half the fat and discard. When sausage is brown, add the remaining butter and blend well with the meat. Cook *gemelli al dente,* drain, and add to the pan with the sausage meat. Toss meat and pasta together. Sprinkle on the cheese and toss again. Serve in individual dishes, with more grated cheese on the side. Serves 4 to 6.

VERMICELLI CON FILETTO DI POMODORO E SALSICCIA
(Vermicelli with Tomato and Sausage)

    3 cups Filetto di Pomodoro (page 68)
    1 pound sweet Italian sausage
    1 tablespoon butter
    1 teaspoon olive oil
    1 pound *vermicelli*
    1 cup grated Parmesan cheese

Make *filetto di pomodoro* and keep warm. Take casings from sausage and sauté the meat in the butter and olive oil (oil keeps the butter from burning), breaking up the meat as it cooks. No other seasoning is necessary in the meat, as the sauce is rather spicy. When sausage is browned, add it to the warm sauce, stir well, and simmer for 10 minutes. Cook *vermicelli* in rapidly boiling water until *al dente;* drain. Toss gently with half of the cheese, top with the sausage and *filetto* sauce, and serve. Pass the rest of the cheese. Serves 4 to 6.

MACCHERONCELLI CON SALSICCIA
(*Baked Macaroni with Sausage Meat*)

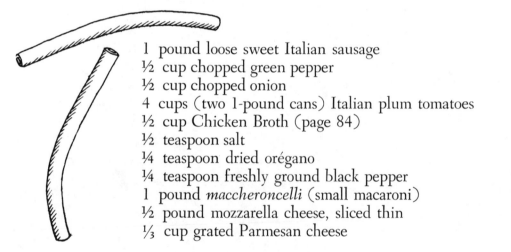

1 pound loose sweet Italian sausage
½ cup chopped green pepper
½ cup chopped onion
4 cups (two 1-pound cans) Italian plum tomatoes
½ cup Chicken Broth (page 84)
½ teaspoon salt
¼ teaspoon dried orégano
¼ teaspoon freshly ground black pepper
1 pound *maccheroncelli* (small macaroni)
½ pound mozzarella cheese, sliced thin
⅓ cup grated Parmesan cheese

Preheat the oven to 400° F. Cook the sausage in a skillet until brown; set aside. Drain all but 2 tablespoons of the sausage fat, and sauté the green pepper and onion in what remains, until soft. Add tomatoes put through food mill, chicken broth, salt, orégano and pepper to the skillet and cook until most of moisture has evaporated, about 20 minutes. Cook *maccheroncelli al dente;* drain. Arrange layers of the pasta, sausage and sauce, and mozzarella slices in a baking dish, until everything is used. Sprinkle with the Parmesan and bake until brown. Serves 4 to 6.

PASSO DI SELLA, in the Dolomites—Trentino-Alto Adige

PERCIATELLI CON SALSA DEI POMIDORO E SALSICCIA
(*"Pierced" Pasta with Tomato Sauce and Sausage*)

> 1 garlic clove, peeled and whole
> 1 tablespoon olive oil
> 1 pound sweet Italian sausage
> 2 cups (one 1-pound can) Italian plum tomatoes, put through food mill
> 1 teaspoon salt
> ½ tablespoon dried orégano
> Liberal amount of milled black pepper
> 1 pound *perciatelli*
> ½ cup freshly grated Parmesan cheese

Sauté the garlic in the oil until golden, mash in the pan, then discard. Cut sausage in its casing into 3-inch pieces and sauté these until brown on both sides. Add tomatoes and salt, stir well, cover pan, and cook for 45 minutes. Remove cover, lower fire, add orégano and pepper and stir well; cook until some of the liquid has evaporated from sauce. Cook *perciatelli al dente;* drain. Toss with cheese and serve in individual dishes topped with a generous spoonful of the sauce. Serve sausages as next course, with a vegetable and salad. Serves 4 to 6.

REGININI CON SALSICCIE
(*Baked "Little Queens" with Sausages*)

> 1½ pounds sweet Italian sausage
> 2 garlic cloves, minced
> 2 white onions, minced
> 2 tablespoons olive oil
> 4 cups (one 2-pound can) Italian plum tomatoes

½ cup water
½ teaspoon dried sweet basil
1 pound *reginini* (small pasta tubes)
1 pound ricotta cheese
½ cup grated Parmesan cheese

Sauté sausage with garlic and onions in the oil until onions are soft; slice sausage thin. Stir in tomatoes, water and basil. Bring to a boil, reduce heat, and simmer until liquid is absorbed, about 1 hour. While sausage mixture simmers, cook *reginini* in boiling salted water until *al dente;* drain. Mix ricotta cheese in a bowl with 3 tablespoons water. Heat oven to 350° F.; grease a large casserole and arrange a layer of pasta on the bottom; top with layer of meat sauce, a layer of ricotta, a sprinkle of Parmesan. Bake, uncovered for 30 minutes. Serves 4 to 6.

PENNE ALLA GIOVANNINO
(*"Quill Pens" Giovannino*)

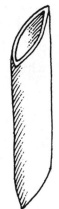

Four 4-inch hot Italian sausages, casings removed
Four 4-inch sweet Italian sausages, casings removed
1 tablespoon olive oil
8 slices of prosciutto, chopped
4 cups (one 2-pound can) Italian plum tomatoes with basil leaf
1 pound *penne*
¼ cup grated Parmesan cheese
¼ cup grated Romano cheese

Cook the sausage meats in the oil until brown; if very fatty, pour off half of the fat. Add prosciutto and the tomatoes that have been pushed through a food mill. Simmer, stirring, for 15 minutes. Cook for another 10 minutes to reduce and thicken sauce. Cook *penne al dente,* drain, and toss with the cheeses. Serve in hot soup bowls with the sausage sauce spooned over right from the pan. Serves 4 to 6.

LASAGNE AL FORNO ALL'AMEDEO
(*Amedeo's Baked Lasagne*)

This is an unusual lasagne *recipe given to me by a chef who worked for an Italian industrialist; thus it bears the chef's name.*

> 1 recipe Pasta Fresca all Uovo (page 42)
> 3 tablespoons olive oil, in all
> 2 small white onions, chopped
> 2 tablespoons chopped Italian parsley
> ½ pound top round of beef, ground twice
> ⅓ cup milk
> 1½ cups Basic Tomato Sauce (page 63)
> 1 recipe Béchamel Sauce (page 73)
> 1 cup grated Parmesan cheese

Roll out the pasta dough to ⅛-inch thickness and cut into strips 2½ by 5½ inches for *lasagne;* dry as recommended (page 43). Drop two at a time into rapidly boiling salted water to which 1 tablespoon of the oil has been added to keep the pasta from sticking. Cook for 4 minutes; remove with slotted spoon to dry on paper towels. Repeat until pasta is all cooked. Sauté onions, parsley and beef in remaining oil until onion is soft but beef still pink. Stir in the milk; when it is well blended, add the tomato sauce and simmer for 20 minutes.

Meanwhile, prepare the Béchamel sauce. Butter a large heatproof glass baking dish. Carefully spread out in the dish a layer of the pasta strips, cover with meat sauce, and top with grated Parmesan. Repeat the layer of pasta, cover with Béchamel sauce, and sprinkle with cheese. Then again, a layer of pasta, meat sauce and cheese, then another covered with Béchamel and cheese. Brown in 450° F. oven for 15 minutes, until sauce bubbles and top is pale brown. Serves 4 to 6.

AGNOLOTTI ALLA ROMANA

As I remarked earlier agnolotti *are* ravioli, *but the name changes when the famous pasta squares are stuffed with meat (and sometimes made round instead of square). Properly,* ravioli *are filled only with eggs, cheeses and vegetables.*

> 2 cups ground beef
> 6 slices of Genoa salami
> 1 garlic clove
> Dash each of salt and pepper
> 2 eggs, beaten
> 4 tablespoons grated Parmesan cheese
> 1 recipe Pasta Fresca for Ravioli (page 44)
> 3 cups Mushroom and Cheese Sauce (page 74)

Finely mince (or put through food chopper) beef, salami and garlic. Place in a large bowl, add salt and pepper, and beat in the eggs and cheese. Prepare the dough as suggested on page 44. Place a teaspoon of the filling in the center of each square, cover with the other sheet of dough, then firmly press between the mounds of filling. Cut into squares with a pastry cutter. Place on a dry white cloth, cover with another cloth, and dry for 40 minutes, or according to directions. Prepare mushroom and cheese sauce. Cook squares in gently simmering water until they float to the surface. Test for doneness by tasting one. Remove with slotted spoon; drain on paper towels. Place in hot soup bowls and serve with hot mushroom and cheese sauce spooned atop each square. Serves 4 to 6.

Note: Do not have water boiling violently or it will break up the *agnolotti* before they have cooked. They are usually but not always done when they float to the surface. Test often and return to the pot if not properly done.

AGNOLOTTI ALLA NIZZA
(*Agnolotti Nice Style*)

2-pound rump of beef
1 teaspoon salt
Milled black pepper
3 tablespoons butter
2 tablespoons olive oil
1 cup red wine
6 beets
1 egg
1 white onion, minced
½ cup grated Gruyère cheese
1 recipe Pasta Fresca for Ravioli (page 44)

Sprinkle the beef rump with salt and pepper and brown in 2 tablespoons of the butter and the oil. Lower heat, cover pot, and simmer for 1 hour. Add the wine, stir in well, cover pot again, and cook for 1 to 1½ hours, until meat is tender. Remove meat and cool. Simmer the liquid in the pot, stirring often, until it is thickened; set aside. Cook beets and peel. Finely mince beef and beets (or put through grinder) and place in a large bowl. Blend in the egg. Sauté the onion until soft in the remaining tablespoon of butter; blend this into the mixture along with 2 tablespoons of the cheese and salt and pepper to taste.

Prepare dough for *ravioli*. Fill one sheet with the beet-and-beef mixture, cover with the second sheet of dough, press, and dry according to directions. Cook in simmering water until the filled *agnolotti* float to the top. Test. Remove with slotted spoon, drain, and serve in hot bowls. Spoon the sauce from the meat pot atop, sprinkle with remaining cheese, and serve immediately. Serves 4 to 6.

AGNOLOTTI ALL'ANTONIO

1 recipe Pasta Fresca for Ravioli (page 44)
6 slices of prosciutto
4 slices of mortadella
1 veal sweetbread, blanched and cleaned
1 egg, beaten
¼ teaspoon salt
Milled black pepper
Pinch of grated nutmeg
6 mushrooms, sliced
4 tablespoons butter
6 tablespoons peas
4 quarts Chicken Broth (page 84)
4 tablespoons grated Parmesan cheese

Prepare pasta dough according to directions. Finely mince (or put through food chopper) prosciutto, mortadella and sweetbread. Place in a large bowl, stir in the beaten egg, salt, pepper and nutmeg, blending well. Fill and dry the *agnolotti* according to directions. Sauté mushrooms in butter for 10 minutes. Lightly cook peas in a small amount of salted water, drain, and add to mushrooms and butter. Bring chicken broth to a gentle boil, drop in the *agnolotti,* and cook until they float to top. Test. Do not drain. Butter an ovenware serving dish; take *agnolotti* directly from the broth and arrange in the buttered dish. Spoon mushrooms and peas over them and sprinkle with Parmesan; place in broiler for 5 minutes. Serves 4 to 6.

CAPPELLETTI ALLA ROMANA
("*Little Hats*" *Roman Style*)

I am told that the Roman cappelletti *differ from others, being larger and having a raw rather than cooked filling. Also, they are usually cooked in broth.*

1 recipe Pasta Fresca for Ravioli (page 44)
1 small calf's brain
½ boned chicken breast, minced
2 slices of prosciutto, chopped
2 slices of mortadella, chopped
¼ pound lean pork, ground
1½ teaspoons salt
Liberal amount of milled black pepper
2 eggs, beaten
2 tablespoons Marsala wine
2 quarts Chicken Broth (page 84)
¼ cup grated Parmesan cheese
Melted butter

Prepare dough, but do not yet roll out into sheets. Parboil the calf's brain, remove skin and membrane, and mince. In a bowl mix all meats together, season with salt and pepper, and blend in eggs and Marsala. Mix well. Roll out pasta dough into sheets; cut into 2½-inch circles. Place a teaspoon of the raw-meat filling in each, fold across into half-moons, then pull edges together into "little hat" shapes. Dry for 20 minutes. Bring the broth to a simmer and drop in the *cappelletti,* a few at a time. Remove them when they are tender, usually in less than 15 minutes, with a slotted spoon; drain. Serve as first course with a light sprinkling of Parmesan and hot melted butter. Serves 4 to 6.

TORTELLINI ALLA BOLOGNESE

Here are the "little twisted ones," the copy of Venus's navel, the favorite pasta of Bologna.

½ turkey breast (4 pounds), boned
4 small slices prosciutto
1 medium-size veal sweetbread, blanched and cleaned
¼ pound lean pork
¼ pound lean beef

7 tablespoons butter, in all
¼ pound Parmesan cheese, in all, grated
2 egg yolks, beaten
Salt
Pinch of grated nutmeg
Light pinch of ground cinnamon
Liberal amount of milled black pepper
1 recipe Pasta Fresca for Tortellini (page 44)
4 quarts Chicken Broth (page 84)
1 cup heavy cream

Cut the turkey breast, prosciutto, sweetbread, pork and beef into pieces. Melt 4 tablespoons of the butter in a large saucepan, and in it sauté the meats until pieces of sweetbread are cooked. Remove from stove; cool. Put mixture through a meat grinder twice so that all is very finely ground. Place in large bowl and stir in half the cheese, the beaten egg yolks, a little salt, the nutmeg, cinnamon and some pepper; blend well.

Prepare the pasta dough and cut it into circles for *tortellini* (page 45); fill with the stuffing mixture and dry. Bring the chicken broth to a gentle simmer, not violent or it will break up the pasta. Heat remaining butter in a large saucepan or flameproof serving dish over low heat. Now carefully drop filled *tortellini,* a few at a time, into the gently simmering broth, and simmer until they are cooked through, but *al dente,* about 12 minutes. Remove with a slotted spoon, drain, and place in the saucepan with the melted butter. Pour in the cream and sprinkle remaining cheese over the *tortellini,* gently stirring with a wooden spoon until butter, cream and cheese have blended into a smooth sauce. Serve immediately in hot bowls, and pass additional grated Parmesan at table. Serves 8 as a first course.

 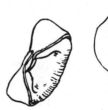

FIDENZA, the west porch of the Cathedral—Emilia-Romagna

CANNELLONI VERDI
(*Baked Green Cannelloni*)

>1 recipe Pasta Verde (page 45)
>1 cup Béchamel Sauce (page 73)
>2 cups Bolognese Sauce (page 71)
>1 tablespoon olive oil
>1 pound ricotta cheese
>10 slices of lean prosciutto, finely chopped
>½ cup grated Parmesan cheese
>½ cup grated Romano cheese
>1 garlic clove, minced
>2 tablespoons chopped Italian parsley
>2 egg yolks, beaten
>1 teaspoon salt
>Milled black pepper
>3 tablespoons melted butter

Prepare the green pasta dough, cut it into 4-inch squares, and dry for 1 hour. Prepare the sauces. Cook 2 squares of pasta at a time in boiling salted water with the olive oil added to keep pasta from sticking. As each 2 squares are cooked *al dente,* remove, drain well, and dry on paper towels. Continue until all pasta has been cooked. Drain the ricotta in a strainer, place in a bowl, and blend in the prosciutto, Parmesan and Romano, garlic, parsley, beaten egg yolks, salt and pepper. Mix well. In the center of each pasta square place a heaping tablespoon of this filling; then roll carefully into a tube. Place filled tubes, without touching, side by side in a buttered heatproof glass baking dish; brush them with melted butter. Lightly cover them with Béchamel sauce, then with Bolognese sauce, pouring the remainder of the sauce on either side. Brown in a 400° F. oven for 15 minutes. Serve the rest of the sauces in boats on the side. Serves 4 to 6.

MANICOTTI ALLA TOSCANA
(Baked Manicotti Tuscan Style)

1 recipe Pasta Fresca all'Uovo (page 42)
4 cups Basic Tomato Sauce (page 63)
4 tablespoons butter
1 tablespoon olive oil
1 garlic clove, minced
6 mushrooms, minced
1 pound beef round, ground twice
1 teaspoon salt
Liberal amount of milled black pepper
½ pound ricotta cheese
¼ pound Parmesan cheese, grated

Prepare pasta dough, cut into 3-inch squares, and dry for 1 hour. Prepare tomato sauce, simmer. Heat 3 tablespoons of the butter and the oil in a saucepan; sauté garlic until soft. Add mushrooms, beef, salt and pepper and sauté until brown, stirring often. Stir in the ricotta and half of the Parmesan, blending well. When *manicotti* are dry, spread a liberal tablespoon of beef mixture on each square and roll up tightly, carefully pressing edges together and sealing; if necessary moisten the edges with water to make sealing more effective; filling has to be completely sealed in or it will be lost during boiling of the pasta. Cook *manicotti al dente* in gently boiling salted water, remove with skimmer, and drain. Arrange a layer in a buttered baking dish. Cover with tomato sauce and sprinkle with Parmesan; arrange another layer crosswise, cover with sauce, and sprinkle with Parmesan. Bake in preheated 350° F. oven for 25 minutes, until cheese browns and sauce bubbles. Serves 6.

TUFOLI IMBOTTITI CON CARNE
(*Baked Meat-stuffed Tufoli*)

1 pound veal, ground
1 pound pork, ground
2 shallots, chopped
1 egg, beaten
½ cup bread crumbs
1 tablespoon raisins, minced
½ tablespoon salt
2 tablespoons olive oil, in all
½ cup grated pepato cheese
1 pound *tufoli* (very large tubes)
3 cups Basic Tomato Sauce (page 63)

Mix together meats, shallots, beaten egg, bread crumbs, raisins, salt, ½ table-spoon of the oil and the grated cheese; mix well. Sauté mixture in another ½ tablespoon of oil in a frypan for 15 minutes, stirring and blending well. Remove from heat and let cool. Cook *tufoli* in boiling salted water with remaining tablespoon of olive oil added to keep these large pasta from sticking. Cook for 6 minutes, or until half done; drain. When cool enough to handle, spoon the meat mixture into the tubes, filling them. Oil a baking dish or casserole, place *tufoli* in it, side by side but not touching, and cover each with a liberal spoonful of tomato sauce. Bake, uncovered, in 400° F. oven for 15 minutes. Serve remaining sauce from a sauceboat. Serves 4 to 6.

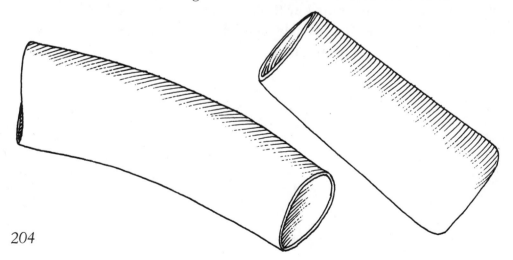

SPIEDINI ALLA ROMANA
("Little Skewers" Roman Style)

I had this specialty of the ancient city on a bed of noodles, and recommend it highly as an unusual way to serve that American favorite, spaghetti and meatballs.

1½ pounds good beef, preferably sirloin, ground twice
2 tablespoons grated Romano cheese
2 tablespoons grated Parmesan cheese
½ cup bread crumbs
4 eggs, in all, beaten
1 tablespoon chopped Italian parsley
1 garlic clove, finely minced
½ teaspoon salt
Milled black pepper
½ pound mozzarella cheese
½ pound Genoa salami, unsliced
12 small skewers
½ cup flour
½ cup very dry bread crumbs
6 tablespoons butter, in all
4 tablespoons olive oil
1 pound *fettucce* (wide *fettuccine*)

In a large bowl place beef, both cheeses, bread crumbs, 2 of the eggs, the parsley, garlic, salt and pepper. Blend thoroughly, then form oblong rolls 1 inch thick, 3 inches long. Cut mozzarella and salami into 1-inch cubes. Place a meat roll on a skewer, crosswise, then a piece of mozzarella, then one of salami, another beef roll, another cube of cheese and one of salami. Thread all skewers this way. Dip the skewers into the flour, then into remaining beaten eggs, then into the dry bread crumbs. Sauté in 4 tablespoons of the butter and the oil in a deep saucepan, turning the skewers until meat, cheese and salami are golden. Cook *fettucce al dente*, drain, and toss with remaining butter. Serve on individual plates, with 2 skewers to each person atop the *fettucce*. Serve 6.

BAVETTINE CON BRACIOLINE DI MANZO
(Bavettine with Stuffed Beef Rolls)

This is a popular Italian dish which can be made in a number of ways, with beef, pork, veal, even with breast of chicken.

> 2 pounds round steak
> 5 cups Basic Tomato Sauce (page 63)
> ½ pound salt pork
> 4 slices of prosciutto
> 2 tablespoons chopped Italian parsley
> Pinch each of salt and pepper
> 2 tablespoons grated Parmesan cheese
> 2 tablespoons olive oil
> 1 pound *bavettine* (very narrow *linguine*)

Have butcher cut the beef into pieces 8 by 9 inches, ½ inch thick, and pound the pieces to flatten them as for veal scaloppine. Prepare the tomato sauce and bring to a simmer. Mince the salt pork, prosciutto and parsley. Sprinkle lightly with salt and pepper, mix in the cheese, and mince everything again until it is a fine paste. Spread this liberally over the flat pieces of beef. Roll from short end into compact rolls and tie with string. Sauté the *bracioline* (beef rolls) in the oil, turning often, until brown. Add them, with the oil they have cooked in, to the tomato sauce and stir well. Simmer, uncovered, until meat is tender and sauce thickened. Cook *bavettine al dente;* drain. Serve in hot soup bowls with tomato sauce liberally spooned atop. Cut one of the *bracioline* into ½-inch rounds and center 2 slices on each dish of pasta. Serve remaining beef rolls, with more sauce, as entrée, with a salad. Serves 6.

RIGATONI CON FETTA DI MANZO
(*Rigatoni with Pot Roast*)

Here is an all-time Italian favorite that I have had in Rome, in Florence, Naples, and Genoa, each time on a Sunday, correcting the misconception that tomato and beef cooked this way is confined to the South.

2 tablespoons olive oil
2 garlic cloves, mashed
1 teaspoon salt
Liberal amount of milled black pepper
3-pound beef chuck roast
4 cups (one 2-pound can) Italian plum tomatoes
1 bay leaf
Pinch of dried rosemary
1 cup red wine
6 mushrooms, sliced
1 pound *rigatoni* (grooved pasta tubes)

Heat the oil in a large pot; sauté garlic, moving it around in the oil until it is brown; discard garlic. Sprinkle salt and pepper on meat and sear it in the oil on all sides over high flame. Lower flame and stir in tomatoes, bay leaf, rosemary and wine; cover pot and simmer for 2 hours, stirring often and basting meat, until it is fork-tender. Lift meat to a warm platter. Add the mushrooms to the pot and simmer for 10 minutes, stirring with a wooden spoon as they cook. Cook *rigatoni al dente,* drain, and place in a hot bowl. Spoon one third of the sauce over and toss well. Serve in hot soup bowls with liberal spoonings of sauce. The pot roast, sliced, serves as entrée with salad and vegetables. Serves 6.

Another great meat dish should be mentioned here. It is Italian through and through, but I have eaten it only in New England. See Catherine Spadaccino's Foggia Beef Roll on page 65.

OSSI BUCHI ED ORZO ALLA MILANESE
(Veal Shanks and Orzo Milanese)

6 veal shanks, each 2 inches thick
¼ cup flour
4 tablespoons olive oil
2 tablespoons butter
1 teaspoon salt
Milled black pepper
Pinch of dried rosemary
1 garlic clove, chopped
2 large white onions, chopped
1 large carrot, chopped
1 large celery rib, chopped
2 cups dry white wine
1 cup Basic Tomato Sauce (page 63)
1½ cups Chicken Broth (page 84)

Dust the pieces of veal with flour and place them in a pan with 2 tablespoons of the olive oil and the butter; sprinkle with salt and mill in pepper. Cook over medium heat, turning the veal until all sides are brown. Add more oil if needed. Place the veal shanks on their sides, so marrow doesn't drop out, in a large deep pot. Add remaining oil and sprinkle lightly with rosemary, then with the garlic, onions, carrot and celery. Cover the pot and simmer for 15 minutes.

Take off cover, add wine, tomato sauce and chicken broth. Stir well, cover pot again, and simmer on top of stove for 1½ hours, or until veal is fork-tender and sauce thickened. Stir often. Meanwhile, prepare the pasta.

Orzo Milanese:

2 tablespoons butter
2 small white onions, chopped
1 garlic clove, minced
2 cups *orzo* (pasta that looks like barley or rice)
5 cups Chicken Broth (page 84), warm
⅓ cup grated Parmesan cheese
¼ teaspoon ground saffron

209

GRAVEDONA, Baptistry of Santa Maria del Tiglio—Lombardy

Melt the butter in a pan, add onions, and simmer until soft; stir in garlic. Add the *orzo* and stir well into butter and onion and garlic until the pasta kernels are coated. Blend in 1 cup of broth and stir gently as the *orzo* absorbs the liquid, adding more broth as it is needed; 10 minutes should see the pasta cooked. Now stir in the cheese and saffron; add more chicken broth, stir, and simmer until broth is absorbed and pasta is still *al dente*.

Serve *orzo* in the center of a large platter surrounded with the *ossi buchi,* the veal sauce on the side. Each serving should have a veal shank and a large spoonful of *orzo* with sauce spooned over it. Provide marrow spoons, so that each guest can pry out that tasty tidbit from the veal bone. Serves 6.

Note: To give the veal added piquancy, mix together 1 tablespoon chopped parsley, 1 minced garlic clove and 1 tablespoon grated lemon rind. Lightly sprinkle over each veal shank before serving. This is called *gremolata* in Milan.

SPAGHETTINI E COSCIOTTI D'AGNELLO
(*Spaghettini with Lamb Shanks*)

4 carrots, chopped
2 celery ribs, chopped
4 tablespoons butter
3 pounds lamb shanks, cut into 2-inch pieces
Salt
Milled black pepper
1 tablespoon flour
1 cup canned Italian plum tomatoes
1 cup dry white wine
1 cup water
1 teaspoon chopped fresh thyme
1 bay leaf
1 pound spaghettini
2 strips of lemon rind, chopped
1 tablespoon chopped parsley

Sauté vegetables in 2 tablespoons of the butter. Add the meat and season generously with salt and pepper. When the vegetables are soft and the meat brown, add remaining butter blended with the flour; stir and cook until the flour browns. Add the tomatoes, wine and water to cover meat; add the herbs; simmer for 1 hour. Fifteen minutes before serving remove meat from pot and strain the sauce. Cook spaghettini *al dente,* drain, and toss with sauce. Serve in individual bowls. Before serving lamb as an entrée, sprinkle with chopped lemon rind and parsley. Serves 4.

SPAGHETTI CON CAPRETTO IN UMIDO
(Spaghetti with Kid Stew)

This is a peasant dish I had in a farmhouse just outside Foggia several years ago when caught there in a snowstorm, the first in years; it was just the dish for the day.

>3 tablespoons butter
>3 tablespoons olive oil
>2 garlic cloves
>3 small white onions, chopped
>2 pounds of lean kid (or lamb), cubed
>1 cup Chianti or other dry red wine
>4 cups (one 2-pound can) Italian plum tomatoes with basil leaf
>1½ teaspoons salt
>Liberal amount of milled black pepper
>2 tablespoons chopped parsley
>2 celery ribs, chopped
>1 large potato, peeled and diced
>1 pound spaghetti

Heat butter and oil in a large deep saucepan. Add garlic and onions and sauté until garlic is brown; discard garlic. Stir in the meat cubes; brown. Stir in the wine slowly, mixing well with the meat with a wooden spoon. Add the tomatoes, salt, pepper, parsley, and celery; simmer for 40 minutes. Add the potato and cook, uncovered, until sauce is thickened and potato and meat tender. Cook spaghetti *al dente*, drain, and toss with half of the meat stew. Serve in hot soup bowls with a liberal amount of sauce atop each portion. Serves 4 to 6.

TAGLIATELLE VERDI CON MAIALE USO PIEMONTESE
(*Green Noodles with Pork Piedmont Style*)

> 1 fresh pork shoulder
> 2 white truffles, sliced thin
> Milled black pepper
> 3 tablespoons butter
> 1 teaspoon salt
> 4 slices of prosciutto, chopped
> 2 small white onions, chopped
> 2 celery ribs, chopped
> 2 small carrots, chopped
> 1 tablespoon chopped parsley
> Pinch of dried sweet basil
> 2 cups (one 1-pound can) Italian plum tomatoes, pushed through food mill
> 1 cup white wine
> 2 cups Chicken Broth (page 84)
> 1 recipe Pasta Verde (page 45) or 1 pound commercial green noodles

Have butcher skin, bone, and split the pork shoulder so it will lie flat. Trim off most of the outside white pork fat leaving a thin layer. Place truffle slices over entire meat surface and liberally mill black pepper over meat. Roll up tightly and tie with soft white string into a compact roll. Heat butter in a large pot and brown pork roll in it on all sides. Sprinkle with salt and pepper, add the prosciutto, onions, celery, carrots, parsley and basil, and stir in the tomatoes, wine and broth. Cook, covered, on top of stove over low flame for 2 hours. Remove cover and cook for 1 hour longer, stirring often until meat is fork-tender and sauce thickened.

Meanwhile, prepare green pasta dough and cut into *tagliatelle* (page 43); dry. Cook *al dente* and drain. Serve noodles in hot soup bowls, with liberal amounts of the pork sauce spooned atop each portion. Cut wafer-thin slices from the pork shoulder; place 3 atop each dish of pasta. Meat roll, untied and sliced, serves as entrée with a fresh vegetable and salad. Serves 6.

PORCELLINO RIPIENO ARROSTITO
(*Roast Stuffed Suckling Pig*)

This is a dish I saw prepared at a wedding in Florence; it is an impressive one that everyone should have at least once. Six piglets were cooked there, but I have reduced the recipe so that only one piglet is required.

 1 suckling pig (8 to 10 pounds)
 2 teaspoons salt
 3 garlic cloves, peeled and halved
 1 pound *mezzani* (medium-size macaroni)
 Pinch of grated nutmeg
 ¼ cup grated Parmesan cheese
 1 cup light cream
 1 teaspoon crushed red pepper

Wash the piglet well; scrape its skin with a sharp knife, and sprinkle it inside and out with salt. Insert the tip of a pointed knife in the skin in 6 places, preparing slits large enough to insert ½ garlic clove in each. Cook *mezzani* one third done, very very chewy, and drain well. Sprinkle lightly with nutmeg, add cheese and cream, and toss. Stuff the piglet with the pasta and sew the opening so it is completely sealed. Dust piglet with the crushed red pepper and place in an uncovered roasting pan. Roast in a preheated 500° F. oven until the meat is brown. Then lower heat to 350° F., cover the pan, and cook the piglet for at least 3 hours, basting with pan juices frequently, until it is tender inside and crisp outside. Serve whole, on a large hot platter, and carve at the table, giving each person a portion of piglet and a spoonful of *mezzani*. At the wedding, a crisp cold salad of hearts of romaine and orange slices accompanied it. Serves 6.

Chapter VIII

Poultry & Game
with PASTA

*A*n early pasta recipe that I had translated in Italy's *Museo Storico degli Spaghetti*, the museum at Pontedassio, went, "First catch a nice fat chicken," and as I read it I could envision a hefty Italian woman dressed in black, chasing a squawking chicken, cleaver in hand. Another, detailing a favorite of mine, *fettuccine* with hare sauce, advised, "Shoot a hare—"and here my imagination went all out, with creeping man, smoking gun and leaping game. And, in the end, pasta with butter and frustration.

But with such things now made easy, the makings for what I consider among the very best of all pasta and sauces, those of poultry and game (mainly because the main course is often lifted from the pasta sauce itself)

are as close as your butcher shop or specialty meat market that offers everything from a haunch of venison to a mallard duck.*

　　If you come upon a recipe that appeals to you, but for which you cannot
bag exactly the game specified, try it anyway with the meat of domesticated
bird or beast. Once you have caught your chicken or hare in your own way,
here are a few things you may want to do with them.

FUSILLI E POLLO ALLA ROMANA
("Twists" and Chicken Roman Style)

I've had this for dinner at trattorie *in Rome several times with a green salad
and a bottle of Frascati. It's a favorite there and also in my home.*

　　2　tablespoons olive oil
　　3　tablespoons butter
　　1　stewing chicken (5 pounds), trussed
　　1　teaspoon salt
　　Liberal amount of milled black pepper
　　1　leek, sliced thin
　　Pinch of dried rosemary
　　2　cloves
　　1½　tablespoons chopped parsley
　　1　large ripe tomato, peeled and diced
　　2　cups Chicken Broth (page 84)
　　1　pound *fusilli*

Heat the oil and 2 tablespoons of the butter in a large pot. Add the chicken,
season with salt and pepper, and brown on all sides over medium-high
flame. Add the leek, rosemary, cloves and 1 tablespoon of the parsley. Continue to brown chicken and herbs, turning bird often. Don't rush this stage

* The most delicious game birds I have been able to find (oven ready) are available
from Mrs. Howard Capp, Birdcliff Game Farm, Wingdale, New York. Price list will be
sent upon request. Highly recommended are wild turkey, mallard duck, chukar partridge,
quail, baby and mature pheasant, baby and mature guinea hens.

as slow cooking is the way to achieve final flavoring. Stir in the tomato, mixing well. Add half of the broth, cover pot, and simmer for 1 hour. Remove cover, stir, turn chicken on its side, and pour in remaining broth. Cover pot, simmer for 30 minutes, and turn chicken on its other side. Simmer for 30 minutes longer. Remove chicken from pot and simmer the sauce, uncovered, stirring often, until sauce is smooth and thick. Rub remaining butter over chicken, sprinkle with remaining parsley, and place in a low oven. Cook *fusilli al dente,* drain, and stir directly into the chicken sauce, mixing well. Serve *fusilli* on a large hot platter with the whole chicken, untrussed, in the center. Serves 6.

PASTA E POLLO ALLA CONTADINA
(Chicken and Spaghetti Farmer's Style)

> 2 tablespoons butter
> 4 slices of prosciutto, finely minced
> 1 teaspoon salt
> Milled black pepper
> 1 chicken (3 pounds)
> 1 garlic clove, quartered
> ½ teaspoon dried rosemary
> 12 plum tomatoes, peeled and diced
> 1 cup Chicken Broth (page 84)
> 1 pound spaghetti

Heat butter in a large pot, stir in minced prosciutto, and sauté until soft. Sprinkle salt and pepper over chicken. Make 8 slits in the bird; insert the garlic pieces in 4, rosemary in 4. Brown on all sides. Add the tomatoes and simmer, covered, for 1½ hours, until tender, basting with warm chicken broth every 20 minutes. Remove chicken for serving as entrée. Simmer sauce, uncovered, until it is smooth and thickened, stirring often. Cook spaghetti *al dente;* drain. Serve in hot soup bowls with hot chicken-tomato sauce liberally spooned atop each portion. Serves 6.

PERCIATELLI E POLLO ALLA PIZZAIOLA
("Pierced" Pasta and Chicken with Tomato Sauce)

2 garlic cloves, minced
4 tablespoons olive oil
1 young fryer chicken, cut-up
1 teaspoon salt
Liberal amount of milled black pepper
12 plum tomatoes, peeled and diced
½ teaspoon dried orégano
3 basil leaves, chopped, or ½ teaspoon dried sweet basil
1 pound *perciatelli*

Sauté garlic in the oil until soft. Toss chicken pieces in garlic and oil in the pan, sprinkle with salt and pepper, and cook over medium-high heat until chicken is well browned on both sides. Add tomatoes, orégano and basil, cover pan, and cook for 40 minutes, stirring often, until chicken is tender but not falling apart. Remove chicken to a warm platter for second course. Cook remaining sauce, uncovered, for 5 minutes, until it thickens, stirring often. Cook *perciatelli al dente,* drain, and toss with half the sauce. Spoon the remainder of sauce over each serving. Serves 4.

RIGATONI CON POLLO ALLA ZINGARA
(Rigatoni with Chicken Gypsy Style)

2 tablespoons butter
2 tablespoons olive oil
1 chicken (3 pounds), cut into serving pieces
½ cup dry white wine
2 garlic cloves
Pinch of ground sage
Pinch of dried rosemary

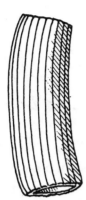

1 teaspoon salt
Liberal amount of milled black pepper
2 cups Chicken Broth (page 84)
3 anchovy fillets
½ tablespoon wine vinegar
6 plum tomatoes, peeled and diced
½ pound *rigatoni* (grooved pasta tubes)
Grated Asiago cheese

In a deep saucepan heat butter and oil; sauté the chicken pieces in it, browning them evenly. Pour in the wine and continue cooking, uncovered, until wine evaporates. Add the garlic, sage, rosemary, salt, pepper and broth. Cover pan and simmer for 1 hour, or until chicken is fork-tender. Transfer chicken to a warm platter in a low oven. Meanwhile soak the anchovies in cold water to desalt them; drain. Chop the anchovies, then crush into a paste in the vinegar. Stir this into the sauce; add the tomatoes. Simmer over a low fire, uncovered, stirring often, for 20 minutes, or until sauce is smooth and thickened. Cook *rigatoni al dente*, drain, and place in a large hot bowl. Pour in two thirds of the sauce; toss well. Serve immediately in hot soup bowls. Pass the cheese at table. Chicken, topped with the remaining sauce, comes as second course. Serves 4.

FETTUCCINE ALLA TEDESCA
(*Fettuccine German Style*)

6 tablespoons butter, in all
1 tablespoon olive oil
1 chicken (4 pounds)
1 teaspoon salt
Liberal amount of milled black pepper
4 tablespoons brandy

1 recipe Pasta Fresca all'Uovo (page 42)
½ cup grated Parmesan cheese
½ cup heavy cream, warmed
1 white truffle, grated

In a large pot heat 4 tablespoons of the butter and the oil. Brown the chicken in this, seasoning it with salt and pepper. Bake the chicken in a covered pan in a 350° F. oven for 2 hours, or until fork-tender, basting the bird often with its own juices and with the brandy. Remove and cool. Skin and bone chicken, cutting meat into small strips. Return strips to the brandy-flavored drippings in the roasting pan, blend, and simmer, uncovered, for 10 minutes.

Meanwhile prepare pasta dough, cut into *fettuccine* (page 43), and let them dry for 1 hour. Cook them *al dente;* drain. Place in a large hot bowl and toss with the remaining butter and the cheese. Add the warm cream and the chicken strips in their sauce; toss again, with wooden forks. Serve immediately in hot bowls. Sprinkle some grated truffle atop each portion, and pass more grated cheese at table. Serves 4 to 6.

CANNELLONI ALLA GIORGIO
(*George's "Large Reeds"*)

1 recipe Pasta Fresca all'Uovo (page 42)
1 chicken (3 pounds)
4 teaspoons salt
½ recipe Mornay Sauce (page 73)
2 egg yolks, beaten
Liberal amount of milled black pepper
⅓ cup grated Pecorino cheese
⅓ cup grated Parmesan cheese
½ cup bread crumbs
2 tablespoons olive oil
2 tablespoons butter

Prepare the fresh pasta dough, cut into squares, and dry (page 43). Cover chicken with water and add 3 teaspoons salt; cook for 1½ hours, or until fork-tender. Remove; cool. Discard skin and bones and dice the chicken meat. Prepare Mornay sauce. Blend in chicken, egg yolks, remaining salt, pepper, and cheeses. Simmer, uncovered, stirring often with a wooden spoon, until sauce is extremely thick. Chill. Cook the dried pasta squares and drain. Spoon chicken filling on each pasta square, roll up, and sprinkle with bread crumbs. Sauté in olive oil and butter until golden. Serves 6.

CAPELLINI E POLLO
(Baked Fine Vermicelli and Chicken)

```
1  large chicken (4 pounds), roasted
½  pound mushrooms, sliced
10  tablespoons butter, in all
½  cup flour
4  cups Chicken Broth (page 84)
1½  cups milk
½  cup heavy cream
Salt and pepper
½  pound capellini
½  cup bread crumbs
½  cup grated Asiago cheese
```

Cut meat from chicken into cubes. Sauté mushrooms in 2 tablespoons of the butter for 5 minutes. Melt remaining butter and blend in flour, broth and milk. Cook over low heat until sauce begins to thicken, stirring frequently. Add cream and season well with salt and pepper. Cook *capellini al dente* (for no more than 4 minutes); drain. Arrange in a greased casserole; arrange chicken and mushrooms over them and pour sauce over all. Sprinkle bread crumbs and cheese on top and bake in 450° F. oven until sauce bubbles and crumbs brown. Serves 4 to 6.

BERGAMO, the Colleoni Chapel—Lombardy

FETTUCCELLE CON FILETTI DI POLLO E PEPE NERO
("Little Ribbons" with Fillets of Chicken and Black Pepper)

2 whole chicken breasts, filletted
8 tablespoons butter, in all
1 teaspoon olive oil
1½ teaspoons salt
Liberal amount of milled black pepper
1 pound *fettuccelle* (narrow *fettuccine*)

Cut boned chicken fillets into pieces the size of your thumbnail. Sauté in 6 tablespoons of the butter and the oil (to keep butter from burning) in a fry-pan for 15 minutes. When chicken is done, but still juicy—don't overcook—add salt and mill in much black pepper. Stir well, adding more butter if needed; chicken should be moist. Remove from fire, but keep warm. Cook *fettuccelle al dente;* drain. Toss with remaining butter, then with half of the chicken mixture. Serve in individual dishes with the remaining chicken sauce spooned atop. Serves 4 to 6.

RIGATONI E PETTO DI POLLO
(Rigatoni and Chicken Breast)

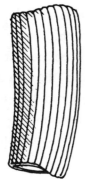

1 pound *rigatoni* (grooved pasta tubes)
½ chicken breast, boned
¼ pound butter
¼ pound Parmesan cheese, grated
2 egg yolks, beaten
1 cup heavy cream
1 teaspoon salt
Liberal amount of milled black pepper

Cook *rigatoni* for 10 minutes in boiling salted water; drain. Grind raw chicken twice. Blend butter, half of the cheese, the egg yolks, cream, salt, pepper, and chicken. Place pasta in a large pot and stir in the chicken mixture, blending well. Simmer for 15 minutes, stirring often, until *rigatoni* is *al dente*. Serve immediately in hot rimmed soup bowls. Pass the remaining cheese at table. Serves 4 to 6.

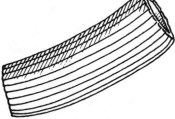

SPAGHETTINI CON PETTO DI POLLO E PISELLI
(*Spaghettini with Chicken Breast and Peas*)

    1 boned chicken breast, cubed
    2 tablespoons olive oil
    ½ teaspoon salt
    Milled black pepper
    1 cup (one 8-ounce can) baby peas
    1 pound spaghettini
    3 tablespoons grated Parmesan cheese
    1 egg, beaten

Sauté chicken cubes in the oil until golden; season with salt and pepper. Heat peas in their liquid; pour liquid into saucepan with chicken and simmer, uncovered, for 5 minutes. Add peas and more black pepper, stir, and simmer for 5 minutes. Cook spaghettini *al dente,* drain, and place in a large hot bowl. Just before serving blend cheese and beaten egg and stir into the chicken and peas. Add half of this to the hot spaghettini and toss well with wooden forks. Serve in hot bowls with the remainder of the sauce spooned atop individual portions. Serves 4 to 6.

CANNELLE CON PURÉ DI POLLO
(*"Small Reeds" with Puréed Chicken*)

> 2 slices of bread
> 1 cup milk
> 1 whole chicken breast
> 1 cup Beef Broth (page 85)
> Pinch of grated nutmeg
> ½ teaspoon salt
> Milled black pepper
> 2 tablespoons butter
> 3 tablespoons Marsala wine
> ½ pound *cannelle*
> 1 egg yolk, beaten
> ½ lemon

Soak the bread in the milk and squeeze almost dry. Mince the raw chicken breast and pound in a mortar with 1 tablespoon of the broth and the bread. Put chicken and bread through a food mill. Season with nutmeg, salt and pepper and stir into the butter in a saucepan. Sauté for 5 minutes. Add Marsala and remainder of broth; simmer, uncovered, stirring often, for 15 minutes. Cook *cannelle al dente*; drain. Take chicken sauce from stove and stir in beaten egg yolk and the juice from the lemon half, blending well. Place over low flame for 2 minutes while you blend. Divide pasta among 4 hot rimmed soup bowls; liberally spoon chicken sauce atop each portion. Serves 4.

MATERA—Basilicata

BAVETTE CON BRACIOLINE DI POLLO ALLA GIOVANNINO
(*Chicken Rolls with Bavette*)

> 2 whole chicken breasts, boned
> 8 slices of prosciutto
> 6 walnuts, ground
> 12 *pignoli* (pine nuts), ground
> ¼ cup grated Parmesan cheese
> 1½ teaspoons salt
> Liberal amount of milled black pepper
> ½ teaspoon monosodium glutamate
> 1 tablespoon minced parsley
> 1 garlic clove
> 2 tablespoons butter
> 1 tablespoon olive oil
> 4 cups (one 2-pound can) Italian plum tomatoes,
>   pushed through food mill
> 1 teaspoon dried sweet basil
> 1 pound *bavette* (narrow *linguine*)

Cut each chicken breast into quarters. Between sheets of wax paper pound the pieces with a wooden mallet or flat side of a cleaver into thin, but intact, scallops. Place 1 slice of prosciutto on each scallop; sprinkle lightly with all the ground walnuts and *pignoli,* a little Parmesan, some salt and pepper, the monosodium glutamate and parsley. Tie with string into compact rolls. Sauté the 8 chicken rolls with the garlic in the butter and oil over medium-high flame, turning often, until they are brown; remove garlic. Lower heat; stir in tomatoes, basil, remaining salt and more pepper. Simmer, uncovered, stirring often, until chicken rolls are tender and sauce smooth and thickened. Cook *bavette al dente;* drain. Place in a large hot bowl and toss with remaining cheese and half of the tomato sauce. Serve in hot bowls with 2 chicken *bracioline* and a liberal amount of remaining sauce atop each portion. Serves 4.

LINGUINE CON FEGATINI DI POLLO
(Linguine with Chicken Livers)

> 2 white onions, chopped
> 2 slices of bacon, diced
> 2 tablespoons olive oil
> 1 teaspoon salt
> Milled black pepper
> 2 cups (one 1-pound can) Italian plum tomatoes
> ⅛ teaspoon crushed red pepper
> ½ pound chicken livers, quartered
> 1 tablespoon butter
> 1 pound *linguine*

Sauté the onions and bacon in the oil until soft. Add the salt, pepper and tomatoes, breaking up the tomatoes with a wooden spoon as they simmer for 20 minutes. Stir in the red pepper. Continue cooking until sauce is thickened and has body and flavor; taste for flavor. In another saucepan sauté quartered livers in the butter for 5 minutes, turning so livers are well buttered. Add to the sauce, stir in well, and simmer for 5 minutes. Cook *linguine al dente;* drain. Serve in ramekins or soup bowls with sauce and livers spooned atop. Serves 4 to 6.

BUCATINI CON VENTRIGLI DI POLLO ALLA NAPOLETANA
(Bucatini with Chicken Gizzards Neapolitan Style)

Most of us consider chicken gizzards cat food. I did too until I had the following dish in Naples. Now it is one I make often.

> 12 chicken gizzards
> 1 onion
> 1 carrot

229

4 teaspoons salt, in all
3 tablespoons butter
1 garlic clove
2 basil leaves, chopped
1 tablespoon chopped parsley
4 cups (one 2-pound can) tomatoes, pushed through food mill
¼ teaspoon crushed red pepper
1 pound *bucatini* (thin macaroni)

Boil chicken gizzards with onion, carrot and 3 teaspoons of the salt in water to cover in a stewpot for 1 hour. Remove gizzards, cool; remove skins and membranes. Dice the lean dark meat and place it in a saucepan with the butter and garlic. Sauté until garlic is soft, then discard garlic. To meat and butter add basil, parsley, tomatoes, 1 teaspoon salt and the red pepper. Simmer, uncovered, stirring often, for 20 minutes, or until sauce is smooth and thickened and diced meat tender. Cook *bucatini al dente,* drain, and toss with half of the tomato-meat sauce. Serve in hot bowls with remaining sauce liberally spooned atop each portion. Serves 6.

FARFALLETTE CON REGAGLIE DI POLLO
("Little Butterflies" with Chicken Giblets)

¾ pound chicken giblets (half livers)
1 small white onion, minced
4 tablespoons butter
3 tablespoons olive oil
½ cup white wine
1 cup canned tomatoes, mashed
1 bouillon cube
Salt
1 cup heavy cream
1 pound *farfallette*
4 tablespoons grated Asiago cheese

230

Wash the giblets; cut them into pieces the size of a fingernail; set livers aside. Sauté the onion in 2 tablespoons of the butter and the oil. When onion is soft, stir in the gizzards and hearts; simmer for 15 minutes while adding the wine, a spoonful at a time. When the wine is used up, stir in the tomatoes and add the bouillon cube and salt to taste. Blend well, cover pan, and simmer for 1½ hours, stirring in, over this period, half of the cup of cream.

At the end of 1½ hours, stir in the livers; taste and adjust the seasoning; simmer for 10 minutes longer. Cook the *farfallette al dente;* drain. Place in a hot bowl, pour in the sauce, the rest of the cream, warmed, the cheese and remaining butter. Toss well with wooden forks. Serve immediately in very hot bowls. Serves 4 to 6.

CAPPONE ALL'ARISTOCRATICA
(*Stuffed Baked Capon*)

1 recipe Mornay Sauce (page 73)
1 capon (6 pounds)
1 carrot
1 white onion
1 teaspoon salt
½ pound elbow macaroni
2 tablespoons grated Parmesan cheese

Prepare Mornay sauce. Simmer capon with carrot, onion and salt in plenty of water until tender, 1½ to 2 hours. Remove intact and cool. Cook macaroni *al dente*, drain well, and toss with half of the Mornay sauce. Stuff capon with the pasta, sewing or skewering cavity. Place capon in a buttered baking dish, spoon remaining Mornay sauce over it, and sprinkle with cheese. Bake, uncovered, in a preheated 375° F. oven until brown. Serves 6.

GAMBA DISOSSATA DI CAPPONE ALLA TOSCANA
(Boned Leg of Capon Tuscan Style)

I tried this recipe in the home of a writer friend in Florence, and liked it so much that I have prepared it often since. He used the tasty wild mushrooms, porcini, which imparted a special flavor, but ordinary mushrooms do well too.

> 2 capon legs (or plump chicken legs)
> 2 eggs, beaten
> 4 tablespoons butter, in all
> 2 tablespoons olive oil
> 1 teaspoon salt
> Liberal amount of milled black pepper
> 1 garlic clove, mashed
> 6 large mushrooms, quartered
> ½ lemon
> 1 white truffle, sliced thin
> 1 pound *fettuccelle* (narrow *fettuccine*)
> 2 tablespoons grated Parmesan cheese
> 3 tablespoons heavy cream

Skin and bone capon legs and pound the meat as for scaloppine. Dip into beaten eggs and sauté in 2 tablespoons of the butter and the oil over medium-high flame until golden. Sprinkle with salt and pepper; add the garlic and mushrooms. Turn the capon legs once and simmer for 5 minutes. Discard garlic. Take capon from saucepan and cut into julienne strips. Replace in saucepan, squeeze lemon juice over all, and stir in the sliced truffle; blend. Simmer for 5 minutes, uncovered, stirring constantly. Cook *fettuccelle al dente;* drain. Place in a large hot bowl and toss with the cheese, remaining butter, melted, and the cream. Add half of the sauce and toss again. Serve immediately in hot bowls with the remaining capon sauce spooned atop individual portions. Pass more grated Parmesan at table. Serves 4 to 6.

LINGUINE FINE CON FILETTI DI TACCHINO
(Fine Linguine with Turkey Fillets)

This I had in Alberto Wirth's fine Victoria Hotel in Rome. Knowing that I am un tifoso di pasta, *my friend Alberto had one of the turkey fillets cut into thin strips and tossed with a dish of* linguine fine *as first course. We finished with that classic Bolognese dish of turkey breast so popular in Rome.*

> 4 cups Basic Tomato Sauce (page 63)
> 1 breast from an 8-pound turkey
> 2 eggs, beaten
> 1 cup seasoned bread crumbs
> 3 tablespoons olive oil
> 3 tablespoons butter
> ½ pound lean prosciutto, sliced thin
> 2 tablespoons grated Parmesan cheese
> 1 small ball of mozzarella cheese
> 1 pound *linguine fine*

Prepare the tomato sauce; simmer. Cut the turkey breast into slices ⅓-inch thick. Dip each slice first into beaten eggs, then into bread crumbs; do this lightly; use not too much of either so that neither egg or bread dominates the flavor. Sauté the slices in oil and butter until golden brown, turning once. Butter a casserole or baking dish and arrange the sautéed slices in it. Place a slice of prosciutto on each slice of turkey, sprinkle lightly with Parmesan, and then lay a slice of mozzarella on each. Bake in a preheated 375° F. oven for 15 minutes, or until cheese melts and turkey is tender. Cook pasta *al dente*, drain, and place in a large hot bowl; toss with half of the tomato sauce. Slice one turkey fillet into very thin strips; toss with the pasta. Serve immediately in hot rimmed soup bowls. Follow with the turkey slices, each topped with a small spoonful of tomato sauce, as a main course, accompanied with a green salad and a glass of very cold Soave Bertani, a classic Italian white wine. Serves 6.

ZITI CON PETTO DI TACCHINO ALLA MODENESE
(Baked "Bridegrooms" with Turkey Breast Modena Style)

½ small turkey breast, cubed
2 tablespoons flour
½ teaspoon salt
Milled black pepper
Light pinch of grated nutmeg
3 tablespoons butter
1 white onion, minced
1 celery rib, minced
1½ cups Chicken Broth (page 84)
4 mushrooms, sliced
1 pound *ziti*
1 cup sour cream, warm
¼ cup buttered bread crumbs

Lightly sprinkle the turkey cubes with flour and season with salt, pepper and nutmeg. Sauté in the butter until golden. Blend in onion and celery and sauté until vegetables are soft. Add broth, cover the pan, and simmer until meat is tender, about 25 minutes. Remove cover, stir in mushrooms, and simmer for 10 minutes, stirring often. Cook *ziti al dente,* drain, and place in a large hot bowl. Pour turkey-mushroom sauce over *ziti,* stir in the sour cream, and toss well. Place in a 2-quart casserole and sprinkle bread crumbs atop. Bake in preheated 400° F. oven for 15 minutes, until top is browned. Serves 4 to 6.

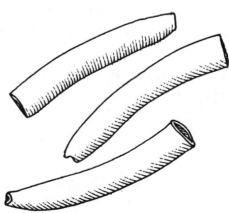

TAGLIOLINI CON PICCIONCELLI
(Baked Narrow Egg Noodles with Squabs)

In my opinion, squabs are the best of poultry and game, being 26-day-old pigeons that have become butterball-fat from being forcefed by their parents. At this age they have never left the nest so they are tender, succulent fare, prized by those who know fine food. Here's one way the Italians team them with pasta.

> 1 recipe Béchamel Sauce (page 73)
> 2 tablespoons butter
> 2 tablespoons olive oil
> 4 slices of prosciuttini (lean ham), diced
> 2 shallots, chopped
> 1 carrot, chopped
> ½ cup chopped celery leaves
> 3 plump squabs
> 1 teaspoon salt
> Liberal amount of milled black pepper
> ½ cup rosé wine
> 2 cups Chicken Broth (page 84)
> Squabs' livers, hearts, gizzards, minced
> 1 pound of *tagliolini*
> ¼ cup grated Asiago cheese

Make the Béchamel sauce. In a deep saucepan, sauté in the butter and oil the ham, shallots, carrot and celery leaves until soft. Add the squabs, and brown, turning on all sides; season with the salt and plenty of black pepper. When birds are well browned, pour in the wine and cook over medium-high flame until it has evaporated. Add the broth, cover the pot, and simmer for 30 minutes, until birds are fork-tender. Remove squabs; cool. Take meat from bones and cube; add with minced giblets to sauce pot and simmer, uncovered, for 10 minutes, stirring often. Cook *tagliolini al dente,* drain, and place in a casserole. Pour the squab sauce, half the Béchamel sauce and all the cheese over the pasta; blend. Cover with remaining Béchamel and brown in 400° F. oven for 10 minutes. Serves 6.

MODENA, the Piazza Grande—Emilia-Romagna

PAPPARDELLE CON PICCIONCELLI
(Broad Egg Noodles with Squab)

> 2 squabs (about 1 pound each)
> ½ teaspoon salt
> Liberal amount of milled black pepper
> 2 tablespoons soft butter
> ½ cup dry white wine
> 1 cup sour cream
> 1 pound *pappardelle*

Clean squabs well, rub with salt and pepper, and spread with soft butter. Place in a baking pan, add the wine, and cook, covered, in 400° F. oven for 1 hour. Remove. Take breasts from squabs and cut into strips ½ inch long, ¼ inch wide. Replace in baking pan, cover with sour cream, and cook, uncovered in 350° F. oven for 15 minutes, until cream has browned. Stir often during this last cooking stage. Cook *pappardelle al dente*, drain well, and toss with squab and sour cream. Serve in warm bowls. Serves 4 to 6.

TORTELLINI DI PICCIONCELLO
(Tortellini of Squab)

Italians use squab often, in many ways. Here is one of the simplest and tastiest in a dish I sampled first in Piacenza.

> 1 recipe Pasta Fresca for Tortellini (page 44)
> 1 squab
> 4 teaspoons salt, in all
> 6 slices of prosciutto
> ¼ teaspoon grated nutmeg

Milled black pepper
¼ cup grated Parmesan cheese
4 quarts Chicken Broth (page 84)
3 tablespoons butter, melted

Prepare the fresh pasta dough. Boil squab in water with 3 teaspoons salt for 35 minutes. Remove, cool, skin; take meat from bones. Mince finely (or put through grinder) squab meat and prosciutto; work meats into a paste, mixing in nutmeg, 1 teaspoon salt, pepper and half of the cheese. Cut dough and fill with this mixture, to make *tortellini* (page 45); shape as suggested and dry. Cook a few at a time in just simmering chicken broth (do not let the broth boil vigorously or it will break open the *tortellini*) until done. Remove with a slotted spoon to a warm platter, cover with hot butter, and sprinkle with remaining cheese. Serve immediately. Serves 4 to 6.

MAFALDA E FARAONA
(Broad Noodles and Guinea Fowl)

The route of the guinea fowl is an adventurous one—from Africa's dark jungles and plains to ancient Carthage, to epicurean Rome, where I first had it, naturally, with pasta.

4 tablespoons butter, in all
2 tablespoons olive oil
2 guinea hens, halved
2 guinea hen livers, minced
2 ounces dried beef, minced
1 onion, minced
1 carrot, minced
1 celery rib, minced
1 tablespoon minced Italian parsley
2 very ripe tomatoes, peeled and diced

Liberal amount of milled black pepper
2 cups Chicken Broth (page 84)
½ pound *mafalda* (a broad noodle, rippled on both
    edges)
¼ cup grated Parmesan cheese

In a deep saucepan heat 3 tablespoons of the butter and the oil, and in it
sauté the guinea hens until brown. Stir in the minced livers, beef, onion,
carrot, celery, parsley, tomatoes, plenty of pepper, and the broth. Simmer for
1½ hours, covered, or until guinea hens are tender. Remove birds to a warm
platter for second course, spooning one third of the sauce over them to keep
them moist. Simmer rest of sauce 15 minutes, uncovered, until smooth and
thickened. Cook *mafalda al dente,* drain well. Place in a large hot bowl, toss
with 1 tablespoon butter and the cheese. Serve immediately in hot bowls with
more sauce spooned atop each portion. Pass more grated cheese at table.
Serves 4.

LINGUINE ALLA CACCIATORA TOSCANA
(*Linguine Tuscan Hunter Style*)

1 duckling
1½ tablespoons salt
Milled black pepper
3 tablespoons chopped parsley
2 small carrots
1 onion
1 celery rib
Duckling's liver
6 tablespoons butter
1 pound *linguine*
½ cup grated Parmesan cheese

Place the duckling in a large pot, cover with water, and add salt, pepper, 2
tablespoons of the parsley, the carrots, onion and celery. Cover, bring to a

boil, lower heat, and simmer for 1½ hours, or until duckling is tender. Remove duckling, saving the water, and cool. Take meat from bones and put through grinder with the remaining tablespoon of parsley, mincing finely. Mince the liver and sauté it for 5 minutes in the butter. Cook *linguine al dente* in the water in which duckling simmered; drain. On a hot serving platter arrange one layer of *linguine,* cover with minced duckling, sprinkle with Parmesan, then cover with minced liver and butter; repeat with at least another layer of all ingredients. Serves 4 to 6.

LASAGNE RICCIE CON ANITRA
("Curly" Lasagne with Duck)

This is one of those rare pasta dishes that is used in Italy as the main course. But lasagne *with sauce and meat often is considered a meal in itself, although I have also had it many times in a small first serving before the entrée. Here is a recipe I enjoyed after a duck shoot in Italy's northern lakes region. Only the duck breasts were used; there is little meat on the legs and wild duck wings are too tough for the palate.*

> 1 duck liver
> 2 duck breasts
> 4 tablespoons butter
> 1 tablespoon olive oil
> 4 small white onions, chopped
> 4 cups (one 2-pound can) Italian plum tomatoes
> 1 cup red wine
> Pinch of dried rosemary
> Pinch of dried orégano
> 1½ teaspoons salt
> Milled black pepper
> 1 pound *lasagne riccie*

Chop and put aside the duck liver; cut each half breast into quarters. Brown duck pieces in the butter and oil; remove. Add the onions and sauté until soft. Stir in the tomatoes; simmer for 20 minutes. Return the duck to the pan and blend in the wine, rosemary, orégano, salt and pepper. Now simmer, uncovered, for 1 hour, or until duck is tender, stirring often. Cook *lasagne riccie al dente;* drain with slotted spoon. Place the pasta on a large warm serving dish. Stir the chopped duck liver into the sauce; simmer for 5 minutes. Spoon the hot sauce and duck pieces over the noodles. Serves 4 to 6.

ARZAVOLA E SALSA COI FUNGHI
(Wild Duck and Mushroom and Cheese Sauce)

> 2 tablespoons butter
> 2 tablespoons olive oil
> 1 white onion, chopped
> 2 whole Mallard duck breasts, boned
> Milled black pepper
> 8 slices of prosciutto
> 4 cups Mushroom and Cheese Sauce (page 74)
> ½ pound spaghettini
> 4 tablespoons grated Parmesan cheese

Heat butter and oil in a pot; sauté onion in it until soft. Add the duck breasts, liberally mill in pepper, and sauté over medium-high flame until brown, turning often. Remove breasts, wrap 4 slices of prosciutto around each, and skewer in place with toothpicks. Return to pot and sauté, turning often, for 15 minutes. Prepare mushroom and cheese sauce. Pour sauce over duck breasts and simmer, uncovered, for 30 minutes, or until breasts are fork-tender. Remove breasts; cut 2 wafer-thin slices from each breast, and add the slices to the pot with the mushroom and cheese sauce. Place remaining breasts on a warm platter, to be sliced and served as entrée with vegetable and salad. Cook spaghettini *al dente,* drain, and place in a warm bowl. Toss with the cheese and serve immediately in hot soup bowls with liberal spoonings of the mushroom sauce atop, and 1 slice of duck centering each portion. Serves 4.

FOLAGHE STUFATE CON LINGUINE
(*Stewed Coots with Linguine*)

This is a dish I had in Pisa after waterfowling on nearby Lake Massacciuoli. Coots are waterfowl with a penchant for fish; consequently it is difficult to tell whether you are eating fish or fowl, so much so, that many Italians believe it is proper to eat them on meatless Fridays. I offer this as I saw it prepared, but suggest that you use a duckling instead of the coots.

> 4 tablespoons butter
> 1 tablespoon olive oil
> 1 white onion, chopped
> 1 carrot, chopped
> 1 celery rib, chopped
> 1 tablespoon chopped parsley
> 2 coots (or 1 duckling)
> 1 teaspoon salt
> Liberal amount of milled black pepper
> ½ teaspoon dried orégano
> 6 cups Basic Tomato Sauce (page 63)
> 1 pound *linguine*
> Grated Asiago cheese

Melt butter and oil in a large pot; sauté onion, carrot, celery and parsley until soft. Add the coots (or duckling), season with salt, pepper and orégano, and brown over high flame on all sides. Reduce flame; add tomato sauce, cover pot, and simmer for 1½ to 2 hours, until birds are fork-tender. Remove birds from pot; cool; take meat from bones and put through grinder. Strain tomato sauce from the cooking pot into a saucepan, stir in the ground poultry; simmer, uncovered, stirring often, for 10 minutes. Cook *linguine al dente;* drain. Serve in hot soup bowls with sauce liberally spooned atop. Pass grated cheese at table. Serves 4 to 6.

AGNOLOTTI BERGAMO CON PERNICI ALLA GIOVANNINO

(Giovannino's Agnolotti Bergamo with Partridges)

1 recipe Pasta Fresca for Ravioli (page 44)
5 red-legged partridges or grouse
5 garlic cloves
8 tablespoons butter
4 tablespoons olive oil
1 tablespoon salt
Much freshly milled black pepper
2 white onions, chopped
2 tablespoons chopped raisins
2 eggs, beaten
5 tablespoons grated Parmesan cheese
4 tablespoons dry bread crumbs
1 tablespoon flour
3 tablespoons warm water
4 tablespoons red currant jelly

Prepare *ravioli* dough and set aside. Rub the partridges with 3 of the garlic cloves, mashed. Then spread 1 tablespoon soft butter over each bird. Place remaining garlic and the oil in a roasting pan and brown garlic on top of stove; remove garlic. Place partridges in the pan, sprinkle with salt and pepper, and brown the birds well. Cover the roasting pan and cook the birds in a 400° F. oven for 1 hour, or until they are tender to the fork. Remove 4 birds to a warm platter for main course. Cool the remaining bird and remove meat from bones; discard skin and bones. Grind the partridge meat or mince finely and sauté with the onions in 3 tablespoons of the butter until the onions are soft. Take from the fire and stir in the raisins, beaten eggs, cheese and bread crumbs. Sprinkle with salt and pepper and blend well.

Roll out pasta dough into thin sheets. Spoon teaspoons of the partridge mixture on one sheet of dough, placing the mounds 2 inches apart; place the other sheet of dough on top and carefully press around each mound of filling. Cut around the mounds with a pastry cutter or sharp knife, making 2-inch

243

circles. Press the edges of each one again, sealing; dry for 20 minutes. Cook *al dente* in simmering salted water, about 8 minutes. Lift out the *agnolotti* with a slotted spoon.

Now place the partridge roasting pan on top of the stove over a low fire. Stir in the flour with a wooden spoon; scrape the brown particles from sides of pan, and stir into a smooth paste with the juices remaining in the pan. Add the warm water and currant jelly, stirring and blending everything well. Spoon 1 teaspoon of this sauce over each hot dumpling and serve immediately. Split the remaining partridges, re-warm in remaining sauce in the roasting pan, and serve half of a bird per person for the main course. Serves 6 to 8.

LUMACHE CON PERNICIOTTE
(*"Snails" with Young Partridge*)

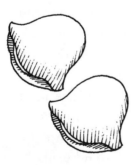

    2 tablespoons olive oil
    2 tablespoons butter
    2 partridges
    Pinch of dried rosemary
    2 shallots, minced
    Partridge livers and hearts, minced
  10 black olives, pitted and sliced
    1 teaspoon salt
    Liberal amount of milled black pepper
    4 cups Chicken Broth (page 84)
    1 pound *lumache*
    1 tablespoon butter
    ¼ cup grated Asiago cheese

Heat oil and butter in a large pot and sauté the partridges in it, browning evenly. Stir in the rosemary, shallots, minced livers and hearts, olives, salt, pepper and broth. Cover pot and bake in 350° F. oven for 1 hour, basting often, until the partridges are fork-tender. Remove the birds; cool. Skin the birds and take meat from bones; cut into 1-inch strips. Place them in the sauce and simmer all on top of the stove, uncovered, for 15 minutes, stirring often until sauce is smooth and thickened. Cook *lumache al dente;* drain. Place in a large hot bowl, toss with the butter, then with the cheese. Serve immediately in hot rimmed soup bowls, with partridge strips in sauce liberally spooned atop each portion. Pass more cheese at table. Serves 6.

SPAGHETTI CON SALSA DI FAGIANO ALLA "POOR SHOT"
(*Spaghetti with Pheasant Sauce*)

In Italy, especially in Rome, during the late fall and early winter, game of many kinds can be seen hanging in front of the trattorie—*wild boar, rabbits, pheasants, partridges, hare. From them come many a tasty pasta sauce. I was fortunate enough to be in on the bagging of the game and making of one such sauce—in this case, the game was a big cock pheasant. Shooting on the estate of a friend of a friend in the North, near Bologna, one of us shot too quickly as the big bird rose cackling hoarsely, the sun flaming on his iridescent ruff. "That one is for the pot and pasta," our host said to the embarrassed gunner. That night, using just the breast meat of the shot-riddled bird which he had soaked in heavily salted water, then drained, he prepared a sauce to remember.*

    1 pheasant breast, boned
    1 small white onion, chopped
    4 tablespoons butter
    1 tablespoon olive oil
    1 teaspoon salt
    ¼ teaspoon crushed red pepper
    2 basil leaves, chopped
    6 very ripe tomatoes, peeled and diced
      Giblets of the bird, including liver
    1 pound spaghetti

Cut the pheasant meat into pieces the size of your thumbnail. Sauté the onion in the butter and oil over medium flame until soft. Stir in the diced pheasant and the salt. Simmer until the meat is brown, stirring constantly with a wooden spoon. Blend in the red pepper, basil leaves and tomatoes, breaking up the tomatoes with a wooden spoon as they cook. Simmer, uncovered, for 25 minutes, until sauce is satiny and the meat tender. Chop the giblets and stir in; simmer for 15 minutes. Cook the spaghetti *al dente*, drain, and place in a warm bowl. Spoon in half of the pheasant sauce and toss gently with wooden forks. Serve in hot soup bowls, with a heaping spoon of the remaining sauce over each serving. Serves 4 to 6.

SPAGHETTI E FAGIANO ALLA GRECO
(*Spaghetti and Pheasant Greek Style*)

I call this unusual dish Greek because when I had it, on an Italian shooting preserve, it was cooked by a chef from Athens, proving that pasta has no nationality, its appeal is truly international.

> ½ cup flour
> ½ tablespoon salt
> Generous amount of milled black pepper
> 1 pheasant, cut into pieces
> 3 tablespoons olive oil
> 8 white onions, chopped
> 2 garlic cloves, minced
> 2 cups Chicken Broth (page 84), warmed
> 1 pound spaghetti

Place the flour, salt and much pepper in a paper bag. Shake the pheasant pieces in the bag until they are evenly floured. Sauté in the oil until the meat is brown; remove the pheasant pieces to a heatproof glass casserole or roaster. Stir the onions and garlic into the oil, scraping the sides and bottom of the pan with a wooden spoon to dislodge browned particles. When onions are soft, stir in the warm broth; simmer until you have a smooth brown gravy. Pour the gravy over the pheasant, cover, and cook in a 350° F. oven for about 25 minutes, until meat is fork-tender. Cook spaghetti *al dente*, drain, and place in a warm bowl. Remove pheasant to a warm platter for second course. Spoon half of the sauce that remains over the spaghetti and toss gently with forks. Serve remaining sauce atop individual bowls of spaghetti. Serves 4 to 6.

FETTUCCE RICCIE E FAGIANO ALLA PASQUALE
(Pasquale's "Curly Ribbons" with Pheasant)

> 1 large pheasant, cut into serving pieces
> 3 tablespoons olive oil
> 2 tablespoons chopped parsley
> 2 garlic cloves, minced
> ⅛ teaspoon minced fresh rosemary
> 10 medium mushrooms, sliced
> 4 tablespoons butter
> 1 large beefsteak tomato, peeled and diced
> ½ cup white wine
> 1½ cups Chicken Broth (page 84)
> 1 teaspoon salt
> Milled black pepper
> 1 pound *fettucce riccie*

Brown pheasant in the sizzling oil, stirring in parsley, garlic and rosemary. When completely browned, pour off oil, add mushrooms, butter and tomato; simmer for 8 minutes. Blend in wine and chicken broth and sprinkle in salt and pepper; stir well. Simmer, covered, until pheasant is tender, about 30 minutes. Cook *fettucce riccie al dente;* drain. Serve in hot soup bowls with the pheasant sauce spooned over. Serve pheasant for second course with a salad and vegetable. Serves 4 to 6.

ORTA—Piedmont

TAGLIOLETTE CON QUAGLIE
(*Noodles with Quail*)

Italians eat just about anything that flies except crows, vultures, hawks and owls, and they are considered Europe's most avid bird watchers. Warblers, buntings, thrush, larks, finch, most birds that we fill our bird feeders for, are fair game. And I must admit the birds come to table as superb fare. In the larger cities there are even vendors (somewhat like our so-called "hot-dog stands") that sell tiny birds, broiled on a spit, and glasses of wine. But in deference to the Audubon Society and bird lovers, I will omit the many recipes for the birds of the field, and concentrate on game birds. One of the best, the most delicate, is the quail. The following I had in Turin on a nest of noodles and it is a superlative entrée.

> ½ pound salted butter
> 8 quail, dressed
> 1 cup heavy cream
> 1 pound *tagliolette*

Melt butter in a deep saucepan, add the quail, and sauté over medium-high flame, continually basting the little birds, inside and out, until they are fork-tender and golden-crisp; probably 25 minutes will do it. Remove to a warm platter. Stir the cream into the melted butter. Simmer, stirring constantly, until mixture forms a smooth and thick sauce. Cook *tagliolette al dente;* drain. Place on a large hot serving platter; arrange the quail on the noodles and pour the butter-cream sauce over all. Serve 2 quail on a nest of noodles to each guest. Serves 4.

LINGUE DI PASSERI E BECCACCE CON SALSA ALLA MILANESE
(*"Sparrows' Tongues" and Woodcock with Milanese Sauce*)

Woodcock are big-billed, darting game birds with breasts of delicately flavored dark meat. Here's the way I had them in Milan.

> 7 tablespoons butter, in all
> 4 woodcock (if you are man enough to bag them)
> 6 mushrooms, minced
> 2 anchovies, minced
> ½ tablespoon flour
> 1 cup Chicken Broth (page 84)
> ½ cup white wine
> ¼ cup caper vinegar
> ½ teaspoon Dijon mustard
> ½ teaspoon salt
> Pinch of cayenne pepper
> 1 pound *lingue di passeri*
> 1 teaspoon capers

In a deep saucepan melt 4 tablespoons of the butter and braise woodcock until evenly browned. Add minced mushrooms and anchovies; simmer. Make a *roux* by blending remaining butter and the flour in a saucepan; stir in broth, wine, caper vinegar, mustard, salt and cayenne, blending well. Pour this over woodcock; cover pan and simmer, stirring often, for 45 minutes, or until birds are tender. Remove woodcock, retaining only the breasts; keep warm. Simmer sauce, uncovered, stirring, until it is smooth and thickened. Cook *lingue di passeri al dente,* drain, and place in a large hot bowl. Strain sauce; add the capers. Pour half of the sauce over the pasta and toss well. Serve immediately in hot rimmed soup bowls, with 1 woodcock breast, covered with sauce, atop each portion. Serves 4.

CONCHIGLIE CON CONIGLIO IN UMIDO
("Shells" with Rabbit Stew)

Rabbit is a dish often served in Rome, usually on Saturday, the same day the Romans serve their famous tripe (see page 178). Here's a rabbit and pasta stew I had there.

> 1 young rabbit, boned (save bones)
> 4 tablespoons butter
> 12 small onions, peeled
> 10 small carrots, scraped
> 4 tablespoons flour
> 1 tablespoon salt
> Liberal amount of milled black pepper
> 1 teaspoon prepared mustard
> 1 bay leaf
> 2 cups Chicken Broth (page 84)
> 1 cup tomato juice
> 1 pound *conchiglie*

Cut rabbit into cubes. Brown the bones in the butter. Add the rabbit meat; brown. Place rabbit cubes in a large casserole; add onions and carrots. Blend flour, salt, pepper, mustard, bay leaf, broth and tomato juice. Pour into the saucepan with the butter and rabbit bones; simmer, uncovered, stirring often, for 15 minutes. Discard bones. Pour sauce over the rabbit and vegetables in casserole; cover. Bake in preheated 325° F. oven for 2 hours. Cook *conchiglie al dente*; drain. Remove cover from casserole and spoon pasta around the border, pushing it into the sauce. Increase heat to 400° F.; bake for 15 minutes, until sauce is bubbling. Serves 6.

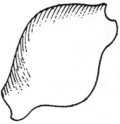

LINGUINE CON CONIGLIO E FUNGHI
(*Linguine with Rabbit and Mushrooms*)

    4 small white onions, chopped
    1 garlic clove, minced
    4 tablespoons olive oil
    1 young rabbit, cut up
    1 teaspoon salt
Liberal amount of milled black pepper
12 small plum tomatoes, peeled and diced
Pinch of grated nutmeg
    1 clove
  ⅓ teaspoon dried red pepper
    1 pound mushrooms, sliced
    1 pound *linguine*

Sauté onions and garlic in the oil until soft. Place rabbit pieces in the pan and sprinkle with salt and pepper; toss rabbit in the oil and onions, coating it, and brown over medium-high heat. Blend in tomatoes and stir in nutmeg, clove and red pepper. Cover, but stir often, and cook for 35 minutes, until rabbit is fork-tender. Remove to a warm platter for a second course.

    Stir sliced mushrooms into the sauce and cook, uncovered, for 8 minutes. Cook *linguine al dente,* drain, and toss with half of the sauce. Spoon the remainder over individual portions of pasta. Serves 4 to 6.

MOSTACCIOLINI CON CONIGLIO
(*"Tiny Moustaches" with Rabbit*)

    1 young rabbit
    2 tablespoons of butter
    2 tablespoons chopped prosciutto fat
    1 white onion, chopped

1 celery rib, chopped
1 bay leaf, broken up
1 teaspoon salt
1 teaspoon flour
2 cups Chicken Broth (page 84)
1 pound *mostacciolini*
¼ cup grated Parmesan cheese

Remove lean meat from rabbit and dice; sauté in the butter, stirring in ham fat, onion, celery and bay leaf. Sprinkle in salt and simmer until ham fat is crisp and onion soft. Add the flour, sprinkling in evenly, then the broth. Cover the pan and simmer until rabbit is tender, about 20 minutes. Remove cover, increase heat, and stir sauce, cooking until it is thickened. Cook *mostacciolini al dente,* drain, and toss in a bowl with the cheese, using forks. Add half of the rabbit sauce and toss again. Serve in rimmed soup bowls with a spoon of the sauce over each serving. Serves 4 to 6.

TAGLIATELLE CON CONIGLIO
(*Broad Egg Noodles with Rabbit*)

6 slices of prosciutto
1 small onion
1 carrot
1 tablespoon chopped parsley
5 tablespoons butter, in all
1 tablespoon olive oil
1 young rabbit, cut into serving pieces
1 teaspoon salt
Liberal amount of milled black pepper
4 ripe tomatoes, peeled and diced
2 cups Chicken Broth (page 84)
½ tablespoon flour
1 pound *tagliatelle*
¼ cup grated Parmesan cheese

Finely mince prosciutto, onion, carrot and parsley. Sauté in 3 tablespoons of the butter and the oil until onion is soft and ham beginning to crisp. Add the rabbit, season with salt and pepper, and brown evenly on all sides over medium-high flame. Reduce heat, add tomatoes and broth, and simmer, covered, for 1½ hours, or until meat is fork-tender. Remove rabbit pieces and cool; take meat from bones and chop coarsely. Make a *roux* or smooth golden butter paste by melting remaining 2 tablespoons butter and stirring in the flour. Stir this and the coarsely chopped rabbit meat into the tomato-vegetable sauce; simmer, uncovered, for 10 minutes, until the sauce is smooth and thickened. Cook *tagliatelle al dente;* drain. Place in a large hot bowl, toss with half of the cheese, then with half of the sauce. Serve immediately in hot bowls, passing extra sauce and extra cheese at table. Serves 4 to 6.

PAPPARDELLE CON SALSA DI LEPRE
(*Wide Egg Noodles with Hare Sauce*)

Pasta with hare sauce is a favorite of mine. I've had it in many places in Italy, but the memorable ones come from Chianti and La Fontanella in Rome, both specializing in game cookery as practiced in Tuscany. This, I believe, is the classic hare sauce.

    1 small hare, boned (save the bones)
    3 tablespoons butter
    2 tablespoons olive oil
    2 carrots
    3 shallots
    1 garlic clove
    1½ teaspoons salt
    Liberal amount of milled black pepper
    1 teaspoon dried tarragon
    2 large very ripe tomatoes, peeled and diced
    1½ cups red wine

Liver of the hare, chopped
2 chicken livers, chopped
1 pound *pappardelle*
¼ cup grated Romano cheese

Brown the hare bones in 2 tablespoons of the butter and the oil in a deep saucepan. Finely mince carrots, shallots and garlic; stir in; simmer, uncovered, for 15 minutes. Mince hare meat, or put through grinder. Remove hare bones from saucepan, add minced hare to remaining vegetables, stirring well, and season with salt, pepper and tarragon; brown. Add the tomatoes and wine, cover the pot, and simmer for 2 hours, stirring often. Remove cover and simmer for 15 minutes, until sauce is brown, smooth and thickened. Add the livers; simmer 4 minutes. Cook *pappardelle al dente,* drain, and toss with remaining butter and half of the cheese. Serve in hot bowls with hare sauce liberally spooned atop; pass more cheese at table. Serves 4 to 6.

FETTUCCE CON LEPRE
(*Wide Fettuccine with Hare*)

Hare, especially if it isn't young, is a rather dry meat; the Germans offset this by larding. The Italians have several ways of moistening the meat. Here's one method I learned in Ravenna.

1 recipe Mornay Sauce (page 73)
2 ounces dried beef
1 small white onion
1 carrot
1 celery rib
3 tablespoons butter
1 tablespoon olive oil
1 small hare, boned
Pinch of grated nutmeg

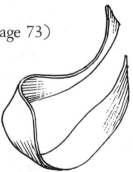

Milled black pepper
Liver and kidney of hare, diced
1 pound *fettucce* (wide *fettuccine*)

Make the Mornay sauce. Finely mince the dried beef, onion, carrot and celery; sauté in butter and oil until onion is soft. Cube the hare meat and sauté in the same pan until brown. Sprinkle in nutmeg and pepper, blending well. Add the liver and kidney and sauté for 5 minutes. Blend in the Mornay sauce and simmer, uncovered, until sauce is smooth and thickened and ingredients well blended. Cook *fettucce al dente;* drain. Place in a large hot bowl, pour in half of the hare sauce, and toss well. Serve immediately in hot bowls with the remaining sauce liberally spooned atop the portions. Serves 4 to 6.

LEPRE ALLA FIORENTINA
(Hare in the Florence Style)

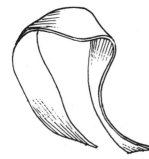

1 loin of hare
4 tablespoons olive oil
3 carrots, chopped
3 celery ribs, chopped
3 white onions, chopped
½ teaspoon salt
Milled black pepper
1½ cups red Chianti
4 very ripe tomatoes, peeled and diced
2 garlic cloves
4 rosemary leaves
2 sage leaves
3 slices of bacon, chopped
2 anchovies, chopped
1 pound *fettucce* (wide *fettuccine*)
1 tablespoon butter
¼ cup grated Parmesan cheese

Brown the hare in the oil, turning often. Lower flame and add the carrots, celery and onions; season with salt and pepper and simmer, stirring often, for 15 minutes. Add the wine, tomatoes, garlic, rosemary, sage, bacon and anchovies; blend well. Simmer, uncovered, basting often, for 1½ hours, or until meat is tender and sauce is dark brown and thickened. Remove hare, cube the meat, and return it to the sauce; simmer. Cook *fettucce al dente*, drain, and place in a hot bowl with the butter; toss. Add the cheese; toss again. Serve in hot soup bowls with hare sauce liberally spooned atop each portion. Serves 4 to 6.

TAGLIATELLE VERDI CON CAPRIOLO
(*Green Noodles with Venison*)

1 recipe Pasta Verde (page 45)
2 garlic cloves, chopped
2 tablespoons chopped parsley
14 very thin slices of prosciutto
3-pound loin of vension, well hung
2 tablespoons olive oil
8 mushrooms, sliced
1 cup red wine
2 white onions, chopped
2 carrots, chopped
2 celery ribs, chopped
12 small very ripe plum tomatoes, peeled
1 clove
2 cups boiling water
1 teaspoon salt
½ cup grated Parmesan cheese

Prepare the green pasta dough, cut into *tagliatelle* (page 43), and dry. Mix half of the garlic and half of the parsley and mince together. Roll 10 slices of prosciutto in the mixture until they are well coated. Lard the

258

venison; make deep incisions in the meat; push the prosciutto into the slits. Chop remaining prosciutto. Sauté remaining garlic and parsley and the chopped prosciutto in the oil in a heavy pot. When ham fat is crisp, put in the venison and brown on all sides over a medium flame. Add the mushrooms and wine, cover the pot, place over low flame, and simmer for 10 minutes. Stir in the chopped onions, carrots and celery, blending in well. Cook for 15 minutes, lifting the meat and stirring with a wooden spoon to dislodge browned particles that have stuck to the bottom of the pan. Now add the whole plum tomatoes and the clove, stirring them in well. Simmer for 20 minutes, covered, stirring often. Pour in the boiling water and add the salt, stirring in well. When venison is fork-tender remove to a warm platter for the second course.

Stir sauce in pan well and strain through cheesecloth or a fine strainer. Replace in pan and simmer for 15 minutes, uncovered. Cook *tagliatelle al dente;* watch carefully as fresh pasta cooks more rapidly than dry. Drain, place in a warm bowl, and toss with the cheese, using wooden forks. Serve in hot rimmed soup bowls with strained venison sauce lavishly spooned over each serving. Serves 4 to 6.

Chapter IX

Near GRIMALDI—Calabria

Vegetables with PASTA

$\mathcal{T}$he versatility of pasta was never more clearly pointed out to me than one evening when I arrived at my mother-in-law's, hungry for a dish of spaghetti. Nonplussed for exactly thirty seconds because she had no sauce prepared, she went into her garden and picked a head of cauliflower. She quickly boiled it, separating it into little "flowers" when it was tender. These she put into a frypan with one quarter pound of butter and liberally milled black pepper over it, stirring gently until cauliflower and butter were blended and steaming hot. Then she covered the pan, turned the fire very low, and in another pot cooked the spaghetti less than *al dente*. Drained, it was then put with the butter and vegetable and tossed right in that pan. It was a delicious, fresh-tasting meal right from the garden.

Many superb pasta sauces are growing in your garden, dishes that can come to table as fresh as springtime and as stimulating as summer.

LINGUINE CON ASPARAGI
(*Linguine with Asparagus*)

> 18 tips of fresh young asparagus
> 1 teaspoon salt
> ¼ pound butter
> Milled black pepper
> 1 pound *linguine*
> ½ cup grated Parmesan cheese

Carefully cook the asparagus tips in salted water to cover until they are almost done; do not let them break up; just over 5 minutes should do it; drain. Replace asparagus in the pot with half of the butter; mill in black pepper and shake the pan well so asparagus is butter coated. Cook *linguine al dente;* drain. Toss in a warm bowl with remaining butter and the cheese; mill in black pepper and toss gently again. Serve in hot soup bowls with the asparagus tips atop, evenly divided among the servings. Serves 4 to 6.

BUCATINI CON BROCCOLI ALLA CALABRESE
(*Bucatini with Broccoli Calabrian Style*)

This is a specialty of Calabria that I always have at least twice when in the area.

> 1 large bunch of broccoli
> 2 garlic cloves, minced
> 4 tablespoons olive oil
> 2 pounds ripe tomatoes, peeled and cut into strips
> 4 tablespoons mixed raisins and pine nuts, minced
> 1 pound *bucatini* (thin macaroni)
> 2 tablespoons minced parsley

Clean broccoli and rinse well; boil in salted water until tender; drain. Remove flowerets and place on a warm platter. Sauté garlic in the oil until brown; add tomatoes and simmer for 15 minutes, uncovered. Add raisins and pine nuts, stir in well, and simmer for 5 minutes. Cook *bucatini al dente*, drain, and place in a large hot bowl. Add the broccoli flowerets, pour the sauce over, and toss well but carefully with wooden forks. Serve immediately in hot soup bowls, sprinkled with parsley. Serves 6.

CAPPELLI DI PRETE CON BROCCOLI
(*Baked "Priests' Hats" with Broccoli*)

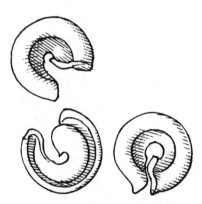

1 large bunch of broccoli
7 quarts water
2 tablespoons salt
2 garlic cloves
5 tablespoons olive oil, in all
4 tablespoons butter
1 pound *cappelli di prete*
1 cup grated Asiago cheese

Remove all leaves from the broccoli and separate heads from stalks. Separate the heads into flowerets or buds. Cook the leaves and stalks in the water with the salt for 10 minutes. Add the broccoli flowerets and cook them for 5 minutes. Remove the broccoli stems and leaves, discard; save the water. Put the drained flowerets in a pan with the garlic, 3 tablespoons of the oil and the butter; cook for 5 minutes. Cook the *cappelli di prete* in the broccoli water until less than *al dente*; drain. Oil a casserole with the remaining olive oil and arrange a layer of pasta in it. Place a layer of broccoli flowerets over the pasta and sprinkle with cheese; repeat until broccoli and pasta have been used; end with a heavy sprinkling of cheese atop. Bake for 10 minutes in 375° F. oven. Serves 4 to 6.

TAGLIATELLE CON CAVOLO
(*Noodles with Cabbage*)

>1 pound hot Italian sausage
>1 medium head of cabbage, shredded
>Much freshly milled black pepper
>Salt
>1 pound *tagliatelle*

Remove casing from sausage and break meat into pieces. Sauté sausage until well cooked; drain, saving 3 tablespoons of the fat. Place the fat, the cooked sausage and ½ cup water in a saucepan. Add the shredded cabbage, plenty of black pepper and 1 teaspoon of salt, or to taste. Cover the pan tightly and cook over low fire for 20 minutes. Cook the *tagliatelle* until *al dente*, drain, and add to the cabbage and sausage. Toss lightly until well mixed. Serves 4 to 6.

SPAGHETTI CON CAVOLO VERZA ALLA LOMBARDA
(*Spaghetti with Savoy Cabbage Lombard Style*)

>2 tablespoons butter
>2 tablespoons olive oil
>¼ pound bacon, minced
>4 ripe tomatoes, peeled and diced
>1 white onion, minced
>½ garlic clove, minced
>1 tablespoon minced Italian parsley
>1½ teaspoons salt
>Liberal amount of milled black pepper

Near BRIENNO, on Lake Como—Lombardy

1 small head of Savoy cabbage, washed and diced
1 quart Beef Broth (page 85)
½ pound spaghetti
6 tablespoons grated Parmesan cheese

Melt butter, add oil, and sauté minced bacon in it until nearly brown. Stir in tomatoes, onion, garlic and parsley and season with salt and pepper. Simmer, uncovered, for 15 minutes. Add cabbage and broth, cover, and simmer for 45 minutes. Add spaghetti and cook, uncovered, stirring gently with a wooden fork, for 15 minutes, or until pasta is *al dente*. Serve immediately in hot rimmed soup bowls with Parmesan sprinkled atop. Serves 4.

TAGLIOLINI FRESCHI CON CAROTE
(Fresh Noodles with Carrots)

1 recipe Pasta Fresca all'Uovo (page 42)
3 tablespoons butter
3 tablespoons olive oil
6 mushrooms, sliced
4 carrots, diced and cooked *al dente*
8 thin slices of prosciutto, cut into julienne strips
Grated Parmesan cheese

Prepare fresh pasta dough and cut it into noodles ¼ inch wide. Dry for 1 hour. While they are drying, prepare the sauce. Heat butter and oil and in it sauté the mushrooms, carrots and ham for just 5 minutes; remove from heat. Cook noodles *al dente;* drain, saving 4 tablespoons of the boiling pasta water. Reheat sauce and stir in saved pasta cooking water; blend well. Serve noodles immediately in hot bowls with the sauce spooned atop. Pass cheese at table. Serves 6.

CONCHIGLIE CON CAVOLFIORE
(*"Shells" with Cauliflower*)

1 small cauliflower, leaves still attached
1 teaspoon salt
½ pound *conchiglie*
4 tablespoons butter
Liberal amount of milled black pepper
½ cup grated Parmesan cheese

Place cauliflower in a 4-quart pot, cover with water, and add the salt. Simmer, covered, for 15 to 20 minutes, or until cauliflower is just tender. Lift it from the water and cool; take flowerets from cauliflower and put them aside on a warm platter. Return base of cauliflower to pot. Add *conchiglie*; cook *al dente*. Remove cauliflower, then drain pasta. Place in a large hot bowl, stir in butter, mill in black pepper, and mix well. Add the cauliflowerets and toss. Serve immediately in hot rimmed soup bowls with Parmesan liberally sprinkled atop. Serves 4.

MEZZANI CON MELANZANE
(*Baked Macaroni with Eggplant*)

½ pound broken *mezzani* (medium-size macaroni)
1 large eggplant, peeled and diced
5 cups Basic Tomato Sauce (page 63)
1 mozzarella cheese, sliced thin

Cook the *mezzani al dente;* drain. Arrange a layer of pasta in bottom of a baking dish, top with a layer of eggplant, then tomato sauce, then slices of cheese to cover; repeat until eggplant, sauce, cheese and pasta are used. Bake in 325° F. oven for 30 minutes. Serves 4 to 6.

AGRIGENTO, the Temple of Hercules—Sicily

PERCIATELLI CON MELANZANE ALLA SICILIANA
("Pierced" Pasta with Eggplant Sicilian Style)

 3 tablespoons olive oil
 2 garlic cloves, mashed
 1 eggplant, peeled and cubed
 ½ small chili pepper, diced
 1 sweet red pepper, diced
 2 tablespoons minced parsley
 ½ teaspoon salt
 Liberal amount of milled black pepper
 8 cups (two 2-pound cans) Italian plum tomatoes, put
   through food mill
 6 anchovy fillets, drained and minced
 1 pound *perciatelli*

Heat oil; sauté garlic in it until brown, then discard garlic. Add eggplant cubes, peppers, parsley, salt and pepper; simmer for 10 minutes, uncovered, stirring often. Blend in tomatoes; simmer, uncovered, stirring often, for 30 minutes, or until sauce is smooth and thickened. Stir in the anchovies and simmer for another 10 minutes. Cook *perciatelli al dente;* place in a large hot bowl, pour in half of the sauce, and toss well with wooden forks. Serve immediately in hot rimmed soup bowls with the remaining sauce lavishly spooned atop. Serves 6.

RIPIENO DI MELANZANE CON CHICCHĪ DI RISO
(Baked Eggplant Stuffed with "Grains of Rice")

 ½ cup *chicchi di riso*
 1 large eggplant
 3 tablespoons olive oil

269

    1 large white onion, minced
    3 large ripe tomatoes, peeled and diced
    ¼ pound beef round, ground twice
    1½ teaspoons salt
    Liberal amount of milled black pepper
    4 tablespoons grated Asiago cheese

Cook the grains of pasta less than *al dente;* drain. Halve the eggplant and remove pulp, keeping shell intact. Sauté together in the oil the eggplant pulp, onion, tomatoes and beef; season with salt and pepper and simmer for 10 minutes, blending the mixture well. Remove from heat and stir in the pasta. Fill the eggplant shells with the mixture and top with grated cheese. Place 1 cup hot water in a casserole and arrange the eggplant halves in it. Bake in preheated 400° F. oven for 20 minutes, or more, until eggplant is tender. Cut each eggplant half into sections to serve. Serves 4.

BUCATINI CON LATTUGA ARRICCIATA
(*Bucatini with Escarole*)

    1 large head of escarole, washed and chopped
    2 tablespoons olive oil
    2 tablespoons butter
    1 teaspoon of salt
    Liberal amount of milled black pepper
    1 pound *bucatini* (small macaroni)
    6 tablespoons grated Parmesan cheese

Cook the escarole, covered with water, until tender; drain well. Heat olive oil and butter until butter is melted. Place escarole in a large hot bowl, add olive oil and butter, salt and pepper; blend. Cook *bucatini al dente,* drain, and place in bowl with hot escarole; toss well, using wooden forks. Serve immediately in hot bowls with cheese sprinkled atop. Serves 6.

FARFALLETTE CON FAVE GRANDI
(*"Little Butterflies" with Beans*)

2 cups fresh shelled lima beans
1 teaspoon salt
4 slices of lean bacon
1 pound *farfallette*
1 tablespoon butter

Half cover beans with water and add the salt; cook, covered, until nearly done, but firm, not soft; drain. Cut bacon into small pieces and sauté until crisp. Pour off half of the grease; combine drained lima beans with the bacon and mix. Cook *farfallette* until *al dente*; drain well. Toss in a warm bowl with the butter, add lima beans and bacon, and toss again. Serve individually in warm bowls. Serves 4 to 6.

SPAGHETTI CON FAVE PICCOLE
(*Spaghetti with Lima Beans*)

½ pound spaghetti, broken into 1-inch pieces
3 cups cooked baby limas
1 white onion, thinly sliced
1 large celery rib, chopped
2 cups Basic Tomato Sauce (page 63)
1 tablespoon minced fresh basil
1 tablespoon butter
¼ cup grated Parmesan cheese
Two 4-inch sweet Italian sausages, sliced

Cook the spaghetti pieces *al dente*; drain. Blend limas, onion, celery, tomato sauce and basil; stir in spaghetti. Butter a baking dish and pour in the mixture. Sprinkle the cheese on top and arrange the sausage slices; bake, uncovered, in a preheated 375° F. oven, for 15 minutes, until sausage browns and mixture bubbles. Test a piece of sausage and a piece of onion; when they are done, it is time to remove from oven. Serves 6.

CAPELLINI CON FUNGHINI
(*Fine Vermicelli with Small Mushrooms*)

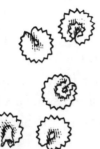

24 whole button mushrooms, washed
¼ pound butter
Liberal amount of milled black pepper
1 pound *capellini*
3 tablespoons grated Parmesan cheese

Sauté the mushrooms in the butter for 10 minutes, or until soft, milling in much black pepper. Cook *capellini al dente;* be careful, as this is a fragile pasta and probably will be ready in less than 5 minutes; drain. In a large hot bowl, place half of the mushroom and butter sauce, add the *capellini* and toss; sprinkle in the grated cheese and toss again. Serve immediately in hot rimmed soup bowls, with the remaining mushroom-butter sauce spooned atop. Pass more grated cheese at table. Serves 4.

FARFALLONI CON FUNGHI ALLA MARIA LIMONCELLI
(*"Big Butterflies" with Mushrooms*)

1½ pounds fresh mushrooms
5 shallots, chopped
½ cup butter
½ cup Chicken Broth (page 63)

272

½ tablespoon salt
¼ teaspoon dried red pepper
1 pound *farfalloni*
½ cup grated Romano cheese

Wash mushrooms and chop them, stems and all, without peeling. Simmer shallots in butter until soft. Add mushrooms and chicken broth and simmer, stirring often, for 45 minutes. Add salt and red pepper, stir in well, and cook for a further 5 minutes. Cook *farfalloni al dente*, drain, and place in a large hot bowl. Add cheese and toss. Pour mushroom sauce over the pasta and toss well but gently. Serves 4 to 6.

BUCATINI ALLA DOMENICANA
(*Bucatini with Anchovies and Mushrooms*)

4 ounces dried mushrooms
12 anchovies
3 tablespoons olive oil
2 tablespoons water
¼ teaspoon salt
1 garlic clove
1 pound *bucatini* (thin macaroni), broken into 3-inch lengths
1 tablespoon minced parsley
⅓ cup bread crumbs

Soak the dried mushrooms in warm water until they are flexible and some-what puffed into shape; drain, rinse in cold water, drain again; mince. Rinse the anchovies well in cold water, drain, and mash. Simmer the mushrooms in 1 tablespoon of the olive oil, the water and the salt for 10 minutes. Push through a sieve with half of the cooking liquid and put aside. In a saucepan sauté the garlic in 1 tablespoon of the oil until brown; discard the garlic. Add the mushrooms and liquid and the anchovies; simmer for 5 minutes and remove from fire. Cook *bucatini* in lightly salted water until *al dente,* drain, and place in a casserole. Cover the *bucatini* with the mushroom-anchovy sauce; sprinkle with parsley. Brown the bread crumbs in the remaining olive oil and sprinkle over casserole. Bake in a preheated 400° F. oven for 10 minutes. Serves 4 to 6.

SPAGHETTINI CON PISELLI E UOVA
(*Spaghettini with Peas and Eggs*)

> 1 pound spaghettini
> 6 tablespoons grated Parmesan cheese
> 1½ teaspoons salt
> Liberal amount of milled black pepper
> 2 cups fresh shelled peas, cooked *al dente* and drained
> 3 eggs, beaten

Cook spaghettini *al dente;* drain, saving ⅓ cup of the cooking water. Return spaghettini and water to the pot and over low flame quickly blend in 2 tablespoons of the cheese, the salt, pepper, peas and eggs; toss well; remove from fire before eggs set. Serve immediately in hot rimmed soup bowls with remaining cheese sprinkled atop. Serves 6.

STELLE E PISELLI
(*"Stars" and Peas*)

> 4 tablespoons butter, in all
> 2 tablespoons olive oil
> 4 slices of prosciutto, diced
> 2 tablespoons minced Italian parsley
> 2 small white onions, minced

8 cups Beef Broth (page 85)
1½ cups fresh shelled peas
1 teaspoon salt
Liberal amount of milled black pepper
½ pound *stelle*
6 tablespoons grated Parmesan cheese

Melt butter, add oil, and sauté in this the *prosciutto,* parsley and onions, until onions are soft and ham is almost crisp. Stir in 4 cups of the broth and the peas, and season with salt and pepper. Simmer, covered, for 20 minutes, stirring often. As liquid is absorbed, add more broth, a cup at a time. Now add the *stelle* and more broth and simmer until pasta is *al dente*. Serve immediately in hot rimmed soup bowls. Dot with remaining butter and sprinkle with Parmesan. Serves 6.

TAGLIATELLE CON PISELLI
(*Noodles with Peas*)

3 white onions
2 celery ribs
6 slices of bacon
2 tablespoons butter
2 tablespoons olive oil
1 pound fresh peas, shelled
6 very thin slices of prosciutto, cut into julienne strips
1 tablespoon minced parsley
1 teaspoon salt
Liberal amount of milled black pepper
1 cup Chicken Broth (page 84)
1 pound *tagliatelle*
¼ cup grated Parmesan cheese

Mince finely onions, celery and bacon; sauté in butter and oil until onions are soft. Add the peas, prosciutto strips and parsley; season with salt and pep-

275

per. Simmer for 5 minutes; add broth, cover pan, and simmer for 20 minutes, or until peas are tender. Cook *tagliatelle al dente,* drain, and place in a large hot bowl. Sprinkle cheese on the pasta and toss well. Add half of the sauce and toss again. Serve immediately in hot soup bowls with remaining sauce spooned atop. Serves 6.

VERMICELLI CON PEPERONI VERDI
(Vermicelli with Green Peppers)

> 1 white onion, minced
> 1 garlic clove, minced
> 2 tablespoons olive oil
> 3 tablespoons butter
> 4 small sweet green peppers, cored, deseeded and diced
> 1 cup Chicken Broth (page 84)
> 1 teaspoon salt
> Liberal amount of milled black pepper
> 1 pound *vermicelli*
> 4 tablespoons grated Asiago cheese

Sauté onion and garlic in oil and butter until onion is soft; add peppers and simmer for 10 minutes. Add the broth, salt and pepper; stir well and simmer, uncovered, for 15 minutes. Cook *vermicelli al dente;* drain. Add the pepper sauce and toss well, using wooden forks. Serve immediately in hot rimmed soup bowls with cheese sprinkled atop. Serves 6.

FETTUCCINE FRESCHE CON SPINACI
(Baked Fresh Fettuccine with Spinach)

  1 recipe Pasta Fresca all'Uovo (page 42)
  2 pounds fresh spinach
  1 white onion, minced
  1 garlic clove, minced
  8 slices of prosciutto, diced
  2 tablespoons butter
  2 tablespoons olive oil
  2 tablespoons flour
1½ cups light cream
Juice of 1 lemon
  1 teaspoon salt
Liberal amount of milled black pepper
  4 tablespoons grated Parmesan cheese

Prepare the fresh pasta dough, cut it into *fettuccine* (page 43), and dry. While it is drying, cook spinach without water in a covered pan until soft. Drain spinach and press out all liquid from it; put through a food chopper. Sauté onion, garlic and prosciutto in butter and oil until onion is soft. Add the flour and blend it in; stir in the cream slowly until the sauce is smooth. Blend in spinach and lemon juice and season with salt and pepper. Cook noodles much less than *al dente* (for they will be cooked further); be careful as fresh pasta cooks quickly. Drain, place in a large hot bowl, pour the spinach sauce over, and toss. Place in a buttered baking dish or casserole and sprinkle with cheese. Bake in a preheated 375° F. oven for 10 minutes, until cheese browns and sauce bubbles. Serves 6.

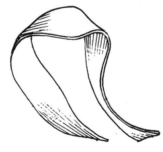

RAVIOLI CON SPINACI E RICOTTA
(Ravioli with Spinach and Ricotta)

1 recipe Pasta Fresca for Ravioli (page 44)
½ pound spinach
½ pound ricotta cheese, drained
1 egg
2 cups grated Parmesan cheese
1 teaspoon salt
Milled black pepper
¼ teaspoon grated nutmeg
¼ pound butter, melted

Prepare the fresh pasta dough. Wash spinach thoroughly and cook in a covered pan without water until tender; drain spinach and press out all liquid. Put drained spinach and ricotta through a food chopper and place in a bowl. Blend in the egg and 1 cup of the Parmesan and season with salt, pepper and nutmeg; mix well. Roll out dough into thin sheets; place a teaspoon of filling on bottom sheet every 2 inches; cover with the second sheet of dough and cut into squares with a pastry cutter. Dry for 45 minutes. Cook a half dozen at a time in simmering salted water. Remove *ravioli* with a slotted spoon as they are done; drain on paper towels. Serve immediately drenched with hot melted butter. Pass remaining Parmesan at table. Serves 4 to 6.

The following are four similar, yet subtly different, simple tomato sauces for four different pastas, each with its special texture.

FETTUCCE AI POMIDORO ALLA MARIA
(*Maria's Fettucce with Tomatoes*)

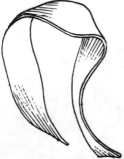

10 plum tomatoes, peeled and diced
5 tablespoons butter
2 tablespoons olive oil
1 teaspoon dried orégano
1 tablespoon chopped parsley
1 teaspoon salt
1 pound *fettucce* (wide *fettuccine*)
½ cup grated Parmesan

Chop the tomatoes and simmer them, uncovered, with the butter, oil, orégano, parsley and salt for 20 minutes. Cook *fettucce al dente*; drain. Place in individual dishes and spoon the tomato sauce directly from the pan over the pasta. Pass the Parmesan at table. Serves 4 to 6.

BAVETTE ALLA CIOCIARA
(*Bavette Peasant Style*)

1 garlic clove, minced
2 tablespoons olive oil
6 very ripe tomatoes, peeled and diced
¼ teaspoon crushed cherry pepper
½ teaspoon salt
1 pound *bavette* (narrow *linguine*)

Sauté garlic in oil until soft; add diced tomatoes and simmer for 15 minutes. Stir in cherry pepper and salt and simmer for another 15 minutes. Cook *bavette al dente;* drain. Place in pan with the tomato-garlic sauce and toss right in the cooking pan. Serves 4 to 6.

CONCHIGLIE ALL'INFERNO
(*"Shells" with Hot Sauce*)

2 garlic cloves, minced
2 tablespoons olive oil
8 cups (two 2-pound cans) Italian plum tomatoes
1 teaspoon salt
3 tablespoons chopped fresh basil
1 teaspoon crushed red pepper
1 pound *conchiglie*
1 tablespoon butter
½ cup grated Asiago cheese

Sauté minced garlic in the oil until soft. Put tomatoes through food mill and add them to the garlic-oil with the salt, basil and red pepper, stirring well. Simmer, uncovered, stirring often, until water has evaporated and sauce thickened. Cook the *conchiglie* in rapidly boiling salted water until *al dente*. Remove the shells with a skimmer or slotted spoon, draining them. Place in warm bowl with the butter and cheese; toss. Add half of the sauce and mix well with the pasta. Serve in warm bowls, each portion topped with a dollop of the remaining sauce. Have plenty of wine close at hand to keep the flame down. Serves 4 to 6.

TRIPOLINI ALLA ANTONIO
(*Tripoli "Bows" Antonio*)

2 garlic cloves, minced
1 tablespoon chopped parsley

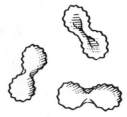

2 tablespoons olive oil
6 ripe tomatoes, peeled and diced
1 teaspoon salt
1 pound *tripolini*
½ cup grated Parmesan cheese

Sauté garlic and parsley in the oil until soft; add diced tomatoes and salt. Cook, uncovered, for 35 minutes over low fire. Meanwhile, cook *tripolini* *al dente*; drain. Pour sauce over pasta and toss with the cheese. Serves 4 to 6.

FUSILLI BUCATI AI POMIDORO VERDI
(Thin Macaroni "Twists" and Green Tomatoes)

6 medium-sized green tomatoes, slightly yellowish, just
    beginning to ripen
1 cup flour
1 tablespoon salt
Liberal amount of milled black pepper
6 tablespoons olive oil
1 pound *fusilli bucati*
2 tablespoons butter, melted

Slice tomatoes into ½-inch slices; flour each slice on both sides and season with salt and pepper; cook in hot olive oil until each side is evenly browned. Cook *fusilli bucati al dente*; drain. Toss with the melted butter, mill in black pepper, and toss again, gently. Place in hot soup bowls, with 3 slices of crisp green tomato atop each serving. In eating, the diner breaks the tomato up with his fork and stirs it into the pasta, releasing its liquid and flavor. Serves 4 to 6.

LINGUINE E ZUCCHINI ALLA MARIA LUISA
(Maria Luisa's Linguine and Zucchini)

2 medium-size zucchini
4 tablespoons butter
4 tablespoons olive oil
1 tablespoon salt
Much freshly milled black pepper
1 pound *linguine*

Cut zucchini into thin slices about the size and thickness of a fifty-cent piece. Sauté in 2 tablespoons of the butter and the oil until they are deep gold in color. Drain zucchini on paper towels; sprinkle lightly with salt and mill pepper over the slices. Cook *linguine al dente*, drain, and toss with remaining 2 tablespoons butter. Mill black pepper over the pasta and toss again. Serve in individual hot soup bowls, with slices of hot zucchini atop. Serves 4 to 6.

DITALINI E FAGIOLI
("Little Thimbles" and Beans)

2 onions, chopped
1 garlic clove, minced
3 tablespoons olive oil
6 cups Basic Tomato Sauce (page 63)
2 cans (1 pound, 4 ounces each) *cannellini* beans
1 cup water
2 teaspoons salt
Milled black pepper
Pinch of red pepper
½ teaspoon dried orégano
¼ pound *ditalini*
¼ cup grated Parmesan cheese

283

Cook onions and garlic in the oil until onions are soft. Add tomato sauce, undrained beans, water and seasonings. Cover and simmer until mixture thickens, about 30 minutes. Cook *ditalini* less than *al dente,* on the chewy side. Drain; stir slowly into the bean and tomato sauce. Sprinkle with Parmesan and serve in hot soup bowls. Serves 4 to 6.

CONCHIGLIETTE CON FAGIOLI ALLA SORRENTO
("Tiny Shells" with Beans alla Sorrento)

    2 cups dried Great Northern beans
    2 teaspoons salt
    2 small celery ribs, chopped
    2 small white onions, chopped
    3 tablespoons olive oil
    6 ripe tomatoes, peeled and diced
    1 tablespoon chopped Italian parsley
    4 fresh basil leaves, chopped, or 1 teaspoon dried sweet basil
    ½ pound *conchigliette*

Soak the beans in water for 6 hours; drain. Place the beans in 4 quarts of water, add 1 teaspoon of salt, and cook until beans are *al dente*—firm, but nearly done, about 1 hour; drain.

Sauté the celery and onions in the oil until soft. Sprinkle in remaining salt, then add the tomatoes, parsley and basil. Simmer for 15 minutes, uncovered, breaking up the tomatoes with a wooden spoon as they cook. Add beans to the pan with the tomatoes and vegetables; stir in well. Cook the *conchigliette al dente*, drain, and add to the bean mixture. Serve in hot soup bowls. Serves 4 to 6.

VENICE—Veneto Euganea

LUMACHINE CON PATATE
("Small Snails" with Potatoes)

This is a farmer's lunch that I had one cold day outside Foggia—an unusual teaming of potatoes and pasta.

2 white onions, chopped
2 tablespoons olive oil
2 tablespoons butter
1 pound potatoes, peeled and cubed
2 pounds very ripe tomatoes, peeled and diced
1½ teaspoons salt
Liberal amount of milled black pepper
1 tablespoon minced Italian parsley
1 pound *lumachine*
6 tablespoons grated Romano cheese

Sauté onions in the oil and butter until soft; stir in potatoes and simmer, covered, for 15 minutes. Blend in tomatoes and season with salt, pepper and parsley. Simmer, covered, for 25 minutes; then uncovered for 10 minutes, stirring often. Cook the *lumachine al dente;* drain. Blend pasta into the tomatoes and potatoes, mixing well, add 4 tablespoons Romano and blend. Serve immediately in hot rimmed soup bowls with remaining cheese sprinkled atop. Serves 6.

BAVETTE CON LEGUMI MISTI
(Bavette with Mixed Vegetables)

2 tablespoons olive oil
4 tablespoons butter, in all
2 small white onions, chopped
2 small carrots, chopped

4 cups (one 2-pound can) Italian plum tomatoes with
   basil leaf
1 teaspoon salt
Milled black pepper
1 small eggplant, unpeeled
3 tablespoons *pignoli* (pine nuts)
1 pound *bavette* (narrow *linguine*)

Heat the oil and 2 tablespoons of the butter; sauté the onions and carrots
in this until onions are soft. Stir in the tomatoes, breaking them up with a
wooden spoon as they cook. Add salt and pepper and cook, uncovered, over
a medium flame for 25 minutes, stirring constantly, until sauce is smooth
and velvety and thickened. Cut unpeeled eggplant into bite-sized pieces
and sauté the pieces in remaining 2 tablespoons butter. Stir in the pine
nuts and cook until the eggplant is tender. Stir eggplant mixture into the
tomato sauce. Simmer for 5 minutes, uncovered. Cook *bavette al dente;*
drain. Serve in hot individual rimmed soup bowls, with the tomato-eggplant
sauce spooned over. Serves 4 to 6.

VONGOLETTE ALLA GIARDINIERE
(*"Little Clam Shells" Garden Style*)

3 celery ribs
2 medium zucchini
1 small eggplant
2 green peppers
3 white onions, chopped
6 ripe tomatoes, diced
2 tablespoons olive oil
1½ teaspoons salt
Milled black pepper
1 pound *vongolette*
½ cup grated Asiago cheese

Cut celery, zucchini, eggplant and peppers into 1-inch pieces. Stir all the vegetables into the olive oil, add salt and pepper, and cook, covered, for 1 hour. Cook *vongolette al dente;* drain. Toss with cheese, then with the hot vegetable sauce. Serves 4 to 6.

TAORMINA, the cathedral square—Sicily

RIGATONI "TUTTO GIARDINO"
(Rigatoni with the Whole Garden)

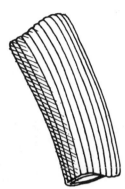

½ cup parsley leaves
1 garlic clove
2 white onions
6 slices of prosciutto
3 small red radishes
3 small carrots
2 small leeks
⅓ cup fresh basil leaves
3 tablespoons butter
3 tablespoons olive oil
1 cup finely chopped cabbage
1 large zucchini, diced
4 ripe tomatoes, peeled and diced
1 cup Chicken Broth (page 84)
1½ teaspoons of salt
Liberal amount of milled black pepper
1 pound *rigatoni* (grooved pasta tubes)
⅓ cup grated Romano cheese
⅓ cup grated Parmesan cheese
6 tablespoons soft butter

Mince finely the parsley, garlic, onions, prosciutto, radishes, carrots, leeks and basil, and mix all together into what Italians call a *soffritto*. Heat butter and oil in a large pot, stir vegetable mixture into it, and simmer until onions and carrots are soft; blend in the cabbage, zucchini, tomatoes, and chicken broth; season with salt and pepper. Simmer, covered, for 20 minutes, stirring often, until vegetables are tender. Cook *rigatoni al dente,* drain, and place in a large hot bowl. Sprinkle the mixed cheeses over the pasta and stir in the soft butter; toss well. Add the vegetable sauce and toss again. Serve immediately in hot soup bowls. Serves 8.

SPAGHETTINI ESTIVI
(*Summer Spaghettini*)

2 pounds ripe tomatoes, peeled and sliced
1 pound spaghettini
1 tablespoon chopped Italian parsley
5 fresh basil leaves, chopped
Juice of 1 lemon
1 tablespoon olive oil
1 garlic clove, quartered
½ teaspoon salt
Milled black pepper

Dip tomatoes into hot water and peel; slice thin. Cook spaghettini *al dente*, drain, and place in a large hot bowl. Add the slices of raw tomato, the parsley, basil, lemon juice, oil, garlic, salt and plenty of pepper. Using wooden forks, toss well. Serve immediately in hot rimmed soup bowls. Serves 4 to 6.

CANNELLE CON SALSA FREDDA
(*"Small Reeds" with Cold Sauce*)

4 very ripe plum tomatoes, peeled and chopped
1 sweet green pepper, seeded and chopped
1 sweet red pepper, seeded and chopped
4 ribs of white celery with leaves, chopped
1 tablespoon salt
Liberal amount of milled black pepper
1 tablespoon capers
1 teaspoon dried orégano
2 tablespoons chopped fresh basil leaves

2 tablespoons wine vinegar
1 tablespoon olive oil
1 pound *cannelle*

Place tomatoes, peppers and celery in a bowl; add salt and black pepper, capers, orégano and basil; stir in vinegar. Pour the olive oil over to make a layer on top, cover bowl, and place in refrigerator overnight.

Next day cook *cannelle al dente,* drain, and serve in very hot soup bowls. Stir the cold sauce well and spoon some of it over each serving at table. This is a dish for hot weather and is surprisingly piquant and good, proving once again that pasta can reach out and grab flavors, hold them and pass them on. Serves 4 to 6.

LINGUINE PRIMAVERILE
(*Springtime Linguine*)

Here's another version of springtime pasta with an uncooked vegetable and seasonings, surprisingly good.

6 very ripe tomatoes, peeled and diced
1 garlic clove, finely minced
8 large fresh basil leaves, minced
2 tablespoons minced Italian parsley
1½ teaspoons salt
Liberal amount of milled black pepper
4 tablespoons fine olive oil
1 pound *linguine*
Grated Romano cheese

In a large bowl blend well the tomatoes, garlic, basil, parsley, salt, a lot of pepper and the oil. Cook *linguine al dente;* drain. Serve immediately in hot bowls with the springtime sauce lavishly spooned atop. Pass cheese at table. Serves 6.

Chapter X

Particular PASTAS

$\mathcal{H}$ere, first, are some of the simplest and therefore among the best of pastas, the ones sauced with olive oil and garlic, butter and cheese, and with added variations on these themes—cream, eggs, anchovies, herbs, nuts, etc. They are followed by a variety of particularly original recipes—those in which cheeses figure importantly; tomatoes stuffed with pasta; a number of unusual baked dishes, including *timballi* (pasta "pies"); and two special sections, one on pasta with truffles and one on the aristocrat of all pastas, *fettuccine*. These recipes do not fit into any general category, but each has a particular quality to recommend it.

Near CORTONA—*Tuscany*

VERMICELLI CON AGLIO ED OLIO
(*Vermicelli with Garlic and Oil*)

Here is a dish you can prepare in 15 minutes, at the outside, and be almost completely assured that no guest has had it before. It is a favorite in many parts of Italy as a snack after the theater, much as scrambled eggs are for us.

> 2 garlic cloves
> 4 tablespoons olive oil
> 1 pound *vermicelli*
> Milled black pepper

Mash garlic with the heel of your hand; sauté in the oil, pressing it down with a wooden spoon and swishing it about the oil until it is well browned; discard garlic. Place oil in a warm bowl. Cook *vermicelli al dente;* watch carefully, for this slender pasta cooks quickly; drain well. Immediately fork into the bowl with the hot oil; mill in pepper and toss with wooden forks. Serve in hot rimmed soup bowls. Serves 4 to 6.

LINGUINE FINE CON OLIO ED AGLIO
(*Fine Linguine with Oil and Garlic*)

Here's another version of a favorite of mine, with a clever way of mixing in the oil.

> 1 pound *linguine fine*
> 12 garlic cloves, peeled
> 7 tablespoons olive oil
> Milled black pepper
> 1 tablespoon minced parsley

Cook *linguine fine. al dente,* drain, and keep warm. Put 2 garlic cloves in each of 6 ramekins; cover with 2 ounces of cooked *linguine.* Pour a brimming tablespoon of olive oil over each dish of pasta, and sprinkle with pepper and a pinch of parsley. Cover each ramekin with another very hot ramekin; let oil and garlic blend with pasta for 5 minutes. Turn each ramekin upside down, so the *linguine fine* is served in the hot dish, and the oil will now be distributed evenly; discard garlic. Serves 6.

LINGUE DI PASSERI CON LE ACCIUGHE ALLA MARIA LIMONCELLI
(Maria Limoncelli's "Sparrows' Tongues" with Anchovies)

 3 tablespoons olive oil
 3 tablespoons butter
 3 garlic cloves
 2 cans (2 ounces each) anchovies, drained
 1 pound *lingue di passeri*

Heat oil and butter in a saucepan. Add garlic and cook until soft; discard garlic. Add anchovies and cook to sauce consistency. Push through a strainer. Cook *lingue di passeri al dente,* drain, and place in a hot bowl. Pour anchovy sauce over and toss gently with wooden forks. Serves 4 to 6.

SPAGHETTI CON LE ACCIUGHE
(Spaghetti with Anchovies)

 3 tablespoons butter
 3 tablespoons olive oil
 3 garlic cloves, minced
 3 cans (2 ounces each) anchovy fillets

⅛ teaspoon crushed red pepper
1 pound spaghetti
4 tablespoons chopped Italian parsley

Heat butter and oil, stir in garlic. Add undrained anchovies, saving six for garnish. Sauté until anchovies have become a paste; stir in the red pepper. Cook spaghetti *al dente,* drain, and place in a hot bowl. Slowly pour anchovy sauce over pasta; the sauce should be warm but not hot or it will make the pasta gummy. Toss gently with wooden forks until well blended. Add the parsley and toss again. Serve in hot soup bowls with one whole anchovy fillet atop each serving. Serves 6.

TAGLIOLINI CON PEPE
(*Noodles with Black Pepper*)

This is a simple dish whipped up in a hunting camp when I was bird shooting in the Po Valley, not too long ago. Despite its limited ingredients, it has surprisingly good flavor, a testament to the natural goodness of pasta.

¼ pound sweet butter
1 pound *tagliolini*
1 tablespoon cracked black peppercorns

Soften butter in a pan until it is warm and half melted; place in a warm bowl. Cook *tagliolini al dente;* drain. Place in the bowl with the butter and toss gently, using wooden forks. Add pepper (open pepper mill for coarse grating, or crack the peppercorns by pounding). Toss again. Serve in hot bowls. Serves 4 to 6.

SPOLETO, *the Church of San Pietro—Umbria*

TAGLIATELLE AL DOPPIO BURRO
(*Noodles with Double Butter*)

    1 recipe Pasta Fresca all'Uovo (page 42)
    5 tablespoons butter
    3 tablespoons heavy cream
    ½ cup grated Parmesan cheese

Prepare the fresh pasta dough, cut it into *tagliatelle* (page 43), and dry. During the last 10 minutes of the drying, melt the butter and stir in cream and cheese. Set aside. Cook the fresh *tagliatelle* carefully; it cooks faster than the dry commercial type. When *al dente,* drain, and place in a hot bowl. Reheat butter, cream and cheese, and pour over the pasta, one fourth at a time, gently tossing it with wooden forks. Serves 4 to 6.

TRENETTE CON PESTO ALLA GENOVESE
(*Narrow Noodles with Pesto*)

This is surely one of the great regional dishes of Italy. Pesto—made with pine nuts, butter and fresh basil, among other things—is served also on other pastas, such as fettuccine, *and is used in soups. The recipe and a variation are given in the chapter on basic and special sauces. See page 80.*

MEZZANI TAGLIATI CON MANDORLE
(*Macaroni with Almonds*)

    1 pound cut *mezzani* (short, medium-size macaroni)
    ½ cup butter, melted
    1 cup heavy cream, whipped

½ pound almonds, finely minced
5 tablespoons grated Parmesan cheese
5 tablespoons grated Romano cheese

Cook *mezzani al dente;* drain. Place in a large hot bowl; add the butter, cream, almonds, and half of the cheeses which have been mixed; toss well. Serve immediately in hot rimmed soup bowls. Pass additional cheese at table. Serves 6.

GEMELLI CON SALSA DI PROSCIUTTO
("Twins" with Ham Sauce)

Here is a pasta that will make the uninitiated who think all spaghetti is the same sit up and take notice. Called "twins" because it is made of entwined twists of pasta, gemelli *start off as a conversation piece. The sauce places it further in the unusual category.*

1 recipe Ham Sauce (page 72)
1 pound *gemelli*
2 tablespoons butter
2 tablespoons grated Asiago cheese

Prepare ham sauce. Cook the *gemelli al dente;* drain well. Place the butter in a warm bowl, pour in the pasta, and add cheese. Toss well with wooden forks. Pour half of the ham sauce over pasta and toss again. Serve in warm bowls with the remaining sauce spooned over individual portions. Serves 4 to 6.

SPAGHETTINI VERDI
(*Green Spaghettini*)

Here is one of the simplest and yet most impressive pastas to present, and, in my opinion, one of the tastiest. Here is the recipe as I got it from a friend in Rome.

6 tablespoons butter
2 tablespoons olive oil
3 garlic cloves, mashed
8 tablespoons minced Italian parsley
1 pound spaghettini
Liberal amount of milled black pepper
¼ cup grated Parmesan cheese

Heat butter and oil in a saucepan; sauté garlic in it until brown, then discard garlic. Stir in the parsley; simmer for 4 minutes. Cook spaghettini *al dente*; drain. Place in a large hot bowl; mill in much black pepper, add the cheese, and toss well. Add hot butter and parsley sauce; toss again. Serve immediately in hot rimmed soup bowls. Serves 6.

LINGUINE CON ACCIUGHE ED UOVA
(*Linguine with Eggs and Anchovies*)

4 tablespoons butter
2 tablespoons olive oil
1 garlic clove, minced
1 can (2 ounces) anchovy fillets, drained
4 tablespoons minced parsley
1 teaspoon capers
4 hard-cooked egg yolks, mashed
2 tablespoons wine vinegar
Liberal amount of milled black pepper
1 pound *linguine*

Heat butter and oil in a saucepan. Stir in the garlic and anchovies; simmer for 8 minutes, until of sauce consistency. Add the parsley, capers and mashed egg yolks. Stir in the vinegar and mill in black pepper. Blend everything well and simmer for 5 minutes. Cook *linguine al dente,* drain, and place in a hot bowl. Pour the sauce over, toss well, and serve immediately in hot soup bowls. Serves 4 to 6.

TAGLIATELLE AL LATTE
(*Noodles with Milk*)

> 1½ quarts milk
> 1 teaspoon salt
> 1 pound *tagliatelle*
> 8 tablespoons butter
> 1 pound ricotta cheese
> Milled black pepper
> ½ cup grated Parmesan cheese
> ¼ cup flour
> 1 bouillon cube
> ½ pound prosciuttini, diced
> 1 cup heavy cream

Pour milk into a pot, add the salt, and bring to boil. Cook *tagliatelle* in the milk, one third at a time, removing them with a slotted spoon and draining them; cook less than *al dente;* they should be firm and chewy. Save the milk. Toss the drained noodles in a warm bowl with 2 tablespoons of the butter. In another bowl season the ricotta with pepper and stir in enough of the milk the pasta cooked in to make the mixture smooth and creamy. Butter a baking dish. Cover the bottom with a layer of noodles and cover noodles with some of ricotta mixture. Sprinkle Parmesan over that and dot with butter. Continue the layers until noodles and ricotta have been used. In another pot melt 3 tablespoons of butter and stir in the flour, making a golden paste. Then slowly stir in 2 cups of the milk in which the pasta cooked. Add the bouillon cube and 1 tablespoon Parmesan, mill in black pepper, and stir until mixture is a rich smooth sauce. Pour this over the noodles and cheese. Sprinkle with remaining Parmesan and dot with remaining butter. Bake in 400° F. oven for 20 minutes. Remove from oven and arrange the diced prosciuttini in a crown on the noodles. Warm the cream and serve at table where each diner can pour a small amount over his dish of hot pasta and cheese. Serves 6.

OSTUNI—Apulia

VERMICELLI CON PROVOLONE
(Vermicelli with Provolone Cheese)

This simple but most tasty recipe I learned from an artist friend in Genoa. Out walking one day, we stopped in the market, admired the yard-long tubes of yellow cheese, thigh-thick, hanging from cords outside a cheese store. The sunlight was on them and they gleamed like giant nuggets of Inca gold. He bought two pounds and had the grocer slice off two pieces which we munched while we finished our walk. Provolone is a nutty cheese with a marvelous flavor, not often used with pasta, but my friend used nothing else. He is a man who does nothing the ordinary way.

    ¼ pound sweet butter
    1 pound *vermicelli*
    1 cup grated provolone cheese
    Liberal amount of milled black pepper

Half melt the butter and place in a warm bowl. Cook *vermicelli al dente;* watch carefully, for the "little worms" cook quickly; test every few seconds. Drain, and place in the bowl with the butter; toss, using wooden forks. Add half of the cheese, mill in pepper, and toss gently again. Add remaining cheese, more pepper, and toss again. Serve in hot bowls. Serves 4 to 6.

SPAGHETTINI CON DUE FORMAGGI
(*Sphaghettini with Two Cheeses*)

1 pound spaghettini
½ cup melted butter
½ cup grated Parmesan cheese
½ cup grated Romano cheese
Much milled black pepper

For this dish of my mother-in-law's, the pasta must be perfectly cooked, precisely *al dente,* and well drained. Pour the butter over it in a hot bowl. Using wooden forks, toss the spaghettini gently. Mix the two cheeses, mill in black pepper, and mix again. Sprinkle half into the bowl with the pasta and toss; serve the rest of the cheese at table. Serves 4 to 6.

ZITI AL FORNO ALLA MERETRICE
(*Baked "Bridegrooms" with Harlot's Sauce*)

4 cups Harlot's Sauce (page 74)
3 tablespoons butter
¼ pound provolone cheese, grated
1 pound *ziti,* broken into 2-inch pieces

Prepare the harlot's sauce. Place 2 tablespoons of the butter and half of the grated cheese in a hot bowl. Cook *ziti* until half done, or very chewy, and drain. Toss with the butter and cheese. Place one third of the hot sauce in a buttered casserole; add the *ziti.* Spoon the remaining sauce over the *ziti,* sprinkle with the rest of the cheese, and dot with remaining butter. Bake in a preheated 400° F. oven for 15 minutes, until cheese is melted and golden and *ziti* are properly *al dente.* Serves 4 to 6.

TUFOLI IMBOTTITI
(Baked Stuffed Tufoli)

    3 cups Bolognese Sauce (page 71)
    ½ cup freshly grated ricotta siciliano cheese, or Parmesan cheese
    1 pound ricotta cheese, drained
    1 cup diced mozzarella cheese
    Liberal amount of milled black pepper
    2 eggs, beaten
    1½ tablespoons chopped Italian parsley
    ½ pound *tufoli* (very large tubes)
    1 tablespoon olive oil, in all

Prepare Bolognese sauce and keep hot. Place all of the cheeses in a bowl and add pepper, eggs and parsley; blend well. Cook *tufoli* in lightly salted water with ½ tablespoon of the olive oil to keep pasta from sticking; cook for 8 minutes, or just less than *al dente*. Remove with a skimmer and drain. When cool enough to handle, fill with the cheese mixture; place *tufoli* side by side in a casserole rubbed with remaining olive oil. Place a liberal spoonful of Bolognese sauce over each *tufolo*. Bake in 400° F. oven for 15 minutes. Pass boat of extra sauce at table. Serves 4 to 6.

MANICOTTI CON QUATTRO FORMAGGI
(Baked Manicotti with Four Cheeses)

    ½ cup freshly grated Asiago or Parmesan cheese
    ½ cup freshly grated Pecorino di Tavola cheese
    ¼ pound mozzarella cheese, diced
    1 pound ricotta cheese
    4 walnuts, chopped
    2 tablespoons chopped Italian parsley

3 eggs, beaten
⅛ teaspoon grated nutmeg
½ tablespoon salt
Liberal amount of milled black pepper
4 cups Mushroom and Cheese Sauce (page 74)
2 *manicotti* per person
1½ tablespoons olive oil

Mix all the cheeses in a bowl; add the walnuts, parsley, eggs, nutmeg, salt and plenty of pepper; blend everything well. Heat the mushroom and cheese sauce. Cook *manicotti*, five at a time, in rapidly boiling salted water to which 1 tablespoon olive oil has been added to prevent the big pasta from sticking to itself or to the pot. Cook for 5 minutes, remove with slotted spoon or skimmer immediately, drain well, and fill with cheese mixture. Repeat until the number of *manicotti* desired are cooked and filled. Place in baking dish greased with remaining ½ tablespoon oil. Spoon liberal portions of the heated mushroom and cheese sauce over all the *manicotti*. Bake in 400° F. oven for 15 minutes. Pass boat of extra sauce at table. Serve 2 *manicotti* per person; the recipe makes enough to fill 10 *manicotti*.

PERCIATELLI CON MOLTI FORMAGGI
(*"Pierced" Pasta with Many Cheeses*)

This is a northern Italian classic. The recipe, from a writer friend there, departs from tradition, requiring that you break the pasta in two before cooking.

4 tablespoons butter
1 teaspoon of olive oil
1½ teaspoons flour
1½ cups cream
3 ounces Gouda cheese
3 ounces Gruyère cheese
3 ounces aged Provolone cheese
3 ounces Fontina or Taleggio cheese

½ cup grated aged Asiago or Parmesan cheese
1½ pounds *perciatelli*
Freshly milled black pepper

Melt half the butter in a saucepan, stir in olive oil, add flour, and blend well. Stir in cream slowly, about a teaspoon at a time. Cook for 7 minutes, stirring all of the time; do not boil. Remove from heat but keep warm. Cut all the cheeses (except Asiago or Parmesan) into slivers, and stir them into butter-cream mixture. Cook *perciatelli al dente,* drain, and place in a hot bowl with remaining 2 tablespoons butter. Toss well, but gently, with two wooden forks. Put cream-cheese mixture back on fire, and stir well until cheeses are all just about melted. Pour this over the pasta in the bowl, toss well with two wooden forks. Mill in pepper, toss again. Pass the grated Asiago or Parmesan at the table. Serves 6.

RAVIOLI CON CINQUE FORMAGGI
(Ravioli with Five Cheeses)

1 recipe Pasta Fresca for Ravioli (page 44)
12 ounces Parmesan cheese, grated
½ pound ricotta cheese, drained
6 ounces Romano cheese, grated
6 ounces Emmentaler cheese, grated
6 ounces Gruyère cheese, grated
1 egg, beaten
1 cup heavy cream
¼ teaspoon grated nutmeg
2 tablespoons minced parsley
Liberal amount of milled black pepper
¼ pound butter, melted

Make fresh pasta dough and roll into sheets. Set aside half of the Parmesan to use later and blend all the rest of the cheeses. Stir in the egg, cream, nutmeg and parsley; mill in much black pepper; mix well. Spread out the

307

bottom sheet of dough; place a spoon of cheese filling every 2 inches. Cover with the second sheet of dough, press firmly around fillings, and cut into squares with a pastry cutter. Cook a few *ravioli* at a time in gently boiling salted water, removing with a slotted spoon when cooked; drain. Serve in hot soup bowls, drenched with the melted butter. Sprinkle Parmesan atop. Serves 6.

ZITI TAGLIATI AL FORNO
(Baked "Short Bridegrooms")

Do they serve the perennial American favorite, macaroni and cheese, in Italy? Yes, not usually with elbow macaroni as we do, but with larger varieties such as ziti. Here's a version I had in Naples.

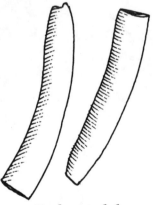

1 pound cut *ziti*
¼ pound butter
4 tablespoons flour
3 cups milk
1 teaspoon salt
Liberal amount of milled black pepper
2 cups grated Parmesan cheese
4 cups (one 2-pound can) Italian plum tomatoes, put through food mill

Cook *ziti al dente;* drain. Melt butter in a saucepan and stir in flour, making a *roux;* slowly blend in the milk, salt, pepper and cheese, simmering and stirring until mixture is a smooth sauce. Place *ziti* in a large hot bowl; pour the cheese sauce over and mix well. In a large baking dish spoon a layer of tomatoes, then a layer of *ziti.* Repeat until all are used; the top layer should be of *ziti.* Bake, uncovered, in preheated 375° F. oven for 20 minutes, or until top is brown and sauce bubbling. Serves 6.

L'AQUILA—Abruzzi

POMODORO RIPIENI DI ORZO
(Baked Tomatoes Stuffed with Pasta "Barley")

6 large firm ripe tomatoes
Pinch of sugar
1 teaspoon salt
Milled black pepper
½ teaspoon dried orégano
½ cup cubed mozzarella cheese
4 tablespoons butter
1 onion, minced
½ pound *orzo*
4 cups Chicken Broth (page 84)
4 tablespoons grated Parmesan cheese

Remove center pulp and seeds from the tomatoes, hollowing them out well. Lightly sprinkle into each a little sugar, salt, pepper and orégano; place 4 cubes of mozzarella in each tomato. Melt butter in saucepan and sauté onion in it until soft; stir in *orzo*, stirring well so each grain of pasta is coated. Pour in 2 cups of the broth, stir well, and simmer until broth is absorbed, adding more broth gradually until *orzo* is about three-quarters cooked, firmer than *al dente*. Blend in the Parmesan, stirring it in well. Spoon *orzo* into the hollowed tomatoes, filling them. Place in a casserole or baking dish with ½ cup of hot broth in the bottom. Bake, covered, in a preheated 400° F. oven for 25 minutes; remove the cover for the last 10 minutes of cooking. Serves 6.

SPAGHETTINI ALL'ABRUZZI
(Spaghettini with White Onions and Bacon)

This is a simple but classic sauce much served in Rome but created in Abruzzi, that province responsible for so many excellent chefs throughout

Italy. It's a deceptive recipe, much tastier than the eye would lead you to believe.

    8 slices of lean bacon
    2 small white onions, minced
    2 garlic cloves, crushed
    1 pound spaghettini
    3 tablespoons freshly grated Asiago or Romano cheese

Cut bacon into very thin slivers, sauté in saucepan with onions (use no other fat) and garlic. When onions are soft and yellow, discard garlic, remove saucepan from fire but keep warm. Cook spaghettini *al dente;* drain, and place in a hot bowl. Return onion-and-bacon pan to fire, and when mixture is very hot, pour right from saucepan onto pasta in the hot bowl. Toss well with two wooden forks, sprinkle on cheese, toss well again. Serve immediately in hot soup bowls. Serves 4.

POMIDORO RIPIENI ALLA SICILIANA
(Baked Stuffed Tomatoes Sicilian Style)

    1 cup small pieces of spaghetti
    6 good-sized tomatoes
    2 small white onions, chopped
    2 tablespoons olive oil
    8 canned sardines, chopped
    1 tablespoon chopped parsley
    1 tablespoon chopped green olives
    1 teaspoon capers, chopped
    2 tablespoons dry white wine
Milled black pepper
Salt
    6 teaspoons bread crumbs
Butter or oil

Cook spaghetti *al dente,* drain, and put aside. Slice off tops of tomatoes and scoop out centers, being careful not to break the skins. Mince pulp and drain. Sauté onions in oil until soft; stir in the minced tomato pulp, sardines, parsley, olives and capers. Blend in wine, mill in black pepper, add salt to taste, and stir in the drained spaghetti. Fill tomatoes with this mixture, lightly sprinkle with bread crumbs, and dot with butter or add a few drops of oil. Bake in a 400° F. oven for 15 minutes, or until tomatoes are cooked through. Serves 6.

GNOCCHI DI SEMOLINO ALLA PERUGINA
(*Semolina Dumplings Perugia Style*)

> ½ cup water
> 2 cups milk
> 1 teaspoon salt
> 4 ounces Italian semolina or fine yellow cornmeal
> 4 tablespoons sweet butter
> 1 raw egg, beaten
> 1½ cups freshly grated Parmesan cheese

Place water and milk in pot and bring to a boil. Take pot from heat, stir in salt, then slowly stir in semolina, a spoonful at a time, mixing well. Replace on low heat and, stirring often, cook for 20 minutes until mixture is smooth and thick. (If too thick, add a small amount of boiling water, stirring well.) Remove from fire, add 1 tablespoon of the butter, then the egg, quickly, blending well. Moisten a large platter or bread board with cold water and spread the *gnocchi* mixture on it in an even smooth layer ½ inch thick. Cool. Cut into 1½-inch circles with cooky cutter. Butter individual ramekins and place 6 or 8 circles in each, slightly overlapping. Dot with remaining butter and sprinkle with Parmesan. Place under broiler until golden, watching carefully so *gnocchi* do not burn. Serve immediately as a first course. Serves 6.

SOUFFLÉ DI CAPELLI D'ANGELO
("Angel's Hair" Soufflé)

    1 recipe Béchamel Sauce (page 73)
    ½ pound *capelli d'angelo*
    3 eggs, separated
    ¼ cup grated Parmesan cheese

Prepare Béchamel sauce. Cook *capelli d'angelo* in rapidly boiling salted water for exactly 60 seconds; remove and drain. In a bowl beat the egg yolks; stir in Parmesan. In another bowl whip egg whites until stiff, then stir into the yolks and cheese and mix in the drained *capelli*. Butter a soufflé dish and pour in the mixture. Bake in 450° F. oven for 15 minutes, until soufflé rises and is browned. Serves 4 to 6.

SFORMATO DI FETTUCCINE VERDI CON ROGNONI E FUNGHI
(Green Fettuccine Mold with Kidneys and Mushrooms)

    1 recipe Mornay Sauce (page 73)
    1 pound green *fettuccine*
    5 tablespoons butter
    ½ cup grated Parmesan cheese
    4 tablespoons bread crumbs
    ½ pound veal kidneys, trimmed and diced
    1 tablespoon flour
    1 teaspoon salt
    Milled black pepper
    1 teaspoon sherry wine
    1 cup Chicken Broth (page 84)
    ½ pound mushrooms, sliced

Prepare Mornay sauce. Cook the *fettuccine* less than *al dente*; drain well. Toss with 2 tablespoons of the butter and 2 of Parmesan; stir in the Mornay sauce and mix well. Pour the noodles and sauce into a 9-inch cooking mold with a 3-inch center well, which has been buttered and then dusted with the bread crumbs. Place in preheated 400° F. oven for 15 minutes. Meanwhile sauté the kidneys in 2 tablespoons of butter for 5 minutes; do not overcook as it toughtens them. Sprinkle lightly with flour, season with salt and pepper, and stir in sherry, broth and mushrooms. Cook just until gravy thickens, stirring it into a smooth sauce. Kidneys should be pinkish and mushrooms crunchy. Turn the pasta mold upside down on a warm platter; fill the center well with the kidneys and mushrooms in their gravy. Serve immediately. Serve from platter at the table. Serves 6.

Note: This mold makes an attractive and versatile luncheon dish, the ring of noodles centered on a platter, the center well filled with anything from creamed chicken, lobster or game, to chicken livers or creamed vegetables.

TIMBALLO DI TUBETTINI E SALMONE
("Tiny Tubes" and Salmon Pie)

The Italians make a pasta pie, or pasta in a pastry shell, called a timballo. *It apparently gets its name from a round musical instrument of that name. This dish I had in a home in the South of Italy and it was actually made with a can of red salmon, perhaps in deference to me, for many Italians sincerely believe that Americans prefer their food from cans. I offer it as I saw it prepared. First, make* half *of the following pastry recipe. (Or make the full recipe and refrigerate half; it keeps well.)*

Pastry for a Two-Crust Pie

> *Full recipe*
>> 2 cups flour
>> 1½ teaspoons salt
>> ¾ cup shortening
>> 5 tablespoons water

Half recipe

> 1 cup flour
> ¾ teaspoon salt
> 6 tablespoons shortening
> 2 to 3 tablespoons water

Sift flour and salt into a bowl, add about two thirds of the shortening, and blend with hands or pastry blender until well mixed. Then add the rest of the shortening and blend all very well. Add the water all at once, mix well with a fork, and work with hands into a smooth ball. Roll out fairly thin between 2 sheets of wax paper until the circle of dough is about 2 inches larger than a 9-inch pie pan. Place the pastry in a pie pan, trim off excess pastry, and flute edge.

Salmon Filling

> 2 tablespoons butter
> 1 small white onion, minced
> 1 can (1 pound) red salmon, with its liquid
> ½ teaspoon salt
> Milled black pepper
> 1 tablespoon chopped fresh dill
> 3 eggs
> ½ cup heavy cream, heated
> 1 cup light cream, heated
> 3 tablespoons *tubettini*

Melt the butter and sauté the onion in it until soft. Stir in the salmon, bones and skin removed, with the liquid; add salt, pepper and dill. Mash the fish with a fork until mixture is smooth. Beat the eggs in a bowl, adding warm heavy and light cream as you beat, or use a blender. Slowly add the smooth salmon mixture from its saucepan to the eggs and cream, beating until smooth. Cook the *tubettini al dente*, drain well, and stir into the salmon and cream. Blend well.

Pour the mixture into the pastry-lined pie pan. Bake in a preheated 400° F. oven for 45 minutes, or until the crust is brown and filling has set. Serves 6.

315

TIMBALLO DI MACCHERONCELLI E POLLO
(*Macaroni and Chicken Pie*)

4 tablespoons olive oil
4 tablespoons butter
4 slices of prosciutto, minced
1 carrot, minced
2 shallots, minced
1 celery rib, minced
1 chicken (3 pounds)
1 teaspoon salt
Milled black pepper
2 cups Chicken Broth (page 84)
1 recipe Pastry for a Two-Crust Pie (page 314)
1 recipe Béchamel Sauce (page 73)
3 chicken livers, chopped
6 mushrooms, quartered
½ pound *maccheroncelli* (small macaroni)
¼ cup grated Asiago cheese

Heat 3 tablespoons of the oil and 3 of the butter in a large pot. Sauté the prosciutto, carrot, shallots and celery until soft. Add the chicken, season with salt and pepper, and brown evenly. Add the chicken broth and braise the chicken, covered, in a 350° F. oven for 2 hours, basting often, until tender. Remove bird; cool.

Prepare pastry; use half to line a 10-inch pie pan. Prepare Béchamel sauce. Sauté chicken livers and mushrooms in remaining butter and oil for 5 minutes. Skin and bone the chicken and cube the meat. Add it to mushrooms and livers. Strain the sauce from the chicken pot into the mixture of chicken, mushrooms and livers. Cook *maccheroncelli al dente*, drain, and place in a large bowl. Stir in the Béchamel sauce and cheese, and the chicken, mushrooms and livers in sauce; blend. Pour into the pastry-lined pie pan; cover with the second sheet of dough, cut off overhanging dough with a pastry cutter, and flute edges. Bake in a preheated 400° F. oven for 20 minutes, or until crust is brown. Serves 4 to 6.

TIMBALLO DI DITALINI
(*"Little Thimbles" Pie*)

Here is another of the famous timballi, *which I had at a friend's in Taranto. In this city of fresh fish and marvelous seafood, the citizens are ostentatiously proud to serve meat, feeling seafood is ordinary. I feel otherwise. This pie came as the luncheon entrée served with a salad and a bottle of Barolo, a dependable red wine.*

1 recipe Pastry for a Two-Crust Pie (page 314)
2 cups Basic Tomato Sauce (page 63)
1 tablespoon olive oil
¼ pound veal, ground
½ teaspoon salt
Milled black pepper
½ pound *ditalini*
⅓ cup grated Parmesan cheese
2 eggs, beaten
¼ cup heavy cream

Make pie pastry, roll it out, and arrange half of it in a 10-inch pie plate. Trim and flute. Roll the remainder into a circle large enough to fit the top of the pan and set aside. Make the tomato sauce.

Heat the oil and sauté veal until brown, sprinkling with salt and pepper. Cook *ditalini* less than *al dente*, drain well, and place in a bowl. Stir in the veal in its oil, the cheese and the tomato sauce, blending well. Pour the mixture into the pastry-lined pie pan. With a whisk beat the eggs and cream well; pour this over the rest of the ingredients in the pie pan. Place the second sheet of pastry atop, seal, cut off any overhanging dough, and flute the edge. Bake in a preheated 350° F. oven for 35 minutes, until crust is lightly browned. Serves 4 to 6.

TRUFFLES

A truffle, in Italian *tartufo,* for those who haven't had the pleasure, is an edible fungus that grows under the ground and is greatly prized by gourmets in Italy and France and, in fact, the world over. They are scented by specially trained dogs and pigs and sold either canned or fresh. Everybody else who assembles a cookbook quotes Brillat-Savarin so I might as well conform: that fastidious old French epicure called them "the diamonds of the kitchen." And he just about had it. Today truffles exported from Italy and France, the only two countries I know where they are found, are exorbitant. For example, a 2-ounce can of either black or white truffles costs $5.50 in the United States. Some think they are worth the price; some think the whole idea preposterous. I think they are worth the price. The French believe the black are the best; most Italians swear by the white. I don't think there is any contest; the white are by far the tastier.

Of course I am somewhat prejudiced, having first had white truffles in Italy's Piedmont region, in Alba, where the finest are found. What these brownish-gray bits of fungi, usually no larger than a walnut, do is to bring a sweet perfume to any dish they decorate, a flavor that is difficult to describe— piquant, different. As for Scotch whisky, you must acquire a taste for them. But once you've had them—thinly sliced over *fettuccine* or riding atop a butter-sautéed boned turkey breast that has had fontina cheese sliced and melted over it in the oven—or had a dish of hot pasta with just butter and white truffles, the way it is served in Alba—then you become a member of the club, and $5.50 for a tiny two ounces of the chief of the tribe *Tuber magnatum* doesn't seem in the least expensive. Try it once and see.

On page 330 is my friend Harris Ravetto's dish of *fettuccine* with truffles. This is the best I ever ate. There follow here three other recipes with truffles, beginning with the one from Alba.

VERMICELLI ALL'ALBA
(Vermicelli with White Truffles and Butter)

1 white truffle
¼ pound butter
1 pound *vermicelli*
½ cup grated Parmesan cheese

Slice the truffle as thin as a razor-sharp knife can. Melt the butter in a pan, stirring in half of the truffle. Cook the *vermicelli al dente,* drain, and place in a warm bowl. Pour in half of the melted butter and truffle and all of the cheese; toss well but gently. Serve in hot soup bowls, with the remaining butter-truffle mixture poured over, and the rest of the sliced truffle atop. Serves 4 to 6.

Note: If the truffle is canned, add the liquid to the butter in the first stage of cooking.

SPAGHETTI CON TARTUFI
(Spaghetti with Truffles)

1 garlic clove
4 tablespoons olive oil
3 anchovy fillets
Milled black pepper
1 pound spaghetti
1 white truffle, minced

Sauté halved and mashed garlic clove in oil until brown; discard garlic. Cut the anchovy fillets into small pieces and add to the oil; mill in pepper. Simmer slowly, stirring until oil and anchovies make a paste. Cook spaghetti *al dente;* drain well. Place in a hot bowl and pour the oil-anchovy sauce over. Use wooden forks and toss well but gently. Serve in hot soup bowls with minced truffle atop each portion. Serves 4 to 6.

SPAGHETTI ALLA CHITARRA CON TARTUFI ED ACCIUGHE

("Guitar Strings" with Truffles and Anchovies)

2 tablespoons olive oil
2 tablespoons butter
2 garlic cloves, mashed
5 anchovy fillets, soaked in cold water and drained
2 large ripe tomatoes, peeled and diced
Light pinch of salt
Liberal amount of milled black pepper
1 pound *spaghetti alla chitarra*
2 black truffles, grated
1 tablespoon minced parsley

Heat oil and butter in a saucepan; add mashed garlic and sauté until brown; remove and discard garlic. Stir in the anchovies; when they have cooked into a sauce, add the tomatoes, salt and pepper. Stir well and simmer, uncovered, for 20 minutes. Cook spaghetti *al dente,* drain, and place in a hot bowl. Sprinkle with grated truffles and toss well with wooden forks. Pour half of the anchovy-tomato sauce over the pasta and toss again. Serve in hot soup bowls with some of the remaining sauce spooned over each portion and parsley sprinkled atop. Serves 4 to 6.

321

CAMOGLI—*Liguria*

FETTUCCINE

The glamour noodle of the pasta tribe is without question *fettuccine,* thus it deserves special treatment here as a "Particular Pasta." Although the Romans ate something very close to this pasta about the year 1200, in America it now seems just to be coming into its own, with the female and home magazines giving much space to recipes for *fettuccine.* But quite a few years ago a man named Alfredo caught the headlines when Douglas Fairbanks and Mary Pickford presented him, in his Roman restaurant, Alfredo alla Scrofa, with a gold fork and spoon, thus honoring him for his dish of *fettuccine* which was tossed at the diner's table with those utensils. Currently there are three Alfredos in Rome, the original being operated by an employee of the gold-fork-and-spoon man.

Perhaps back in the days of Fairbanks and Pickford, the Alfredo *fettuccine* was indeed superb—I am sure that it was. But I have tried the three Alfredos and each time found them wanting, the noodles overcooked, served just barely warm, the service sloppy, the restaurants noisy and full of tourists. And perhaps that is the reason for the decline of their *fettuccine.* One manager told me that they had to cook the pasta soft or the tourists wouldn't eat it. But this sounds like pure alibi to me, like saying that the Chinese have to serve their chicken deep-fried Southern style to please their customers. There is no reason why pasta of any type should be overcooked in Rome, of all places. And mostly it isn't. Excellent *fettuccine* is available in many restaurants and *trattorie* there—and prepared in many ways.

The best *fettuccine* I have eaten was not prepared in Rome, not even in Italy, but in Yorktown Heights, New York, in Ravetto's Restaurant. The method of serving and the recipe for *Fettuccine Ravetto* can be found on page 330. I have seldom seen it equaled, never surpassed.

The classic *fettuccine* is *Fettuccine con Parmigiano e Burro,* simply served with butter and cheese, and black pepper, mixed at the table before the diner's eyes, one of the pleasures of the dish. The noodles should be home-made to be the best. (See Chapter III for the simple steps in preparing, cutting and drying these famous noodles.) Also, they should be cooked *al dente* or less, well drained, and brought to your sideboard in the dining room where the art of mixing the sauce and serving is displayed. They should be tossed in a chafing dish with plenty of butter, and served in hot bowls to your guests as they watch you perform. Following is the classic *fettuccine* dish.

FETTUCCINE CON PARMIGIANO E BURRO
(*Fettuccine with Parmesan and Butter*)

> 1 pound *fettuccine* (preferably homemade)
> ¼ pound butter
> ½ cup grated Parmesan cheese
> Much milled black pepper

Cook the *fettuccine* less than *al dente* for the noodles will cook slightly more when you toss them in the chafing dish with butter and cheese. If the pasta is fresh, be especially careful for it will cook more quickly. Drain well and carry into the dining room where you have the butter melting in the chafing dish. Add the noodles; using two wooden forks toss gently, mixing in the butter. Add the cheese, grated directly from a cylinder-type hand grater; toss. Add more cheese, tossing until the cheese is used up; mill pepper in just before each tossing. Serve immediately in hot soup bowls as first course. Serves 4 to 6.

Note: To make this dish taste exactly right, use nothing but nutty aged Parmesan and for the pepper preferably Tellicherry.

FETTUCCINE ALLA BOLOGNESE

> 2 cups Bolognese Sauce (page 71)
> 1 pound *fettuccine*
> 4 tablespoons butter
> ⅓ cup grated Parmesan cheese

This is a happy mating, one of the great sauces with the prince of noodles. As the sauce is so rich, less cheese and butter are needed, but the procedure is the same. Cook the *fettuccine al dente,* drain, and bring to the chafing dish at the dining-room sideboard. Toss in the melting butter and grate cheese directly onto it. Serve in hot soup bowls, with piping hot Bolognese sauce lavishly topping each serving. Serves 4 to 6.

FETTUCCINE ALLA PIETRO

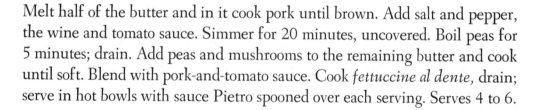

¼ pound butter
½ pound lean pork, finely chopped
1 teaspoon salt
Milled black pepper
½ cup dry white wine
2 cups Basic Tomato Sauce (page 63)
4 tablespoons fresh peas
8 small mushrooms, sliced
1 pound *fettuccine*

Melt half of the butter and in it cook pork until brown. Add salt and pepper, the wine and tomato sauce. Simmer for 20 minutes, uncovered. Boil peas for 5 minutes; drain. Add peas and mushrooms to the remaining butter and cook until soft. Blend with pork-and-tomato sauce. Cook *fettuccine al dente,* drain; serve in hot bowls with sauce Pietro spooned over each serving. Serves 4 to 6.

FETTUCCINE CON PANNA E UOVA
(Fettuccine with Cream and Eggs)

1 pound *fettuccine*
¼ pound butter
½ cup grated Parmesan or Asiago cheese

Much milled black pepper
2 egg yolks
½ cup heavy cream, warmed

Cook *fettuccine al dente,* drain, and add to the chafing dish in which the butter is melting. Have everything else ready at dining-room sideboard—yolks in eggshells, cream, and cheese. Toss the noodles gently with two forks, coating the strands of pasta; from time to time grate in cheese and mill in pepper. When cheese is well mixed add egg yolks, breaking them into the pasta with the wooden stirring fork. Toss the noodles again, then add the cream, and toss again. Serve in hot soup bowls immediately. Serves 4 to 6.

FETTUCCINE CON PISELLI E FUNGHI
(Fettuccine with Peas and Mushrooms)

2 tablespoons fresh peas
⅓ cup mushrooms, sliced
¼ pound butter
1 pound *fettuccine*
½ cup grated Parmesan cheese
Milled black pepper
½ cup heavy cream, warmed

Cook peas lightly in salted water until slightly less than tender; drain. Sauté sliced mushrooms for 3 minutes in the butter in a chafing dish at dining-room sideboard. Cook *fettuccine al dente;* drain. Add to the butter and mushrooms and toss; grate in cheese, mill in pepper, and toss well. Just before serving add the peas and cream and toss again. Serves 4 to 6.

SIENA, the Piazza del Campo—Tuscany

FETTUCCINE CON PROSCIUTTO

    1 pound *fettuccine*
    6 thin slices of prosciutto, cut into julienne strips
    ¼ pound plus 1 tablespoon butter, in all
    ½ cup grated Parmesan cheese
    Milled black pepper

Cook *fettuccine* less than *al dente*. Sauté prosciutto in 1 tablespoon of the butter until crisp. Add pasta and ham to chafing dish in which ¼ pound of butter is melting. With two forks, toss together noodles and crisp ham in the melting butter. Grate in cheese and mill in pepper; toss well. Serve in hot soup bowls. Serves 4 to 6.

FETTUCCINE ROSE
(*Pink Fettuccine*)

Some restaurants in Italy serve fettuccine with just a touch of tomato sauce to give the dish personality. I suggest that you prepare marinara sauce, use what is required for this fettuccine dish, and save the rest in the refrigerator for another meal; it keeps well.

    1 pound *fettuccine*
    4 tablespoons Marinara Sauce (page 69)
    ¼ pound butter
    ½ cup grated Asiago cheese
    Milled black pepper

Cook *fettuccine al dente;* drain well. Bring to dining room with the piping hot marinara sauce. Place noodles in chafing dish with the melting butter; toss; grate in cheese, mill in pepper, and toss. Add the sauce and toss well again with two forks until the pasta is pink. Add the rest of the cheese, toss again, and serve in hot soup bowls. Serves 4 to 6.

FETTUCCINE VERDI CON GAMBERETTI
(*Green Fettuccine with Shrimps*)

> 1 pound green *fettuccine* (preferably homemade; page 45)
> ½ pound small shrimps
> ¼ pound butter
> Milled black pepper
> ½ cup heavy cream, warmed

While the homemade green *fettuccine* is drying, peel shrimps and half-cook them in a small amount of salted water. Remove shrimps and cut them into halves. Cook the fresh *fettuccine* less than *al dente;* drain. Place shrimps in chafing dish with the melting butter, mill in black pepper, and sauté shrimps for 3 minutes. Add the *fettuccine* and toss with shrimps and butter. Add the cream and toss it into the pasta and shrimps just before serving in hot soup bowls. To follow the classic Italian pattern, do not use cheese with this seafood dish. Serves 4 to 6.

FETTUCCINE RAVETTO
(*Fettuccine with Cheese, Cream, Egg and Truffle*)

I have never seen fettuccine *served more skillfully, or had it taste better than at the restaurant of my friend Harris Ravetto, in Yorktown Heights, New*

York. Harris, a tall, slim, handsome fellow who has never made a clumsy movement in his life, performs as gracefully before a table of guests as Toscanini did for an audience at Carnegie Hall. First a waiter wheels in a table with chafing dish aflame, a bowl of fettuccine *freshly cooked* al dente *beside it, next to an eggshell with a yolk gleaming in it. The rest of the ingredients are a little glass pitcher of heavy cream, a hand cheese grater and a large piece of Parmesan, a pepper mill and, in a small silver bowl, one white truffle.*

As you watch, Harris calls the waiter for a half cup of soft butter, puts this in the chafing dish, then the noodles, tossing them gently until they are well mixed with the butter. Now the cream goes in and much black pepper is milled over the fettuccine. *Harris then hand-grates at least a half cup of cheese into the pasta, tosses it again to mix it, adds the egg yolk, tosses lightly again. While the* fettuccine *stays warm in the chafing dish, the flame now lowered under it, Harris deftly slices the white truffle on a small wooden block, shaving it wafer-thin. He adds a few wafers to the pasta, tosses again, then the waiter serves it into hot bowls and pauses before Maestro Ravetto while more white truffle goes atop each serving. I have never had it so good even in Rome. That is the method. Instead of using the chafing dish in the dining room (which is most impressive and eye-pleasing, half the pleasure of any meal), you can use a pot on the stove and do the serving in the kitchen. Ingredients follow.*

1 pound *fettuccine*
¼ pound fresh unsalted butter
½ cup heavy cream
Much freshly milled black pepper
5 ounces Parmesan cheese (about ½ cup grated)
1 egg yolk
1 white truffle, thinly sliced

Serves 4 to 6.

Note: Save the liquid from the truffle if it was canned and add to the *fettuccine* just before serving, tossing it to set the flavor.

Chapter XI

VITERBO, the Piazza del Gesù—Latium

Recipes from Friends, Romans & Countrymen

*T*his may be the most rewarding chapter in the book, resulting as it does from the generosity of others—of friends, chefs, people I have met in passing as I traveled the world, taxi drivers, barbers, hotel clerks, restaurant and hotel owners, hosts and hostesses, even pilots of planes on which I have flown. All the recipes have been carefully tested. Some are credited with the name of the person who contributed it, some with initials, others with just a "friend" or a "chef," depending upon the desires of the donors.

There are too many to thank individually on an acknowledgments page, so I thank them collectively here instead. I am grateful for the time and

effort all of these kind people took to help me put pasta in its proper place—
high on the list of the world's superb foods.

MINA QUARTET

*I begin with four recipes from my sister-in-law, Palmina Thompson, the
youngest of my mother-in-law's three talented daughters but as adept as her
sisters.*

*Although there are recipes for making fresh pasta dough in Chapter III,
two of Mina's are given here, for her way is somewhat different.*

1. BAKED MANICOTTI THOMPSON

Dough:

> 6 eggs
> 3 cups flour
> 2 cups milk
> ½ teaspoon salt

Filling:

> 1½ pounds ricotta cheese, drained
> 2 eggs
> ½ cup freshly grated Parmesan cheese

Sauce:

> 2 cups Basic Tomato Sauce (page 63)

Beat the 6 eggs, add flour, milk and salt, and blend well. Drop 1 tablespoon
of this batter onto a heated griddle and cook lightly on both sides until golden

and set, like a small pancake or crêpe. Continue until batter is used up.

Blend the ingredients for the filling well. Place 1 teaspoon of filling on each *manicotti* pancake and roll up. Place in a baking dish and spoon warm tomato sauce over each little roll. Bake in a 350° F. oven for 30 minutes. Serves 4 to 6.

2. CAVATELLI CON CAVOLFIORE
(Curled Noodle Strips with Cauliflower)

        3 cups flour
        1 egg
        ½ teaspoon salt
        2 tablespoons vegetable shortening, melted
        1 cup water
        1 small head of cauliflower
        2 tablespoons butter, melted
        Liberal amount of milled black pepper

Sift flour and make a well in center. Into this put the egg, salt, and shortening, and half of the water. Slowly whip up, bringing flour from around edges and mixing together; add more water or flour if needed to form a firm ball. Cover ball with a bowl and let rest for 10 minutes. Clean pasta board, and again knead dough until it is elastic and smooth. Cover dough ball again and let stand for another 10 minutes. Now roll out to ⅛-inch thickness. Cut into strips ½ by 1 inch. Shape *cavatelli* by taking each small strip and pressing your index and middle fingers down on it and then pulling them towards you; this will make the little strip curl up. Dry for 45 minutes, then cook *al dente* in 7 quarts of boiling water to which has been added 1 tablespoon of salt.

Boil the cauliflower in lightly salted water until tender; separate into flowerets. Put the melted butter in a warm bowl and add the cauliflower and the *cavatelli*, well drained. Mill black pepper generously over this, toss gently, and serve in hot bowls. Serves 4 to 6.

3. CAPPELLETTI CON POLLO
("Little Hats" with Chicken)

2 whole chicken breasts
1 onion
1 carrot
1 celery rib with leaves
Salt and pepper
½ cup freshly grated Parmesan cheese
1 tablespoon chopped parsley
1 egg, beaten
1 recipe Pasta Fresca for Ravioli (page 44)
Melted butter

Boil chicken breasts, as you would for soup, in water with the onion, carrot, celery rib, and a little salt and pepper. When chicken is tender, remove from broth; strain the cooking liquid and reserve it. Discard skin and bones, and grind or mince the meat. Add half of the cheese, the parsley, egg and 1 teaspoon salt. Blend well.

Make the dough for *ravioli*, roll into sheets, and cut into 2½-inch rounds. Put 1 teaspoon of the filling on each pasta round, then crimp the edges up around the filling closely to make the "little hats," or *cappelletti* that look rather like old-fashioned mob caps. Seal them well; let them dry for 1 hour after sealing. Drop the hats, one by one, into the simmering broth in which the chicken breasts cooked. Cook *al dente* and be careful; fresh pasta cooks quickly. Remove with a slotted spoon to paper towels for draining. Serve in hot bowls with the remaining cheese sprinkled over and with about ¼ teaspoon of hot melted butter over each hat. Serves 4 to 6.

4. VERMICELLI CON VONGOLE
(Vermicelli with White Clam Sauce)

1   garlic clove, halved
⅓   cup olive oil
½   cup clam juice
¼   teaspoon salt
Liberal amount of milled black pepper
⅓   teaspoon dried orégano
1   can (7½ ounces) minced clams
2   tablespoons chopped Italian parsley
1   pound *vermicelli*

Sauté garlic in the oil until golden; flatten the halves, swish well in oil, then discard. Add clam juice, salt, three grindings of pepper and the orégano; simmer for 5 minutes. Now add the canned clams with the juice, stir in well, and cook, uncovered, so liquid will reduce, just under 10 minutes. Stir in the parsley and mix well. Cook *vermicelli al dente*, drain, and toss well with half of the clam sauce. Serve the remainder spooned atop individual servings. Serves 4 to 6.

—*from Palmina Thompson, Elmira, New York*

337

Calabrian hills

AMORINI MADDALENA
(*Maddalena's Beef Soup with "Little Cupids"*)

> 3-pound "arm" chuck beef roast
> 2 potatoes, peeled and diced
> 3 carrots, peeled and diced
> 2 celery ribs with leaves, diced
> 3 small white onions, diced
> 1 pound *amorini*
> ½ teaspoon freshly milled black pepper
> 4 to 6 teaspoons chopped parsley

Cook beef and vegetables in 8 quarts water with 1 tablespoon salt in a covered pot over slow fire for 4 hours, or until the beef is tender but still firm enough to cut without shredding or being stringy. When meat is done, remove to a warm platter for second course. Cook broth over high fire, stirring often, until it has reduced by half. Put broth and vegetables through food mill or strainer into another pot. Cook *amorini al dente,* drain, and add the strained broth. Sprinkle in the black pepper and simmer pasta in broth for 5 minutes. Serve in soup bowls with a teaspoon of chopped parsley afloat each serving. Serves 4 to 6.

Note: This can be attractively varied by using narrow or very fine noodles, and can make a one-dish luncheon by adding half of the beef, diced.

—from my sister-in-law, Maddalena Altman, Elmira, New York

ZUPPA DI VERMICELLI ALLA ROMANO
(*A Roman Soup*)

> 1 medium onion
> ¼ pound ham fat
> 1 garlic clove

1 tablespoon olive oil
4 tomatoes, peeled, seeded, and cut into strips
1 quart water
1½ teaspoons salt
Liberal amount of milled black pepper
¼ pound *vermicelli,* broken into 1½-inch pieces
¼ pound Romano cheese, grated

Mince onion, ham fat and garlic and sauté in the oil in a large pot. When brown, stir in tomatoes, add the water, salt and pepper. Simmer for 15 minutes, then add the *vermicelli* directly to the pot. When it is *al dente,* serve the soup in hot bowls with Romano sprinkled atop. Serves 4 to 6.

—from Carlo, Roman chef

OCCHI DI PASSERI E MINESTRONE DI CAVOLO CAPPUCCIO
("Sparrows' Eyes" and Savoy Cabbage Soup)

½ pound dried peas
1 large Savoy cabbage
4 potatoes, diced
1 turnip, diced
10 cups Chicken Broth (page 84)
½ pound pork, lean and fat, chopped
1 small white onion, minced
1 carrot, minced
1 celery rib, minced
1 tablespoon minced parsley
3 tablespoons butter
2 teaspoons salt
Liberal amount of milled black pepper
½ pound *occhi di passeri*
¼ pound Parmesan cheese, grated

Soak peas in water for 5 hours; drain. Remove stalks and tough portions of cabbage and cut leaves into strips ½ inch by 2 inches. Parboil in salted water for 8 minutes; drain. Place in a 10-quart pot; add the potatoes, turnip and half of the broth. Cover the pot and simmer for 15 minutes. Sauté the pork, onion, carrot, celery and parsley in butter until pork is brown; stir into the cabbage. Add salt and much pepper and simmer for 1½ hours.

Boil the peas separately in salted water until almost tender, drain, and stir into soup pot. Add the rest of the broth and simmer for 15 minutes. Cook *occhi di passeri* separately in boiling salted water until *al dente*, drain, then stir into the soup pot. Serve in hot soup bowls. Pass the Parmesan. Serves 6 to 8.

Note: In Italy much black pepper is used with cabbage.

—from C. S., Foggia

VERMONT SPAGHETTINI

> 1 pound spaghettini
> ¼ pound unsalted butter, melted
> Liberal amount of milled black pepper
> ¼ pound "sharp" aged Vermont Cheddar Cheese, grated

Cook spaghettini in rapidly boiling salted water until *al dente*. Drain with fork-from-pot method and when water is off, place in warm bowl with the butter. Toss, mill in pepper, toss lightly again, then grate the Vermont cheese into the pasta using a flat hand grater. Toss well. Serve in hot soup bowls. Serves 4 to 6.

—from Bob Munson, Roxbury, Connecticut

VERMICELLI AND RICOTTA

1 pound *vermicelli*
3 tablespoons melted butter
½ pound ricotta cheese
Freshly milled black pepper
½ tablespoon chopped parsley
½ cup grated Parmesan cheese

Cook *vermicelli al dente;* drain. Place in a warm bowl with 2 tablespoons melted butter. Stir ricotta in a pan with 1 tablespoon of butter until smooth and warm; pour over hot *vermicelli,* mill pepper over the pasta, sprinkle with parsley and grated cheese, and toss. Serves 4 to 6.

—from Luisa R., Portofino

FETTUCCE AND BROOK TROUT

6 brook trout
7 quarts water
2 small white onions
2 garlic cloves
2 celery ribs, cut into 2-inch pieces
2 teaspoons salt
3 tablespoons olive oil
6 tablespoons butter, in all
1 pound *fettucce* (wide *fettuccine*)
Liberal amount of milled black pepper

Clean the trout and remove heads and fins. Place heads and fins in the water with onions, garlic, celery and salt. Cover and simmer for 1½ hours. Sauté fish in the oil and half of the butter until golden crisp. Remove the center bone or spine from each fish, carefully, pulling out most of the rest of the bones with it. Keep fish on a warm platter. Strain the water the heads and fins were cooked in, return to the stove, and bring to a boil. Cook the *fettucce* in this *al dente;* drain. Melt the remaining 3 tablespoons of butter in a hot bowl and toss the *fettucce* in it. Mill in black pepper; toss again. Serve in hot soup bowls with one boned trout atop each portion. Serves 4 to 6.

—from J. R., Manchester, Vermont

GIANT SHELLS STUFFED WITH LOBSTER

3 cups Red Lobster Sauce (page 77)
1 live lobster (1½ pounds)
18 giant pasta shells (3 per person)
2 tablespoons olive oil, in all
2 tablespoons butter

You need 2 lobsters for this dish, as one is used to make the sauce. Prepare the sauce. Boil the 1½-pound lobster (don't overcook). Remove the meat from the shells, and cut it into thumbnail-size pieces; put aside. Cook pasta shells in rapidly boiling water with only 1 tablespoon of salt and with 1½ tablespoons of the oil added to keep the shells from sticking. When they are firmer than *al dente,* not yet tender, remove the pasta shells one at a time with a skimmer or slotted spoon; drain on absorbent paper and let cool. Stuff each shell with lobster meat. Use also the lobster that you prepared the sauce with to stuff some of the shells. Grease a casserole with the butter and remaining ½ tablespoon of oil (the oil keeps the butter from burning). Place stuffed shells in the casserole and spoon sauce lavishly over each one. Bake in 400° F. oven until sauce bubbles and shells are heated through. Serves 6 as a first course.

—from Maria Luisa Scott, Washington, Connecticut

UDINE, the clock tower—Friuli-Venezia Giulia

LINGUINE CON LUMACHE ALLA PASQUALE
(*Linguine with Snails Pasquale*)

> 2 pounds snails in shells
> 6 cups Marinara Sauce (page 69)
> 1 tablespoon chopped Italian parsley
> 1 pound *linguine*
> 1 tablespoon butter

Scrub each snail well with a stiff brush. Place in a large pot of cold water with weighted cover so snails can't escape; this will bring snails partly out of shell. Soak overnight, then remove and discard any snails that haven't opened. In large pot of boiling salted water cook snails for about 15 minutes. Make marinara sauce; when it is completed, add the drained snails, cover the pan, and cook for 15 minutes. Remove cover, stir well with a wooden spoon, add parsley, and stir. Cook the *linguine al dente,* drain, and toss with the butter in a warm bowl. Spoon ½ cup of sauce over *linguine,* toss, and serve. Follow with the snails in their sauce in soup bowls; use toothpicks to lever the sweet meat from the shells. Serve hot buttered Italian bread and a salad of romaine and Boston lettuce with this. Serves 4 to 6.

Note: Live snails may be obtained from many Italian food stores.

—from my father-in-law, Pasquale Limoncelli

LINGUINE JAMBALAYA

> 2 tablespoons diced bacon
> ½ pound lean ham, diced
> 1 garlic clove, finely minced
> 1 cup finely chopped onions
> 2 tablespoons olive oil
> ½ pound pepperoni sausage, sliced

1 small green pepper, seeded and chopped
8 cups (two 2-pound cans) Italian plum tomatoes, put
    through food mill
1½ teaspoons salt
Milled black pepper
½ teaspoon dried sweet basil
½ cup chopped scallion tops
½ cup finely chopped parsley
1 pound *linguine*
1 pound shrimps, peeled and cleaned
1 dozen oysters and their liquid

Sauté the bacon, ham, garlic and onions in the oil in a 6-quart pot until
onions are soft. Stir in pepperoni, green pepper and canned tomatoes. Stir in
salt, pepper, basil, scallion tops and parsley. Simmer, covered, for 45 minutes,
then uncovered for 15 minutes, stirring often.

Cook *linguine al dente;* drain. Add shrimps and oysters to sauce pot;
simmer, uncovered, for 8 minutes. Serve pasta in hot rimmed soup bowls
(2 ounces per person), the jambalaya liberally spooned atop. Serves 8.

—from F. G. H., New Orleans

SPAGHETTI AND SHRIMPS SAMMY

1 pound fresh shrimps, peeled and cleaned
½ garlic clove, minced
1 white onion, chopped
1 small fresh green pepper, seeded and chopped
1 tablespoon peanut oil
½ teaspoon salt
⅓ teaspoon monosodium glutamate (Chinese variety)
1 pound spaghetti

Cook shrimps until tender but not tough and overdone. Sauté garlic, onion and green pepper in peanut oil until soft. Add cooked shrimps, salt and monosodium glutamate; mix well. Cook spaghetti *al dente*, drain, and toss gently with shrimps and vegetables until well blended. Serve in hot rimmed soup bowls. Serves 4 to 6.

—from Sammy Ashida (formerly with Young's Hotel),
New Milford, Connecticut

CANNERONI CON SALSA DI CARNE
("Large Reeds" with Meat Sauce)

2 pounds boned stewing beef
2 onions, peeled and halved
2 garlic cloves, minced
Salt
Freshly milled black pepper
3 tablespoons olive oil
¼ cup flour
4 ripe tomatoes, peeled and chopped
1 pound *canneroni*
Butter

Place the stewing beef in a saucepan and add water to cover it. Add onions, garlic, and salt and pepper to taste; bring to a boil. Simmer, covered, until meat is tender, for 1 to 2 hours. Shred the meat and reserve it. Measure out 2 cups of the cooking liquid. Heat the oil in a saucepan and add the flour. Stir constantly until flour is golden brown. Stir in the reserved liquid. When the mixture is thickened and smooth, add tomatoes and shredded beef. Simmer for 20 minutes. Cook *canneroni* until *al dente,* drain, and toss with butter. Spoon sauce over individual servings. Serves 4 to 6.

—from P. P., Naples

347

NAPLES, the Palazzo Reale—Campania

QUADRUCCI GIUSEPPE
(*"Small Squares" Giuseppe*)

6 white onions, chopped
2 garlic cloves, minced
2 tablespoons olive oil
¼ pound butter
4 cups (one 2-pound can) tomatoes, put through food mill
1 bay leaf
¼ teaspoon dried orégano
¼ teaspoon dried marjoram
½ teaspoon salt
Liberal amount of milled black pepper
1 pound beef round, ground
1 pound *quadrucci*
¼ cup grated Romano cheese
¼ cup grated Parmesan cheese

Simmer onions and garlic in oil and butter until soft. Add tomatoes and bring to a simmer. Stir in bay leaf, orégano, marjoram, salt and pepper; cook for 20 minutes. Slowly add meat and simmer, uncovered, for 1 hour. Cook *quadrucci al dente*; drain. Mix the cheeses and toss with the pasta. Spoon meat sauce over each serving of pasta and pass more grated cheese at the table. Serves 6.

—*from Joseph H., Buffalo, New York*

TAGLIOLINI DEL BUONGUSTAIO
(*Gourmet's Noodles*)

¾ pound beef sirloin, chopped
2 raw egg yolks
2 shallots, chopped

2 tablespoons fresh caviar
Liberal amount of milled black pepper
1 teaspoon salt
1 pound *tagliolini*
2 tablespoons butter, melted

In a bowl mix beef, egg yolks, shallots, caviar, pepper and salt together well. Cook *tagliolini al dente,* drain, and toss with melted butter in a hot bowl. Place in hot soup bowls with a good spoonful of the meat mixture atop each serving. Each person tosses and mixes for himself. Serves 4 to 6.

—*from Paolo Crossi, Rome*

ZITI CON RICOTTA MARIO
(Baked "Bridegrooms" with Cheese Mario)

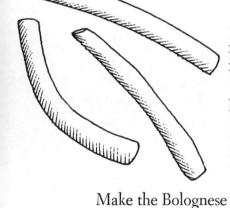

3 cups Bolognese Sauce (page 71)
½ pound fresh ricotta cheese
¼ teaspoon grated nutmeg
1 teaspoon salt
Freshly milled black pepper
1 tablespoon chopped Italian parsley
1 pound *ziti*
1 tablespoon olive oil

Make the Bolognese sauce. Place the ricotta in a strainer and drain; then put in a bowl and mix in the nutmeg, salt, pepper and parsley, mixing well. Break *ziti* into 3-inch pieces and cook in rapidly boiling salted water until less than *al dente,* on the chewy side; drain well. Toss in a bowl with the ricotta mixture, until each piece of pasta is well coated. Oil a baking dish, put in the *ziti,* and cover with warm Bolognese sauce. Bake, uncovered, in a 400° F. oven for 15 minutes. Serves 4 to 6.

—*from Mario, Mario's Restaurant, New York City*

BAVETTINE WITH CHIPPED BEEF

> 1 can (10½ ounces) condensed mushroom soup
> 1 cup Chicken Broth (page 84)
> 6 ounces dried chipped beef
> ½ pound mushrooms, peeled and quartered
> 2 tablespoons unsalted butter
> 1 pound *bavettine* (very narrow *linguine*)

Place the undiluted mushroom soup in a saucepan; heat and stir, slowly adding the broth, until mixture is a smooth sauce. Break chipped beef into small pieces and stir them into the mushroom sauce. Sauté the mushrooms in 1 tablespoon of the butter until half done but still firm and crunchy; add to the sauce and chipped beef, blending well. Cook *bavettine* in unsalted rapidly boiling water until *al dente*. Place in a warm bowl with remaining tablespoon of butter; toss. Add 2 tablespoons of beef sauce and toss again. Serve pasta in warm individual bowls with another tablespoon of sauce atop each portion. This is a very salty dish; this is the reason you don't put salt in the pasta water. It is used by the friend who contributed it as a Sunday lunch, usually after a big Saturday night. It seems to help. Serves 6.

—from Bert Fader, West Nyack, New York

BUCATINI BRUNO

> ½ pound lean pork, chopped
> 1 tablespoon olive oil
> 1 pound beef sirloin, chopped
> 1 teaspoon dried orégano
> 1 teaspoon salt
> Liberal amount of fresh-ground black pepper

    12 ripe plum tomatoes or one 2-pound can of tomatoes
    1 pound *bucatini* (small macaroni)
    ½ cup freshly grated Parmesan cheese
    1 white truffle

Sauté chopped pork well in the oil. When done, add sirloin seasoned with orégano, salt and black pepper. Cook until beef is less than half done, red and still moist. Peel and cook fresh tomatoes or put canned ones through food mill and add to saucepan with the meat. Simmer for 20 minutes, uncovered, stirring well while sauce is cooking.

    Cook the unbroken *bucatini* in rapidly boiling salted water until *al dente*; drain. Toss in a bowl with the cheese, then place in the pan with the meat and tomato mixture; mix gently and toss again. Serve in individual hot bowls with thinly shaved white truffle on top. Serves 4 to 6.

—from Bruno Ranieri, Washington, Connecticut

FUSILLI BUCATI CON FAGIOLI E PEPERONI
(Thin Macaroni "Twists" with Beans and Chilies)

    2 cups dried kidney beans
    ½ pound salt pork
    4 quarts water
    1 tablespoon salt
    2 small green chilies, diced
    4 cups (one 2-pound can) Italian plum tomatoes, put through food mill
    2 cups chopped onions
    1 pound round steak, ground
    1 pound pork, ground
    2 garlic cloves, finely minced
    1 tablespoon olive oil

1 tablespoon chili powder
1 teaspoon ground cuminseed
1 pound *fusilli bucati*
Butter

Soak beans and salt pork in water to cover for 5 hours. Drain and place in a large kettle with the 4 quarts water. Bring to a boil and cook, partly covered, for 1 hour. Add the salt and green chilies. Add tomatoes and onions. Simmer while preparing the other ingredients. Combine round steak, pork and garlic. Cook the meat in the oil, breaking it up with a wooden spoon, for 10 minutes. Add the meat to the beans. Sprinkle with chili powder, cuminseed and salt to taste. Stir well and continue cooking, uncovered, for 1 to 1½ hours, stirring often. Cook *fusilli bucati al dente,* drain, and toss with soft butter. Serve the meat sauce over the pasta. Caution: have plenty of cold beer on hand. Serves 8.

—from Ted R., New Mexico

BAKED LASAGNE

1 garlic clove, minced
3 small white onions, chopped
3 tablespoons olive oil
8 cups (two 2-pound cans) Italian plum tomatoes, pushed through food mill
1 tablespoon sugar
½ teaspoon salt
1 teaspoon dried sweet basil
1 pound ground meat (mixture of beef and pork)
½ pound *lasagne*
½ pound ricotta cheese
½ pound mozzarella cheese
½ cup grated Parmesan cheese

Sauté garlic and 2 chopped onions in 1 tablespoon of the oil; add tomatoes, sugar, salt and basil. Simmer for 1 hour over a low flame until most of the moisture has evaporated. Meanwhile, sauté the third onion in another tablespoon of oil, add the ground meat, and brown all together lightly. Add the tomato sauce.

Cook *lasagne* in boiling salted water with remaining 1 tablespoon oil until *al dente;* drain. Alternate strips of *lasagne* with layers of sauce in a large baking dish. On each layer of sauce spread ricotta, sliced mozzarella and grated Parmesan. End with a layer of sauce. Bake in a 400° F. oven for 20 minutes. Serves 4 to 6.

—from R. D., SAS Pilot, Copenhagen

BAKED LASAGNE MAMMA LUCIA

2 garlic cloves, peeled and left whole
1 Bermuda onion, chopped
4 tablespoons butter
7 tablespoons olive oil, in all
½-pound piece of beef rump
¼ pound mushrooms, sliced
1 cup red wine
3 cans (2 pounds, 3 ounces each) peeled tomatoes, strained
Salt and pepper
1 pound mild Italian sausage (½ pound if you want a less rich stuffing)
1 pound broad *lasagne*
1 cup grated Parmesan cheese
1 pound mozzarella cheese, sliced thin
Miniature Meatballs (see below)
1½ pounds fresh ricotta cheese

Brown garlic and onion in butter and 6 tablespoons of the oil. Place the piece of beef on top and brown evenly. Add mushrooms and brown for 5 minutes, then add wine and cook until it evaporates completely. Remove garlic. Add the tomatoes and season wtih salt and pepper. Bring to a boil over a high flame, then lower heat. Simmer about 2 hours, until sauce is a rich dark red and thickened. Remove beef (it will be good for hero sandwiches).

Sauté sausage in a frying pan for 15 minutes, or until evenly browned, then cut it into small pieces. Make the meatballs. Cook *lasagne* in boiling salted water with remaining tablespoon of oil added to keep noodles from sticking to each other; cook over high heat for 15 minutes, until tender but not soft. Drain off hot water and replace noodles in the pot with a small quantity of cold water, so they won't stick together before the dish is assembled.

Pour a few tablespoons of sauce on the bottom of a square baking pan and place a layer of *lasagne* on it. Sprinkle with grated cheese, and spoon a layer of sauce over that. Then arrange slices of mozzarella, pieces of sausage, and the small meatballs in the pan. Now blend the ricotta with some of the sauce, and spoon some of this over the layer of meats. Repeat this procedure in layers until you have used all the ingredients (but you should have sauce left over). Use only sauce and a sprinkling of Parmesan for the top layer. Bake in preheated 350° F. oven for 20 minutes, and serve immediately. Serve the remaining sauce and more grated Parmesan separately at the table. Serves 6.

The miniature meatballs are made this way:

> 1 cup dry whole-wheat bread cubes
> Milk
> ½ pound beef chuck, ground
> 1 garlic clove, squeezed through a press
> 1 teaspoon minced parsley
> 1 teaspoon grated Parmesan cheese
> 1 egg, beaten
> Salt and pepper
> Butter

Soak the bread cubes in milk to cover for a few minutes, then squeeze the milk from them well until they are almost dry. Mix together bread, ground beef, garlic, parsley, cheese and egg until well blended. Season with salt and pepper. Shape mixture into small meatballs the size of shell almonds, and sauté in a little hot butter until browned.

—Lucia Abbot, Bethlehem, Connecticut

LASAGNE RICCIE IMBOTTITE ALLA MARIA LUISA
(Baked Stuffed "Curly" Lasagne Maria Luisa)

> 1½ pounds *lasagne riccie*
> 4 tablespoons olive oil
> 2 tablespoons butter
> 1 onion, minced
> 1 garlic clove, minced
> 2 pounds beef round, ground twice
> Salt and pepper
> 3 tablespoons chopped parsley
> 4 cups Basic Tomato Sauce (page 63)
> 3 pounds ricotta cheese
> 3 small mozzarella cheeses, sliced
> 1 cup grated Parmesan cheese

Cook *lasagne riccie* in boiling salted water with 2 tablespoons of the oil until slightly less than *al dente;* drain. Rinse in cold water so noodles can be handled.

In remaining 2 tablespoons oil and the butter sauté onion and garlic until onion is soft; add ground beef and salt and pepper to taste and cook for 10 minutes. Add parsley. Put this mixture in a strainer so all excess fat and liquid drains off.

Into a square or oblong casserole pour a small amount of tomato sauce, enough to cover the bottom. Arrange a layer of the pasta in the casserole, one of each of the 3 cheeses, one of the meat mixture, then more sauce. Repeat until casserole is almost full; ingredients expand a little. End with sauce and Parmesan. Bake in a 350° F. oven until bubbling. Serves 12.

—from Maria Luisa Scott, Washington, Connecticut

LASAGNE VERDI ALLA DORIS
(*Green Lasagne Doris*)

        1 recipe Pasta Verde (page 45)
        1 recipe Béchamel Sauce (page 73)
        2 tablespoons butter
        1 medium-sized white onion, chopped
        1 carrot, chopped
        1 small celery rib, chopped
        ¼ pound salt pork, minced
        ½ pound lean pork, ground fine
        Salt
        ¼ cup dry white wine
        3 tablespoons Basic Tomato Sauce (page 63)
        ¼ cup grated Parmesan cheese

Prepare green pasta dough, cut it into 4-inch squares, and dry on cloth for 1 hour. While it is drying make Béchamel sauce. Now sauté in butter the onion, carrot and celery until onion is soft; stir in the minced salt pork and cook until it is almost crisp; then add the ground lean pork; stir well with a wooden fork. Sprinkle lightly with salt and simmer until meat is brown. Blend in wine and tomato sauce, stir well, and simmer, covered, for 15 minutes. Boil pasta squares, two at a time, in boiling salted water; drain. Place a layer of the squares in a buttered baking dish. Spoon a layer of meat sauce over this, make another layer of pasta squares, and cover with Béchamel sauce. Make another layer of pasta, then meat sauce, and end with Béchamel;

top with Parmesan. Bake in a 400° F. oven for 10 minutes, until sauce bubbles and top browns. Serves 4 to 6.

—from Doris Limoncelli, Reston, Virginia

BUCATINI CON POLPETTE D'AGNELLO E SALSA DI UOVA
(*Bucatini with Lamb Meatballs and Egg Sauce*)

 2 pounds lamb, ground
 Salt
 Freshly milled black pepper
 3 eggs, in all
 ¼ cup grated incanestrato cheese
 1 tablespoon chopped parsley
 1 tablespoon chopped raisins
 1 garlic clove
 2 tablespoons olive oil
 ½ tablespoon flour
 ½ cup dry white wine
 Juice of ½ lemon
 1 pound *bucatini* (small macaroni)

Place ground lamb in a bowl and season with salt and pepper to taste. Add 1 egg, beaten, the cheese, parsley and raisins. Blend well and form into tiny meatballs half the size of a walnut. Sauté garlic in the oil until brown; discard garlic. Add the meatballs to the oil and lightly sprinkle with flour. Brown. Add the wine and cover the pot for 3 minutes. Remove cover and stir the meatballs and liquid with a wooden spoon, scraping the cooked particles from the side into the sauce. Beat remaining 2 eggs with lemon juice; add to meat pan, stir well, and simmer for 3 minutes. Cook *bucatini al dente*, drain, and place in a bowl. Pour meatballs and egg sauce over pasta and toss well. Serves 4 to 6.

—from A. De Rossi, Genoa

PORTOFINO—Liguria

FETTUCCINE VERDI E BIANCHE
(*Green and White Fettuccine*)

4 tablespoons butter
1 tablespoon olive oil
4 slices of prosciutto, cut into julienne strips
2 garlic cloves
8 small mushrooms, sliced thin
2 cups Basic Tomato Sauce (page 63)
2 tablespoons cooked or canned fava beans
1 pound *fettuccine* noodles, half green, half white
¼ pound Parmesan cheese, grated

In 2 tablespoons of the butter and the oil sauté the prosciutto. Add the garlic and mushrooms and sauté until garlic is brown; discard garlic. Stir in the tomato sauce and beans; simmer, uncovered, for 10 minutes. Cook *fettuccine al dente*; drain. Place in a bowl with the remaining butter and toss. Serve in soup bowls, with sauce liberally spooned atop. Pass the Parmesan. Serves 4 to 6.

—from "Nick," chef, Naples

BAKED STUFFED GIANT SHELLS

6 cups Basic Tomato Sauce (page 63)
18 giant pasta shells
1 tablespoon olive oil
1½ pounds fresh ricotta cheese, drained
4 tablespoons grated Parmesan cheese
6 slices of prosciutto, finely diced
2 tablespoons minced parsley
1 raw egg yolk
Pinch of sugar
Liberal amount of milled black pepper
½ teaspoon salt

Prepare the tomato sauce; simmer. Cook the shells in salted boiling water with the olive oil; cook to less than *al dente* stage, remove with slotted spoon, drain, and cool. In a large bowl mix ricotta, Parmesan, prosciutto, parsley, egg yolk, sugar, pepper, and salt; blend well. Stuff each shell with some of this mixture. Spoon some tomato sauce into a flameproof glass casserole or baking dish; arrange the stuffed shells in the sauce. Spoon more tomato sauce atop each shell. Bake in a preheated 400° F. over for 20 minutes. Serve 3 shells to each person for a first course. Serves 6.

—from Maria Luisa Scott, Washington, Connecticut

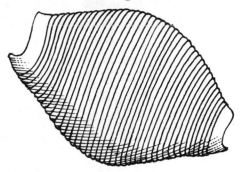

LINGUINE ALLA CARBONARA
(*Linguine with Ham-Egg Sauce*)

> 8 slices of bacon, in thin strips
> 1 tablespoon olive oil
> ½ cup diced lean prosciutto
> 3 egg yolks
> 1 cup grated Parmesan cheese
> 1 pound *linguine,* cooked and drained

Brown the bacon in the olive oil; mix in the ham until slightly browned. Drain off half the fat and discard it. Beat the egg yolks, then stir in ¼ cup of the cheese. Toss hot *linguine* with the bacon mixture, then immediately with the egg-yolk mixture. Serve sprinkled with the remaining cheese. Serves 4 to 6.

—from Fanny Graef, New York City

ROME, *Trajan's Column*

MAGLIETTE RIGATE ROBERTO
("Grooved Links" Roberto)

    1 pound *magliette rigate*
    ¼ pound butter
    ½ pound prosciutto
    3 egg yolks
    ½ cup heavy cream
    ⅓ cup freshly grated Parmesan cheese

Cook the *magliette rigate* in rapidly boiling, lightly salted water until *al dente;* gently remove with slotted spoon or skimmer, but be careful not to break the pasta. In a porcelainized cast-iron pan melt the butter and add the prosciutto cut into thin strips. Sauté for 2 minutes. Beat the egg yolks with the cream. Now place the pasta in the pan with the butter and prosciutto, add the beaten egg and cream, and stir carefully so as not to break the pasta. Place on a low fire and simmer for 30 seconds, continuing to stir gently. Grate cheese over the dish and serve while the sauce is creamy, before the eggs solidify. Serves 4 to 6.

—Bob, a writer friend in Rome

RIGATONI ALL'ARRABBIATA
(Raging Rigatoni)

This is a current favorite in Rome; it is guaranteed to bring a stuffy dinner party alive, drive the pompous to their knees, and raise the languid from their seats.

    6 slices of bacon, chopped
    2 tablespoons olive oil
    4 cups (one 2-pound can) Italian plum tomatoes
    Black pepper
    ½ teaspoon salt

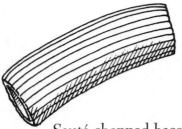

2 large fresh chili peppers (*peperonchino*)
1 pound *rigatoni* (grooved pasta tubes)
2 tablespoons butter
½ cup grated Romano cheese

Sauté chopped bacon in the oil until soft; drain off half the fat and discard it. Add tomatoes, breaking them up with a wooden spoon as they simmer. Mill in black pepper and add the salt. Chop hot peppers and blend into the tomato mixture, stirring well. Simmer, uncovered, for 15 minutes longer until sauce is thickened. Cook *rigatoni al dente;* drain. Place in a warm bowl with the butter and cheese; toss gently with wooden forks. Serve in hot soup bowls with *arrabbiata* fire sauce spooned over each serving. At the elbow of each diner place one large glass of cold water and one large glass of wine. Both will be needed. Serves 4 to 6.

—from Mary Neville, Rome

SPAGHETTI ALLA CARBONARA OLGA

2 small white onions, chopped
4 tablespoons butter
½ cup dry white wine
5 slices of bacon, chopped
3 eggs, beaten
2 tablespoons chopped parsley
½ cup grated Parmesan cheese
Liberal amount of milled black pepper
1 pound spaghetti

Sauté onions in butter until soft. Stir in wine and add bacon; cook until wine evaporates. In a large bowl put beaten eggs, parsley, cheese and black pepper; beat. Cook spaghetti *al dente;* drain. Fork spaghetti from pot into bowl, toss, and garnish with hot onions and bacon. Serves 4 to 6.

—from Olga Ravetto, Yorktown Heights, New York

SPAGHETTI ALL'AMATRICIANA GRAEF
(*Spaghetti with Bacon Sauce*)

½ pound bacon, chopped
2 white onions, chopped
½ cup dry white wine
1½ pounds tomatoes, peeled and diced
½ teaspoon freshly ground black pepper
1 pound spaghetti, cooked and drained
½ cup grated pecorino cheese
½ cup grated Parmesan cheese

Cook the bacon and onions until browned but not crisp. Add the wine, tomatoes and pepper; cook over medium heat until wine has evaporated and sauce has thickened. Spoon over individual dishes of hot spaghetti. Pass mixed cheeses at table. Serves 4 to 6.

—*from Fanny Graef, New York City*

SPAGHETTINI PRIMAVERILE
(*Springtime Spaghettini*)

12 small very ripe plum tomatoes
2 tablespoons olive oil
1 garlic clove, halved
8 slices of bacon, diced
½ cup fresh basil leaves, shredded
3 grindings of fresh black pepper
1 pound spaghettini

Peel tomatoes by plunging into hot water, then stripping off the skins. Squeeze out seeds by holding a tomato in the hand and closing the fist; most seeds will pop out. Do this over the sink. Then dice the tomatoes.

Place the oil and garlic in a frypan and sauté until garlic is golden and soft; then add bacon pieces. Sauté until soft but not crisp. Add diced tomatoes, basil leaves and black pepper. Cook over medium fire, using a wooden spoon to stir and break up tomatoes as they cook. Cook for 25 minutes, uncovered, until water has evaporated from sauce.

Boil spaghettini *al dente* in rapidly boiling lightly salted water; drain. Place directly in serving bowls and spoon tomato sauce on top. This dish has a taste right from the garden. Serves 4 to 6.

—from Fortunato E., Perugia

LINGUINE ALLA LUIGI

3 tablespoons olive oil
2 white onions, chopped
6 mushrooms, sliced thin
6 artichoke hearts, diced
6 chicken livers, diced
3 cups Ham Sauce (page 72)
Pinch of grated nutmeg
1 pound *linguine*

Sauté in the oil the onions, mushrooms and artichoke hearts until soft, about 10 minutes. Stir in the livers; cook for 5 minutes, stirring often with a wooden spoon. Add the ham sauce and the nutmeg, stir well, and simmer for 10 minutes. Cook *linguine al dente,* drain, and toss with half of the sauce. Spoon the remainder generously atop individual servings in hot soup bowls. Serves 4 to 6.

—from Luigi, chef, Parma

Note: The ham sauce in this recipe of course was made from the local ham in Parma, the world's best prosciutto.

MAGLIETTE SPACCATE ALLA TOMMASO
("Split Links" Tommaso)

1 garlic clove, minced
Two 4-inch sweet Italian sausages, sliced thin
3 tablespoons butter
3 tablespoons olive oil
8 small firm mushrooms, sliced thin
2 tablespoons peas, cooked
2 tablespoons lima beans, cooked
½ teaspoon salt
Liberal amount of milled black pepper
1 pound *magliette spaccate*
½ cup grated Parmesan cheese

Sauté the garlic and sausages in butter and oil until sausages brown; add mushrooms and simmer for 10 minutes. Stir in peas and beans and sprinkle in salt and pepper. Cook *magliette spaccate al dente;* drain. Place in a large warm bowl, add half of the cheese, and toss well. Add half of the sauce and toss again. Serve in hot bowls with the rest of the sauce spooned atop and the remaining cheese sprinkled over all. Serves 4 to 6.

—from Tommaso Bona, chef, Rome

TAGLIATELLE VERDI CON FUNGHI
(Green Noodles with Mushrooms)

1 recipe Pasta Verde (page 45)
Two 4-inch sweet Italian sausages
2 medium-sized veal sweetbreads
3 tablespoons butter
4 slices of prosciutto, diced
12 mushrooms, sliced thin

2 large very ripe tomatoes, peeled and diced
1½ teaspoons salt
Liberal amount of milled black pepper
2 cups Chicken Broth (page 84)

Prepare the pasta and cut it into ¾-inch strips for *tagliatelle* (page 43). While it is drying, remove sausage casings and break meat into pieces. Parboil the sweetbreads, remove skin and membranes, and dice sweetbreads. Sauté in butter the sausage pieces, prosciutto and sweetbreads until brown. Stir in the mushrooms and simmer for 5 minutes. Add the tomatoes, salt and pepper and simmer for 10 minutes. Stir in the chicken broth and simmer for 25 minutes, stirring often with a wooden spoon, until sauce becomes smooth and thickened. Cook *tagliatelle al dente*; watch carefully as fresh pasta cooks more quickly than dry; drain. Place in a warm bowl, spoon in 4 tablespoons of sauce, and toss gently. Serve in hot soup bowls with remaining sauce spooned generously atop. Serves 4 to 6.

—from Giorgio, chef, Amalfi

CHICKEN AND LINGUINE LUCIA

1 frying chicken (3 pounds), cut into pieces
Flour
4 tablespoons butter
2 tablespoons olive oil
1 garlic clove, crushed
Salt and pepper
2 large fresh tomatoes, cut into small slices, or 20 cherry
    tomatoes, peeled
1 small can (10 ounces) pitted black ripe olives, halved
¼ pound fresh mushrooms, sliced
½ onion, sliced thin, or 4 scallions, minced
1 tablespoon minced parsley

1 cup dry white wine
1½ cups (one 14-ounce can) peeled tomatoes
1 pound *linguine*

Roll pieces of chicken in flour and brown them evenly in a little of the butter and oil with the garlic in it. Sprinkle with salt and pepper. Pour 1 tablespoon of the oil into a shallow oblong ovenproof casserole and arrange the chicken pieces in it. On top and sides of chicken pieces arrange all the sliced ingredients evenly—sliced tomatoes, olives, mushrooms and onion or scallions. Sprinkle with parsley. Pour the wine over the vegetables and dot with remaining butter. Bake in a 375° F. oven for 45 minutes, turning chicken from time to time. When chicken is tender and has a nice golden color, remove casserole from oven, take out the chicken, and keep it warm.

Pour all the juicy sauce from the casserole into a saucepan and add to it the canned tomatoes. Let the sauce cook briskly for about 10 minutes; crush tomatoes with a spoon while cooking. Cook *linguine al dente*; drain. Place *linguine* in a warm serving bowl, cover with the sauce, and serve. Serve chicken as a second course, with fresh string beans flavored at the last minute with garlic and olive oil and a sprinkle of lemon juice. Serves 4.

—from Lucia Abbot, Bethlehem, Connecticut

FETTUCCE ALLA BIANCA
(Fresh Noodles Bianca)

1 recipe Pasta Fresca all'Uovo (page 42)
2 small white onions, minced
3 tablespoons olive oil
3 tablespoons butter
1 teaspoon salt
½ chicken breast (one side), diced
4 slices of prosciutto, slivered
4 very ripe tomatoes, peeled and diced

369

1½ teaspoons flour
1½ cups white wine
2 large chicken livers, chopped

Prepare the fresh pasta and cut it into ½-inch widths to make *fettucce*. While it is drying, sauté the onions until soft in the oil and butter. Add the salt and diced chicken breast. Simmer until brown. Add prosciutto and tomatoes, sprinkle in the flour, and stir well. Add wine and cook, stirring with a wooden spoon, until moisture evaporates and sauce is smooth, about 20 minutes. Stir in the chicken livers; simmer for 10 minutes, stirring often. Cook the fresh *fettucce* noodles *al dente;* watch carefully as they cook more quickly than the dry. Drain; serve in hot bowls with sauce liberally spooned over each portion. Serves 4 to 6.

—*from Mrs. B. R., Cremona, Lombardy*

FETTUCCE RICCIE GIORGIO
(*"Curly Ribbons" Giorgio*)

1 whole chicken breast, boned
2 tablespoons olive oil
3 tablespoons butter
1 teaspoon salt
Freshly milled black pepper
¼ pound thinly sliced prosciutto
½ cup freshly grated Parmesan cheese
2 tablespoons heavy cream
1 pound *fettucce riccie*

Flatten boned chicken breast under waxed paper with a wooden mallet or cleaver. Put chicken in the oil and butter; season with salt and pepper and turn often; sauté until brown and cooked through, but still moist. Remove and cut into thin strips 1 inch long. Cut the ham into similar strips. Add them both to the saucepan in which the chicken cooked, warming them over low fire and mixing them together. Add half of the cheese and all of the cream. Stir all together well. Cook *fettucce riccie* until *al dente;* drain. Toss in a warm bowl with the mixture of ham, chicken and cream. Serve in individual warm bowls with remainder of cheese on the side. Serves 4 to 6.

—from Giorgio L., Milan

GREEN NOODLE CASSEROLE

> 1 pound green noodles (commercial or homemade)
> 1 package (10 ounces) frozen asparagus spears (optional)
> 2 cans (10½ ounces each) condensed cream of chicken soup, or 1 can cream of chicken and 1 can cream of celery
> 1 cup milk
> Freshly grated Parmesan cheese
> Leftover chicken or turkey
> 1 cup cooked fresh or canned sliced or chopped mushrooms
> Pepper and salt
> Butter

Cook noodles *al dente,* drain, and set aside. Cook asparagus spears according to directions. Mix the soup with the milk. Place all the asparagus in the bottom of a large casserole; cover with a layer of noodles; sprinkle with cheese. Lay chicken or turkey slices or pieces on this and add a layer of mushroom slices. Season with pepper and salt—easy with salt. Pour part of soup mixture over this. Repeat layers of noodles, chicken and mushrooms until casserole is filled to within an inch of top. Sprinkle top liberally with cheese and dot with butter. Bake in a 350° F. oven for approximately 45 minutes, or until bubbly and brown on top. Serves 4 to 6.

Note: Do not repeat the layer of asparagus; this makes it too gooey. Use asparagus only on the bottom.

—from George Herz, West Nyack, New York

SPAGHETTI CON FEGATINI DI POLLO
(*Spaghetti with Chicken Livers*)

This came from the Trulli area, from a little restaurant on a hill outside Alberobello, that astonishing place of the Moorish, whitewashed, conical-roofed houses. The livers used were kid, or young goat, but for obvious reasons I have substituted chicken livers.

> 1 small sweet red pepper, seeded and diced
> 4 teaspoons butter
> 1 teaspoon salt
> ⅛ teaspoon crushed red pepper
> 1 pound chicken livers, diced
> 1 pound spaghetti

Sauté the sweet pepper in butter for 15 minutes; sprinkle in the salt and stir in the crushed red pepper and the chicken livers. Simmer for exactly 5 minutes. Livers, properly cooked, should be pink. Stir well. Cook the spaghetti *al dente*, drain, and toss with half of the liver sauce. Serve in hot bowls; spoon remaining sauce atop individual portions. Serves 4 to 6.

—*from Giovanni, Alberobello*

ALBEROBELLO—Apulia

TAGLIOLETTE CON CONIGLIO
(*Baked Rabbit with Noodles*)

> ½ pound *tagliolette*
> 8 mushrooms, quartered
> 2 tablespoons butter
> 1 tablespoon pine nuts
> 1 whole young rabbit
> 1 garlic clove, mashed
> 4 tablespoons olive oil
> 1½ teaspoons salt
> Liberal amount of milled black pepper
> 2 white onions, quartered
> 3 cups white wine

Cook *tagliolette* until they are half done, very chewy. Drain and place in a bowl. Sauté mushrooms in the butter with the pine nuts; add to the *tagliolette*; toss. Wash and dry the young rabbit; fill with the noodles; sew skin across the cavity so it is completely closed. Rub the rabbit with the mashed garlic and 2 tablespoons of oil; sprinkle with salt and mill pepper over it liberally. In a roasting pan place the remaining oil and the onions; brown the onions with the rabbit on top of the stove over high flame for 10 minutes. Add the wine, cover the pan, and bake in 400° F. oven for 45 minutes, or until rabbit is tender, basting often; add more liquid (hot water) if necessary. Rabbit should be browned and tender but moist. Serve it whole on a warm platter; carve at table and spoon out noodle stuffing to go with each serving of rabbit. Serves 4.

—from Aldo Moro, Taormina

CHITARRA WITH MUSHROOMS AND PURÉED PEAS

6 medium mushrooms, quartered
3 tablespoons butter
1 pound fresh peas, shelled
1 pound *chitarra* ("guitar strings")
Liberal amount of milled black pepper
⅓ cup freshly grated Romano cheese

Sauté mushrooms in the butter until half done, on the firm side. Cook peas in salted water until tender, then purée in a food mill. Place purée in a warm bowl. Cook *chitarra al dente* in boiling salted water; drain. Combine mushrooms with puréed peas, grind in black pepper, and blend. Add pasta and cheese to the bowl with the peas and mushrooms; toss well. Serve in warm bowls. Serves 4 to 6.

—*from Maria Luisa Scott, Washington, Connecticut*

RAVENNA, the Basilica of San Vitale—Emilia-Romagna

MEZZANI TAGLIATI AL FORNO
(Baked Macaroni)

   2 white onions, minced
   2 tablespoons butter
   2 tablespoons olive oil
   8 small mushrooms, sliced thin
   2 tablespoons flour
   2 cups milk
   8 black olives, sliced
   1 teaspoon salt
  ½ cup grated Romano cheese
   1 pound cut *mezzani* (short, medium-size macaroni)
  ¼ cup buttered bread crumbs

Sauté onions in butter and oil until soft. Stir in mushrooms and simmer for 10 minutes. Add the flour, stirring in well, and blend in milk, olives and salt, stirring well with a wooden spoon until the sauce becomes smooth as it simmers. Add half of the cheese and blend in well. Cook cut *mezzani al dente;* drain. Stir into the onion-mushroom sauce. Pour into an ovenproof casserole; sprinkle the rest of the cheese atop, then the bread crumbs. Bake in a 400° F. oven for 20 minutes, or until the sauce bubbles and the top browns. Serves 4 to 6.

—from S. G. L., Ravenna

FETTUCCE FRESCHE ALLA MARIA LUISA

   1 pound Pasta Fresca all'Uovo (page 42)
   3 tablespoons butter
  ½ cup freshly grated Parmesan cheese

375

2 cups sliced fresh small mushrooms
Freshly milled black pepper
4 tablespoons heavy cream

Prepare fresh pasta dough and cut it into ¼-inch strips to make *fettucce*. When dried for 1 hour, cook in rapidly boiling salted water. Watch carefully for fresh pasta cooks more quickly than dry. When *al dente*, remove with a fork, shake off water, and place in a warm bowl with 1 tablespoon of the butter. Toss, add grated cheese, and toss gently again. Sauté mushrooms slightly in remaining 2 tablespoons butter until not quite soft but still firm; do not overcook. Add mushrooms to the pasta. Now mill in pepper, add the cream, and toss again. Serve in hot bowls. Serves 4 to 6.

—from Maria Luisa Scott, Washington, Connecticut

BAKED STUFFED RIGATONI

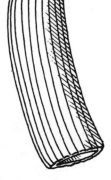

1 white onion, chopped fine
3 tablespoons olive oil
8 cups (two 2-pound cans) Italian plum tomatoes, put through food mill
1 tablespoon sugar
2 teaspoons salt
1 bay leaf
½ teaspoon dried orégano
1 pound ricotta cheese
2 eggs, beaten
2 tablespoons chopped parsley
¾ cup grated Parmesan cheese
⅛ teaspoon black pepper
1 pound *rigatoni* (grooved pasta tubes)

Sauté onion in oil until soft. Add tomatoes, sugar, 1 teaspoon of the salt, the bay leaf and orégano; cover. Simmer for 40 minutes, covered, then for 15 minutes uncovered, stirring often. Combine ricotta, eggs, parsley, ¼ cup Parmesan, remaining 1 teaspoon salt and the pepper. Cook *rigatoni al dente;* drain. Stuff *rigatoni* with cheese mixture. Layer stuffed *rigatoni* and sauce in a square casserole. Sprinkle with remaining Parmesan. Bake, uncovered, in a 400° F. oven for 20 minutes. Serves 6.

—from R. L., barber, Rome

ZITI TAGLIATI AL FORNO
(Baked "Short Bridegrooms")

4 shallots (or scallions fresh from the garden), minced
8 tablespoons butter
8 very ripe tomatoes, peeled and diced
1 teaspoon salt
Liberal amount of milled black pepper
1 cup white Chianti
1 pound *ziti tagliati*
½ cup grated Romano cheese
½ cup grated Parmesan cheese

Sauté the minced shallots in 4 tablespoons of the butter until soft. Stir in the tomatoes, salt and pepper; simmer for 10 minutes. Add the wine and simmer, stirring often, for 25 minutes. Put all through food mill. Stir 2 tablespoons of butter into the purée and simmer into a smooth, velvety sauce. Cook *ziti tagliati al dente;* drain. Place in a large bowl and toss with half of the sauce. Butter a baking dish and pour in half of the pasta. Sprinkle over this half of the Romano and Parmesan which have been well mixed. Add the remaining pasta, spoon the sauce over, and add the rest of the cheese. Fleck the top with the remaining butter. Bake in 400° F. oven, uncovered, for 10 minutes, or until sauce is bubbling and top is brown. Serves 6.

—from T. A., Siena

APPENDIX

PASTA from
Other Nations

$\mathcal{M}$ost countries, America among them, have their own ways with pasta that differ from the Italian. Some are superb, some "different," some quick and easy, others quite involved. Many are worthy of inclusion here. No book of pasta cookery would be complete without some of the tasty dishes that grace the Jewish, Chinese, German, French, Polish, even the Indian tables.

This selection doesn't pretend to cover every country around the world, nor does it represent the complete pasta repertoire of the nations included. But some of the best are here—perhaps one or two that even an Italian will try.

AMERICA

BEEF AND NOODLES

3 pounds beef round (stew-cut)
2 cups Burgundy wine
3 tablespoons fat
1 bay leaf
2 cloves
3 teaspoons salt
Milled black pepper
6 cups water
6 carrots
10 small white onions
1 pound broad noodles
2 tablespoons butter
1½ tablespoons flour
3 tablespoons water

Marinate meat in wine for 5 hours; drain, reserving the wine. In a saucepan melt the fat and brown the meat. Add the wine marinade, all the seasonings and the water. Cover and simmer for 45 minutes. Add carrots and onions and simmer for another 45 minutes. Cook the noodles *al dente,* drain, and toss in the butter; keep warm. With a slotted spoon remove meat and vegetables to a serving casserole. In a saucepan make a smooth *roux* of the flour and 3 tablespoons water; stir it into the liquid in the pot and simmer until thickened; strain. Pour half of this gravy over meat and vegetables, the other half over the buttered noodles. Serve meat and vegetables in the casserole ringed with the noodles. Serves 8.

BAKED MACARONI AND CHEDDAR CHEESE

1 pound elbow macaroni
1 cup grated sharp orange Cheddar cheese
2 cans (10½ ounces each) condensed celery soup
1 cup light cream
½ cup dry bread crumbs
1 tablespoon butter, melted

Cook macaroni *al dente,* drain, place half in a buttered baking dish. Sprinkle half of the grated Cheddar over it; add the rest of the macaroni and cover with the rest of the cheese. Heat soup, stir in the cream, and simmer until well blended; pour over the macaroni. Toss the bread crumbs in the melted butter and lightly sprinkle over the top of the macaroni. Bake, uncovered, in 350° F. oven for 40 minutes. Serves 4 to 6.

NOODLE CASSEROLE

2 tablespoons butter
2 tablespoons olive oil
1 white onion, minced
1 celery rib, minced
½ pound mushrooms, diced
3 tablespoons flour
1½ cups hot milk
1 teaspoon salt
Milled black pepper
½ cup heavy cream
1 cup grated Vermont Cheddar cheese
1½ cups cubed boiled ham
½ pound noodles (*fettuccine* type)
½ cup bread crumbs

In saucepan sauté in the butter and oil the onion, celery and mushrooms until onion is soft. Add flour, stir in hot milk, and blend well. Simmer, stirring, until thickened. Add salt and pepper and cream; stir. Take from heat and blend in cheese and ham. Cook noodles *al dente;* drain. Mix ham and cheese sauce with noodles and arrange in a buttered casserole. Sprinkle bread crumbs on the top. Bake in 350° F. oven for 25 minutes. Serves 6.

NOODLES AND BROWN BUTTER

    1 pound broad egg noodles
    6 tablespoons butter
    ½ cup dry bread crumbs

Cook noodles *al dente;* drain well. Melt butter in frypan and cook until brown; do not burn. Stir in bread crumbs and the drained noodles; toss. Serve in hot bowls. Serves 4 to 6.

OYSTERS TETRAZZINI

    24 fresh oysters
    ¾ cup clam juice
    ½ cup heavy cream
    2 shallots, minced
    5 tablespoons butter
    Pinch of grated nutmeg
    Pinch of dried rosemary
    3 tablespoons flour
    ½ teaspoon salt
    Milled black pepper

    Sprinkling of paprika
    1 pound spaghettini
    ¼ cup grated Parmesan cheese
    ¼ cup grated Cheddar cheese

Shuck oysters; save the oyster liquid and blend it with the clam juice. Place liquid in saucepan, stir in the cream, and bring to a boil; remove from heat. In a second pan sauté shallots in the butter until soft; stir in nutmeg and rosemary. Blend in the flour, mixing into a smooth paste. Add hot oyster-and-clam broth and season with salt and pepper; simmer for 8 minutes, stirring often. Take from heat, stir in oysters, and sprinkle with paprika. Cook spaghettini *al dente,* drain, and arrange in 6 hot ramekins; make a 2-inch depression in center of the pasta. Pour the oyster sauce and 4 oysters into the well in each ramekin; sprinkle Parmesan and Cheddar atop. Place in preheated 400° F. oven for 10 minutes, or until sauce bubbles and top is brown. Serves 6.

CHICKEN DIVAN IN RAMEKINS

    1 recipe Mornay Sauce (page 73)
    2 bunches of broccoli
    6 cups cooked cubed chicken, put through grinder twice
    1 pound *capellini* (fine *vermicelli*)
    ¼ cup grated Parmesan cheese
    3 tablespoons butter

Prepare the Mornay sauce; keep warm. Cook broccoli in boiling salted water until tender, drain, and put through a food mill. Add broccoli purée to the Mornay sauce, blend in the chicken, and mix well. Heat 6 ramekins and butter them lightly. Cook *capellini al dente*; watch carefully, as this is a very thin, fragile pasta and will cook quickly. Drain thoroughly, then place the pasta in the hot buttered ramekins and pour the Mornay-chicken sauce over. Sprinkle with Parmesan and dot with butter. Place under a broiler until the cheese browns and the sauce bubbles. Serves 6.

SPAGHETTI AND MEATBALLS

    2 pounds beef chuck, ground
        twice
    2 tablespoons grated Parmesan
        cheese
    1½ teaspoons salt
    Liberal amount of milled black
        pepper
    ½ cup bread crumbs
    1 tablespoon minced seedless
        raisins
    1 tablespoon minced parsley
    3 eggs
    3 tablespoons butter
    1 tablespoon oil
    8 cups (two 2-pound cans)
        tomatoes, put through food
        mill
    1 pound spaghetti

American cooks usually use a can of tomato paste as a quick sauce thickener, but I have expressed an opinon on that. Using canned tomatoes put through a food mill, and cooking them uncovered, stirring often, accomplishes the same purpose and produces a tastier, lighter sauce.

In a large bowl place beef, cheese, salt, pepper, bread crumbs, raisins, parsley and eggs, blending everything well. Your hands are the best instruments for this. Form meatballs the size of golf balls; sauté them in the butter and oil in a large deep saucepan or pot, turning so they are completely browned. Pour in the tomatoes and simmer, uncovered, stirring often, for 1 hour, or until sauce is smooth and thickened. Cook spaghetti *al dente*; drain. It is the American custom to pour all of the sauce over the pasta and toss so that it is heavily coated. The pasta is served on a large warm platter ringed with meatballs. Serves 8.

SPAGHETTI SOUFFLÉ

    1½ cups broken pieces of
        spaghetti
    1 cup milk
    ⅓ cup butter
    4 eggs, separated
    ½ cup grated Parmesan cheese
    ½ cup grated Cheddar cheese
    ½ cup bread crumbs
    2 tablespoons chopped parsley
    2 small white onions, chopped
    ½ teaspoon salt
    Freshly milled black pepper

Cook spaghetti *al dente*; drain well.

Blend milk and butter in a saucepan, stirring until butter melts. Beat egg yolks and stir slowly into warm milk and butter. Mix in drained spaghetti, cheeses, bread crumbs, parsley and onions; sprinkle in salt and pepper. Blend well. Whip egg whites until stiff and stir into the mixture. Fold the mixture into a buttered soufflé dish. Set in a shallow pan of hot water; bake in 375° F. oven for 30 minutes, or until soufflé rises and browns. Serves 4 to 6.

VEAL AND MACARONI IN SOUR CREAM

    6 loin veal chops
    3 tablespoons flour
    ½ teaspoon salt
    Freshly milled black pepper
    Pinch of dried tarragon
    5 tablespoons butter
    1 pound elbow macaroni
    4 shallots, minced
    2 cups sour cream
    1 small can (6 ounces) tomato
        purée

Dust chops with flour seasoned with salt, pepper and tarragon. Sauté chops in 3 tablespoons of the butter in a saucepan until browned. Cover the saucepan and simmer chops for 25 minutes, or until tender. Cook macaroni *al dente;* drain. Toss macaroni in 1 tablespoon of the butter and place in a casserole; arrange chops on top. Sauté shallots in chop saucepan in remaining 1 tablespoon butter until soft. Blend in

the sour cream and tomato purée, stirring until well blended. Pour sauce over meat in casserole; bake in 375° F. oven for 15 minutes. Serves 6.

PENNSYLVANIA DUTCH CHICKEN NOODLE SOUP

    1 stewing chicken (4 pounds),
        cut up
    6 quarts cold water
    2 white onions, sliced
    8 carrots, sliced
    1 bay leaf
    1 tablespoon chopped parsley
    2 tablespoons salt
    4 cups homemade noodles
        (see below)

Cover the chicken with the water, add vegetables and herbs, and bring to a boil. Reduce heat, add salt, and simmer for 3 hours, or until chicken is tender. Half of the time cook with the pot uncovered, stirring frequently, to reduce the broth. Skim off fat. Remove chicken. Add noodles to broth and cook them *al dente*. Remove bay leaf. Serve noodles and broth in deep hot soup bowls. Chicken with vegetables comes as entrée. Serves 8.

PENNSYLVANIA DUTCH SOUP NOODLES

    2 cups flour
    1 teaspoon salt
    4 eggs, beaten

Sift flour and salt together. Make a well in the center, add the eggs, and blend thoroughly. Knead dough on a floured surface, cover, and let stand for 30 minutes. Roll to ⅛-inch thickness. Turn dough over and continue rolling until very thin. Dry for 1 hour. Cut into lengthwise strips 2½ inches wide. Stack strips on top of one another, and slice into short strips, ⅛ inch wide. Separate noodles and dry for 30 minutes. Makes about 4 cups.

BULGARIA

BALKAN NOODLES

> 1 pound narrow egg noodles
> 12 ounces soft white "farmer's" cheese
> 2 small white onions, minced
> 1 pint sour cream
> 2 garlic cloves, minced
> 1 teaspoon salt
> 1 teaspoon minced fresh mint
> ½ teaspoon cayenne pepper

Cook noodles *al dente;* drain. Blend cheese, onions, sour cream, garlic, salt, mint and cayenne, and toss with the cooked noodles. Bake in a buttered casserole, uncovered, in a preheated 350° F. oven for 20 minutes. Serves 6.

CHINA

VERMICELLI SOUP

> 1½ quarts rich Chicken Broth (page 84)
> 6 ounces *vermicelli,* broken into ½-inch pieces
> 1 tablespoon soy sauce
> 2 hard-cooked eggs, cold, sliced
> ½ cooked chicken breast, cold, sliced thin
> 1 small bunch of raw scallions, including green tails, minced

Cook pasta in boiling chicken broth for 3½ minutes. Add soy sauce to boiling broth and noodles, stir. Serve immediately in soup bowls, garnishing each with 2 egg slices, 2 small slices of chicken, and 1 teaspoon of the minced scallions. Serves 6.

CHINESE CABBAGE, MEATBALL AND NOODLE SOUP

> ½ pound lean pork, ground twice
> ½ pound beef, ground twice
> 1 white onion, chopped
> ½ teaspoon peanut oil
> 2 slices of gingerroot, minced
> 1 teaspoon soy sauce
> ½ teaspoon cornstarch
> ½ teaspoon salt
> 7 cups Chicken Broth (page 84)
> 1 head of *bok choy* (Chinese cabbage)

¼ pound fine noodles (such as
capellini)

Combine the meats, onion, peanut oil,
gingerroot, soy sauce, cornstarch and
salt, blending well. Form into dime-
sized meatballs. Bring broth to a boil
and drop in the meatballs. Keep the
flame low and remove meatballs with
a slotted spoon as they float to the surface. Dice cabbage and add to the
broth; simmer for 6 minutes. Add the
cooked meatballs and the noodles and
cook for another 3 minutes. Serves 4
to 6.

FRIED NOODLES WITH SHRIMPS

   1 pound fine egg noodles
   4 tablespoons peanut oil
  36 shrimps, peeled and deveined
   2 celery ribs, chopped
   2 cups chopped Chinese cabbage
   6 mushrooms, sliced
   ½ cup sliced bamboo shoots
   3 tablespoons soy sauce

Cook noodles for 5 minutes in 4 quarts
water; as noodles come to the surface,
remove and drain. Heat 2 tablespoons
of the oil and cook shrimps and vegetables for 10 minutes, stirring steadily.
Blend in 2 tablespoons soy sauce. Sauté
the noodles in another saucepan in remaining 2 tablespoons of oil hot for 5
minutes. Stir in cooked vegetables and
shrimps and sauté for 5 minutes. Blend
in remaining soy sauce. Serve immediately. Serves 6.

Note: This is a verstatile dish.
Chicken, pork or other ingredients can
be substituted for the shrimps.

PORK AND NOODLES

   2 pounds pork loin, cut into thin
      strips
   2 tablespoons peanut oil
   1 cup Chicken Broth (page 84)
   5 scallions, minced
   1 teaspoon salt
   ½ teaspoon black pepper
   3 tablespoons cornstarch
   4 teaspoons soy sauce
   ½ cup water
   1 pound narrow egg noodles

Sauté pork strips in oil until browned,
add broth and scallions; season with salt
and pepper. Cover; simmer for 15 minutes. Blend cornstarch, soy sauce and
water; add to pork pan. Stir until sauce
thickens. Cook noodles *al dente*; drain.
Serve sauce over the hot noodles. Serves
6.

FRANCE

BRAISED CHICKEN AND NOODLES

   ½ pound narrow egg noodles
   ½ cup grated Emmentaler cheese
   ½ cup heavy cream
   ½ cup sliced mushrooms
   1 teaspoon salt

Milled black pepper
1 roasting chicken (3½ to 4 pounds)
5 tablespoons butter
1½ cups Chicken Broth (page 84)
½ cup grated Parmesan cheese
1 recipe Béchamel Sauce (page 73)

Cook noodles *al dente,* drain, and put in a warm bowl. With a wooden fork gently blend in Emmentaler cheese, cream and mushrooms; sprinkle with salt and pepper; toss. Stuff chicken with noodle mixture, sew skin over cavity, and truss legs and wings. Place the bird in a porcelainized pot with the butter; sprinkle with salt and pepper, and brown on all sides. Add chicken broth, cover the pot, and simmer, basting occasionally for 1½ hours. Take from pot and place in an ovenproof serving dish. Sprinkle the bird with the grated Parmesan and coat with the Béchamel sauce. Put in 500° F. oven for 5 minutes, until Béchamel has a golden glaze. Serves 4 to 6.

BAKED CHICKEN AND NOODLES

1 yellow-skinned boiling chicken (5 pounds)
½ cup heavy cream
1 teaspoon salt
½ teaspoon white pepper
5 egg yolks, beaten
1 pound noodles (such as *tagliolette*)

¼ cup grated Parmesan cheese
1 tablespoon butter
¼ cup grated Emmentaler cheese

Boil the chicken until tender; remove to cool; save the broth. Place 3 cups of the broth in a saucepan and simmer for 5 minutes. Stir in the cream, salt and pepper, then to thicken the sauce, slowly stir in the beaten egg yolks. Discard chicken skin and bones and cut the meat into 2-inch pieces. Cook *tagliolette al dente,* drain well, and toss with the Parmesan. Butter a baking dish and place the *tagliolette* in it. Arrange the pieces of chicken on top and pour the cream sauce over all. Sprinkle the Emmentaler cheese generously atop. Brown in 475° F. oven. Serves 4 to 6.

DOUBLE NOODLES ALSACE

½ pound *fettuccine* or other narrow egg noodles
3 tablespoons butter
4 tablespoons grated Gruyère cheese
½ teaspoon salt
Milled black pepper
2 tablespoons light olive oil

Cook *fettuccine al dente;* drain. Melt the butter and stir in half of the noodles. Blend in the cheese, salt and pepper, and simmer for 3 minutes. Remove from fire and turn into a heated serving dish. Meanwhile sauté the remaining noodles in the oil in a frypan until they are browned, but not too crisp. Ladle these noodles over those in the serving dish; serve in hot bowls. Serves 4.

FISH SOUP WITH SPAGHETTINI

3 pounds whole haddock or halibut
6 small white onions, chopped
3 tablespoons butter
2 garlic cloves, halved and mashed
6 large very ripe tomatoes, peeled and diced
3 quarts water
2 tablespoons chopped parsley
½ teaspoon dried tarragon
½ teaspoon dried sweet basil
1 piece of lemon peel (3 inches long)
¼ teaspoon crushed cherry pepper
1 tablespoon salt
Milled black pepper
¼ pound spaghettini, broken in 2½-inch pieces

Have fish scaled and cut into pieces, including the heads; set aside. Sauté onions in the butter until soft; add garlic and tomatoes, breaking up tomatoes with a wooden spoon as they cook. Cook, uncovered, for 10 minutes. Stir in water, parsley, tarragon, basil, lemon peel, cherry pepper, salt, black pepper and the fish pieces. Simmer, uncovered, for 45 minutes. Cook spaghettini *al dente*; drain. Strain fish soup through cheesecloth or a strainer, forcing, with a wooden spoon, the juices out of fish and tomatoes. Pour strained soup into a clean pan, stir in pasta, and simmer for 5 minutes. Serves 4 to 6.

BAKED NOODLES ANTOINE

1 pound mushrooms, chopped
3 tablespoons butter
1 pound *vermicelli*
2 black truffles, chopped
1 egg yolk
1 teaspoon salt
¼ teaspoon white pepper
½ pound Swiss cheese, grated
1 tablespoon butter

Sauté mushrooms in butter. Cook *vermicelli al dente*; drain. Mix with cooked mushrooms, truffles, egg yolk, salt and pepper; blend well. Place one fourth of the mixture in a layer in a casserole; sprinkle with one fourth of the cheese. Repeat until all of mixture and cheese is used. Place four small lumps of butter on top. Bake in a 375° F. oven for 30 minutes. Raise heat to 425° F. for 10 minutes. Serves 4 to 6.

VERMICELLI WITH HARD-COOKED EGGS

1 recipe Mornay Sauce (page 73)
1 pound *vermicelli*
2 tablespoons butter
6 hard-cooked eggs
4 tablespoons grated Parmesan cheese

Not one person in 10,000 knows how to hard-cook eggs correctly. Usually they are overcooked, the whites rubbery, the yolks orange and hard. Whites should be soft, the yolks light yellow and soft; it is not only better for digestion but much tastier. Here's how: Cover eggs with *cold* water, bring to a boil, then simmer for *exactly* 10 minutes. Remove *immediately* and plunge into cold water.

Prepare Mornay sauce. Cook *vermicelli al dente,* drain, and toss with the butter. Place on a hot ovenproof serving dish. Slice the hard-cooked eggs and arrange them atop pasta. Cover with Mornay sauce, sprinkle Parmesan atop, and brown lightly under the broiler. Serves 6.

GERMANY

GOULASH WITH NOODLES

4 white onions, sliced
6 tablespoons butter, in all
1 pound veal shoulder, cubed
1 pound pork loin, cubed
2 tablespoons flour
2 teaspoons salt
1 teaspoon milled black pepper
1 teaspoon paprika
4 cups Beef Broth (page 85)
1 pound noodles

Sauté onions in 4 tablespoons of the butter until soft; add meats and simmer for 15 minutes. Sprinkle with flour; blend in seasonings and beef broth; stir well. Simmer for 1 hour, uncovered, or until meat is tender and liquid thickened, stirring often. Meanwhile cook the noodles *al dente,* drain, and toss in remaining butter. Serve goulash over buttered noodles. Serves 6.

HUHN IN TOPF MIT NUDELN

(*Chicken in Casserole with Noodles*)

1 chicken (3 pounds)
3 carrots
2 small turnips
1 leek, quartered
3 celery ribs
2 teaspoons salt
Milled black pepper
1 bay leaf
1 pound broad noodles

Put chicken in an 8-quart pot and cover with water. Add vegetables, salt, pepper and bay leaf; simmer for 1½ hours, or until chicken is tender. Remove chicken and vegetables. Take chicken meat from bones, in large pieces. Strain cooking broth and put vegetables through a food mill. Add puréed vegetables to the broth. Cook noodles in this broth *al dente;* drain; save broth to serve as soup. Place chicken pieces atop noodles in hot serving casserole. Spoon 4 tablespoons of hot broth over the chicken and noodles and serve immediately. Serves 6.

GREECE

AVGOLEMONO SOUP

2½ quarts Chicken Broth
(page 84)
½ pound *vermicelli,* broken into
1-inch pieces
3 eggs
½ cup lemon juice
Milled black pepper

Bring broth to a boil, add *vermicelli,* and cook for 10 minutes; remove from heat. Using a wire whisk, beat the eggs; pour in the lemon juice and 2 tablespoons of broth as you beat, and continue beating until eggs are light and fluffy. Stir the mixture into the broth pot, blending well, and mill in black pepper. Serves 8.

GARIDES YAHNI
(*Braised Shrimps with Noodles*)

1½ pounds shrimps
4 onions, sliced
4 tablespoons olive oil
4 cups (one 2-pound can) Italian
tomatoes, put through food
mill
1 teaspoon chopped parsley
1 pound narrow egg noodles
2 tablespoons butter

Cook shrimps in shells in water to cover for 5 minutes. Drain; save 1 cup of the liquid. Shell and devein shrimps. Sauté onions in the oil until soft. Stir in tomatoes, parsley and shrimp broth, and simmer for 20 minutes. Add shrimps and simmer for 5 minutes. Cook noodles *al dente,* drain, and toss with the butter. Serve shrimps and sauce spooned over the noodles. Serves 4 to 6.

SOUPA VOTHINI
(*Beef Soup*)

3 pounds beef shank
4 cups (one 2-pound can)
tomatoes
1½ teaspoons salt
Milled black pepper
3 onions, chopped
2 celery ribs, chopped
4 tablespoons butter
1 cup *orzo* (pasta that looks like
barley or rice)

Place beef in a 4-quart pot and cover with water; bring water to a boil and add tomatoes, salt and pepper. Sauté vegetables in butter for 15 minutes. Add to beef; simmer, uncovered, stirring often, for 1½ hours, or until meat is tender. Strain the liquid and put vegetables through a food mill; stir puréed vegetables and *orzo* into the strained liquid and cook until *orzo* is *al dente.* Remove meat from bones, dice, and add to broth. Serves 6.

389

HOLLAND

GROENTENSOEP
(*Vegetable Soup with Vermicelli and Meatballs*)

    4 quarts water
    1 tablespoon salt
    Liberal amount of milled black
        pepper
    2 pounds pork, cubed
    1 large marrowbone
    2 veal knuckles
    Pinch of dried thyme
    1 bay leaf
    2 large carrots, diced
    1 leek, cut into ½-inch pieces
    2 small firm potatoes, diced
    2 celery ribs, diced
    ½ pound veal, ground
    ½ pound pork, ground
    ¼ pound *vermicelli*, broken into
        1-inch pieces
    4 very ripe tomatoes, peeled and
        diced

In a large pot place the water, salt and pepper, the cubed pork, marrowbone and veal knuckles; when water is simmering add the thyme and bay leaf; simmer, uncovered, over low heat for 3 hours. With skimmer or slotted spoon remove the pork, bones, and bay leaf. Stir in all of the diced vegetables. Simmer for 30 minutes over low fire.

As the soup simmers, prepare tiny meatballs from the ground veal and pork, seasoning them to taste with salt and pepper. Add them to the soup. When the vegetables are almost tender,

add the *vermicelli* and diced tomatoes, stirring them in well. Simmer for 5 minutes. Serves 4 to 6.

Note: Before serving, Amsterdam cooks add 3 tablespoons butter, stir it in well, and then serve the soup immediately.

HUNGARY

TUCOSCSUSZA
(*Noodles with Cottage Cheese*)

    8 slices of bacon, diced
    1 pound egg bows
    2 cups curds or cottage cheese
    1 cup sour cream

Sauté bacon until crisp. Cook egg bows *al dente;* drain. Blend bacon drippings with the pasta. Place in a large bowl and toss with half of the cottage cheese. Place in heated baking dish and cover with remaining cheese and the crisp bacon. Pour on the sour cream. Bake, uncovered, in 400° F. oven for 10 minutes. Serves 6.

INDIA

SPAGHETTI MADRAS

This comes from my friend Muni Nadhan of Madras, India, and it is a roof-raiser. Have plenty of cold wine or beer at hand to put out the fire.

1½ small fresh green hot chili peppers, chopped
1 medium sweet red pepper, chopped
3 tablespoons corn oil
1 tablespoon chopped fresh coriander leaves (Chinese parsley)
½ cup yoghurt
1 pound spaghetti

Sauté the chopped peppers in corn oil for 15 minutes over low fire; add the fresh coriander for the last 2 minutes of cooking. Place yoghurt in a warm bowl and stir in the peppers and corn oil. Cook spaghetti *al dente,* drain, and add to the bowl with the peppers. Toss and serve. Serves 4 to 6.

Caution: Do not serve to people on a bland diet.

SPAGHETTI PARSEE STYLE

1 ounce almonds
1 ounce raisins
¼ pound butter, or ½ cup vegetable shortening, melted
½ pound spaghetti, broken into 2-inch pieces
1 cup less 2 tablespoons sugar
1 cup water
¼ teaspoon grated nutmeg
5 green cardamoms
Small piece of mace

Sauté almonds and raisins in the butter or vegetable shortening until light brown; remove. Add spaghetti to the butter remaining and fry until light brown. Add sugar and water and cook over a high flame for 8 to 10 minutes, or until the water is absorbed. Reduce heat to low, add nutmeg, cardamoms and mace, and mix well. Cover the pan and put a weight on the lid. Keep over a slow fire for 5 minutes, until pasta is tender. Add sautéed almonds and raisins. Serve hot or cold. Serves 8.

JAPAN

NOODLES AND CHICKEN

1 pound fine noodles
½ pound cooked chicken breast
1 tablespoon soy sauce
1 teaspoon salt
Milled black pepper
3 pints seasoned *dashi* (Japanese soup stock available in oriental food shops)
4 eggs, beaten
1 small can (6 ounces) bamboo shoots, cut into ½-inch pieces
4 scallions, cut into 1½-inch pieces
24 small shrimps, peeled

Cook noodles *al dente;* drain. Divide noodles among 6 hot soup bowls. Cut chicken into very thin slices; sprinkle with soy sauce and marinate for 15 minutes. Add salt and pepper to *dashi;* blend in eggs, beating them into the *dashi* with a wire whisk. Arrange noodles with chicken, bamboo shoots, scallions and shrimps attractively; pour egg and *dashi* mixture over the whole. Set the bowls in a pan of hot water, cover each bowl, and steam until a custard forms and is set. Serve very hot in these bowls. Serves 6.

MISO-TAKI
(*Vegetable-Noodle Soup*)

6 ounces dried beans
1 tablespoon vinegar
2 tablespoons soy sauce
9 cups Chicken Broth (page 84)
1 teaspoon salt
½ teaspoon white pepper
8 ounces lean pork, sliced thin
2 onions, chopped
2 carrots, chopped
6 ounces very fine noodles
16 oysters

Soak beans in water for 5 hours; drain. Simmer, covered with water, until tender. Put through food mill; add vinegar and soy sauce, and blend. In another pot bring chicken broth to a boil. Season with the salt and pepper and stir in bean mixture. Add pork and vegetables and cook for 15 minutes. Stir in noodles and cook for 5 minutes. Add oysters and simmer for 4 minutes, stirring often. Serve in hot soup bowls. Serves 6.

JEWISH

CABBAGE WITH NOODLES

2 tablespoons salt
8 cups chopped cabbage
1 cup chicken fat
2 teaspoons sugar
Freshly milled black pepper
1 pound wide noodles

Blend salt and cabbage; marinate for 45 minutes. Drain off all the liquid. Melt chicken fat in a deep saucepan. Stir in the cabbage, sugar and much pepper. Simmer for 35 minutes, until cabbage browns; stir often so it doesn't stick and burn. Cook noodles *al dente;* drain. Add noodles to the cabbage and toss well. Serves 8.

KREPLACH

Dough:

4 cups unsifted flour
4 eggs
2 tablespoons water
1 tablespoon salt

Place the flour on a pastry board and form a center well. Blend in the eggs, water and salt, working them into the flour with the hands. Knead the dough until it is smooth and slightly elastic.

Roll the dough into a thin sheet, as thin as possible; let it dry—not too dry, but until the stickiness and moist feeling has gone. Now cut the dough into 3-inch squares.

Filling: Kreplach can have any number of fillings: kasha, cheese-potato, chicken, ground beef, chicken liver. Chicken liver is typical.

4 tablespoons chicken fat
1 pound chicken livers
1 cup minced white onions
3 hard-cooked egg yolks
2 teaspoons salt
½ teaspoon pepper

Melt the chicken fat; sauté livers and onions for 15 minutes. Remove from fire; cool. Mince (or put through grinder) the livers, onions and egg yolks; mix well, and season with salt and pepper. Place about 1 tablespoon of the mixture on each square of dough. Fold dough into a triangle, wetting the edges with water to seal.

Cook kreplach in gently boiling water—not violently, or it will unseal them; remove with a slotted spoon when they float to the top, then drain. Then, often, they are fried. Or, they can be cooked in rich chicken broth instead of water and are served with the broth in hot soup bowls. Serves 8.

MATZO NOODLES IN CHICKEN BROTH

4 eggs
½ teaspoon salt
4 tablespoons matzo meal
⅓ cup chicken fat
3 quarts rich Chicken Broth
    (page 84)

Whip eggs with salt; blend meal in slowly; mix well. Melt chicken fat in saucepan; pour in enough batter to cover bottom of pan. When cooked on one side, turn and cook the other. Roll each pancake and cut into ⅛-inch strips. Drop into gently boiling chicken broth for 5 minutes. Serve noodles and broth in hot soup bowls. Serves 6 to 8.

BAKED DAIRY NOODLE RING

1 pound egg noodles
2 tablespoons melted butter
3 tablespoons dry bread crumbs
1 pound cream cheese
3 eggs, beaten
⅓ cup sugar
1½ teaspoons salt

Cook noodles *al dente;* drain. Brush a 10-inch ring mold with melted butter; dust with bread crumbs. Blend cheese, eggs, sugar and salt; fold into drained noodles. Spoon into prepared mold. Bake in a 400° F. oven for 30 minutes. Unmold on a warm serving platter. Serves 8.

KOREA

KOREAN NOODLE SOUP

  2 tablespoons sesame seeds
  4 scallions
  ½ pound lean pork, cut into
        wafer-thin slices
  ⅓ cup soy sauce
  8 cups hot water
  ¼ pound fine noodles

In a deep frypan or Dutch oven, with flame very low, brown the sesame seeds; remove and pulverize. Cut off the green tails of the scallions and mince; set aside. Chop the rest of the scallions. Return pulverized seeds to the pan, add the pork slices, the white part of the scallions and the soy sauce. Simmer, uncovered, for 8 minutes. Add the water and the noodles, cover, and simmer for 3 minutes. Uncover pan, blend in the green part of the scallions, stir well, and simmer. Remove from heat when meat is fork-tender. Serve in hot soup bowls. Serves 4 to 6.

PERSIA

DUSHINAR
(*Persian Baked Pasta*)

  1 pound spaghetti, broken into
        2-inch pieces
  4 tablespoons butter
  8 tomatoes, sliced

  4 eggs
  2 cups sour cream
  1 cup light cream
  2 teaspoons cayenne pepper
  2 tablespoons ground walnuts

Cook spaghetti *al dente,* drain, and toss in 2 tablespoons of the butter. Butter a 12-inch casserole and arrange a layer of spaghetti, then one of tomatoes, finishing with a layer of pasta. Beat eggs, blend with sour cream and sweet cream, and beat together for 3 minutes. Pour over the spaghetti. Blend cayenne and walnuts and sprinkle over top of pasta. Fleck with remaining butter and bake, uncovered, in a preheated 375° F. oven for 20 minutes. Serves 6.

POLAND

NOODLES WARSAW

  1 pound sausage meat
  4 tablespoons water
  1 small head of cabbage, shredded
Salt and pepper
  1 pound narrow egg noodles

Cook sausage in a skillet until well browned. Drain, and save 4 tablespoons drippings. Add drippings, water and shredded cabbage to sausage; sprinkle with salt and pepper. Cover and steam for 15 minutes. Meanwhile, cook noodles *al dente;* drain. Add noodles to cabbage mixture and toss. Cook, uncovered, for 8 minutes. Serves 4 to 6.

SPAIN

MACARRONES DE VIGILIA
(*Lenten Baked Macaroni*)

  1 pound mussels in shells
  2 onions, chopped
  4 tomatoes, peeled and diced
  3 tablespoons butter
  2 tablespoons olive oil
  1½ pounds hake or haddock,
      boned and cubed
  1 cup white wine
  1 pound elbow macaroni
  4 tablespoons sharp grating
      cheese

Scrub the mussels and steam them until they open; discard shells and strain the liquid through several layers of cheese-cloth. Sauté onions and tomatoes in 2 tablespoons of the butter and the oil until onions are soft. Add fish cubes and mussels with strained liquid. Simmer for 8 minutes; add wine and simmer for 4 minutes. Cook macaroni *al dente;* drain. Place in a baking dish in layers the macaroni and fish-mussels-sauce. Sprinkle cheese on top, dot with remaining butter, and brown in a 400° F. oven. Serves 4 to 6.

MACARRONES Y MENUDILLOS
(*Macaroni and Giblets*)

  1 pound elbow macaroni
  2 onions, chopped

  ½ pound chicken giblets,
      chopped
  2 ounces smoked ham, chopped
  4 tablespoons butter
  1 tablespoon tomato purée
  1 cup Chicken Broth (page 84)
  ½ cup white wine
  1 teaspoon salt
  Milled black pepper
  3 tablespoons grated sharp cheese

Cook macaroni *al dente;* drain. Sauté onions, giblets and ham in 2 tablespoons of the butter for 5 minutes. Add tomato purée, broth and wine; simmer, uncovered, for 10 minutes. Place macaroni and giblets in layers in a buttered baking dish; season with salt and pepper and sprinkle with cheese. Dot with remaining butter. Brown in 375° F. oven for 10 minutes. Serves 6.

SOPA DE FIDEOS
(*Vermicelli Soup*)

  1 small fresh pork butt
  2 onions
  2 carrots
  1 garlic clove
  2 teaspoons salt
  Liberal amount of milled black
      pepper
  ½ pound *vermicelli*, broken into
      1-inch pieces

Trim most of the fat from the pork butt. Place pork, onions, carrots, garlic, salt and pepper in an 8-quart pot and fill with water. Simmer, covered, for 3 hours, or until pork is tender. Remove pork for entrée. Simmer broth, uncovered, until reduced by half. Strain the broth into another pot; stir in the *vermicelli*; cook over medium-high flame, stirring often, until pasta is *al dente*. Serve immediately in hot soup bowls. Serves 4 to 6.

SOPA DE MACARRONES Y ALMEJAS
(*Macaroni and Mussel Soup*)

2 pounds mussels
2 tablespoons olive oil
3 pints clam juice
½ pound elbow macaroni
2 tablespoons tomato paste
Salt, if needed
Milled black pepper

Scrub mussels well; pat dry. Heat the oil in a saucepan and add the mussels. Heat just long enough for mussels to open. Take mussels from shells and put them with their liquid in a saucepan. Add clam juice and bring to a boil. Add macaroni and tomato paste; season to taste. Cook over medium flame, stirring often, for 20 minutes. Serves 4 to 6.

TURKEY

BURSA DANASI
(*Baked Veal with Noodles*)

2 pounds veal steak, boned and pounded flat
1 garlic clove, minced
Milled black pepper
1 teaspoon salt
1 bay leaf
1 teaspoon dried tarragon
½ cup white wine
4 tablespoons butter
4 tomatoes, peeled and diced
2 onions, minced
6 mushrooms, sliced
2 celery ribs, chopped
1½ cups yoghurt
1 pound narrow noodles

Season veal with garlic, pepper, salt, herbs and wine, and marinate, in the refrigerator, for 5 hours; turn steak after 2 hours. Drain, pat dry with paper towels, and cut into 1-inch cubes. Sauté cubes in 2 tablespoons of the butter until brown, 5 minutes; remove from pan and keep warm. Sauté in remaining butter, tomatoes, onions, mushrooms and celery. Simmer for 15 minutes, stirring frequently. Add yoghurt; heat thoroughly but do not boil. Cook noodles *al dente,* drain, and place in a buttered baking dish. Add veal and cover with the yoghurt-vegetable sauce; cover. Bake in 400° F. oven for 20 minutes. Serves 6.

Leftovers & PASTA

*I*f there is one outstanding lesson that I learned from Maria Limoncelli, the mother of my wife, it is that the most important single ingredient in cooking is imagination. Stir it up along with the food and you will come up with, if not a classic dish, often a memorable one. Pasta and imagination can quickly convert a leftover into a delicacy, put unexpected sparkle into a dull meal. A dab of leftover spinach can become a tasty sauce for spaghetti. A piece of steak, a chicken leg, a slice of cold pork, remaining from another meal, can deliciously fill *ravioli* or *cannelloni*. These stuffed pastas do especially well in the leftover department. Nearly anything can be enhanced and brought to new life encased in fresh pasta dough, boiled or baked, and dressed in a sassy sauce.

397

Even leftover pasta itself (if it has been properly cooked *al dente*) can be used for a filling or to bring personality to another dish. Warming it in a double boiler brings it to life, perhaps to stuff a tomato, drop into a stew or a seafood casserole. Pasta is too versatile and nutritious to waste.

Following are a few ideas for dishes guaranteed to give new life to leftovers. But—and this is a very important point—whenever you have something good in the refrigerator, it could be just the ingredient called for in any number of recipes in previous chapters of this book. A little of this, a little of that—such is the principle of many of the simplest and best pasta sauces. It depends on your point of view whether leftover is really the word for these ingredients. With pasta, and handled properly, leftover is certainly not their flavor.

CAPPELLETTI IN BRODO
(*"Little Hats" in Broth*)

> ½ pound leftover ham, pork, chicken, duck or veal
> 2 tablespoons grated Parmesan cheese
> 1 whole egg, beaten
> ½ teaspoon salt
> Lusty amount of milled black pepper
> Pinch of grated nutmeg (lightly; it is a permeating spice)
> 1 recipe Pasta Fresca for Ravioli (page 44)
> 3 quarts Chicken Broth (page 84)
> Chopped parsley, or melted butter and grated cheese

Grind the leftover meat and mix it with the cheese, egg, salt, pepper and nutmeg. Prepare pasta dough, roll it out, and cut it into 2-inch circles. Put a little mound of the meat mixture into the center of each; fold straight across, then with your fingers bring the edges together and press, forming the dough into a tiny hat. Dry for 25 minutes.

Bring the broth to a simmer and drop in 2 *cappelletti* at a time. When they are all in, cook for 7 minutes. Now you can do one of two things: Either serve the little hats in the broth as a soup, with a sprinkle of parsley over each bowl of soup with its pasta; or you can remove the *cappelletti* with a slotted spoon, drain them well, and serve immediately as a first course, drenching them with hot melted butter and a sprinkling of Parmesan. Serves 4 to 6.

PASTINA WITH MINIATURE MEATBALLS

½ pound leftover chicken
1 tablespoon flour
3 tablespoons butter
1 egg, beaten
1 teaspoon salt
Milled black pepper
Pinch of ground cinnamon
8 cups Chicken Broth (page 84)
4 tablespoons *pastina* (small pasta for soup)
¼ cup grated Parmesan cheese

Put the leftover chicken meat through the grinder, and mix well with the flour, butter, beaten egg, salt, pepper and cinnamon. Form into meatballs the size of marbles. Bring broth to boil, drop in the meatballs, and stir in the *pastina*. Simmer for 10 minutes or less, until *pastina* is *al dente*. Serve in hot soup bowls, sprinkled with Parmesan. Serves 4.

SUMMER SALMON SALAD

2 cups leftover pasta (it must be *al dente!*)
½ tablespoon olive oil (about)
2 tablespoons lemon juice
1 teaspoon salt
¼ teaspoon freshly milled pepper
4 tablespoons chopped scallions
½ cup mayonnaise
1 can (15 ounces) red salmon, drained, flaked and chilled
1 teaspoon dried dillweed
1 cup leftover peas or string beans

Toss the leftover pasta with enough olive oil to coat it. Mix in a salad bowl with lemon juice, salt, pepper, scallions and mayonnaise. Toss the salmon with the dill and arrange in the center. Spoon the peas or beans in a ring around the salmon. Serves 4 to 6.

DAY-AFTER CASSEROLE

2 cups diced leftover lamb or beef
2 tablespoons olive oil
½ cup minced onion
½ cup minced green pepper
1 large eggplant
2 cups (one 1-pound can) tomatoes, well drained
1 cup red wine
⅛ teaspoon ground cinnamon
2 teaspoons salt
½ teaspoon garlic salt
2 cups leftover pasta (*al dente!*)
⅓ cup grated Parmesan cheese

Brown lamb in oil; add onion and green pepper; sauté until tender. Pare and dice eggplant; cook, covered, in 1 inch of boiling salted water for 7 minutes; drain. Stir eggplant, tomatoes, wine and seasonings into lamb. Put in a bowl and refrigerate for 3 hours. Then, stir pasta into this eggplant mixture and place in a 4-quart casserole. Sprinkle with the Parmesan. Bake, uncovered, in a 400° F. oven for 30 minutes. Serves 4 to 6.

399

MEAT LOAF WITH TUBETTINI

This is an excellent way to use up a sizeable piece of meat—about one pound of beef, ham, pork or lamb—left over from another dinner. The meat should be finely ground, perhaps put through the grinder twice.

½ cup *tubettini* ("tiny tubes")
2 small white onions, chopped
2 tablespoons olive oil
2 tablespoons flour
1 teaspoon salt
1 cup light cream
2 eggs
1 pound leftover meat, finely
    ground

Cook *tubettini al dente* in salted water; drain. Sauté onions in oil until soft; blend in flour, sprinkle in salt, and stir in cream; simmer until slightly thickened. Beat eggs well and mix in a bowl with the ground meat and *tubettini*. Add to the cream-and-onion sauce, blending well. Pour into a buttered tin or glass loaf dish and bake, uncovered, in a 400° F. oven for 25 minutes, or until the loaf is firm. Serves 4 to 6.

MONDAY SPAGHETTI

This is a good way to use that leftover Sunday roast (or part of it) on Monday, in a pasta sauce that is quick, easy and excellent.

4 cups chopped leftover roast
2 tablespoons butter
1 tablespoon olive oil
1 white onion, chopped
½ teaspoon dry mustard
1 tablespoon minced parsley
8 cups (two 2-pound cans) toma-
    toes, put through food mill
½ teaspoon salt
Milled black pepper
1 pound spaghetti
¼ cup grated Parmesan cheese

Brown the chopped leftover roast in butter and oil; blend in the onion, mustard, parsley, tomatoes, salt and pepper; stir well. Simmer, uncovered, for 25 minutes, stirring often until sauce is smooth and thickened. Cook spaghetti *al dente,* drain, and toss with half of the cheese. Serve in hot soup bowls with the meat-tomato sauce liberally spooned atop; sprinkle the rest of the cheese on top. Serve immediately. Serves 4 to 6.

BAKED TAGLIATELLE WITH STEAK

2 cups chopped leftover steak
1 tablespoon butter
1 white onion, chopped
1 teaspoon Worcestershire sauce
¼ teaspoon black pepper
1 teaspoon dried sweet basil
1 teaspoon dried marjoram
2 cups (one 1-pound can) toma-
    toes, put through food mill
¼ pound ricotta cheese
⅓ cup grated Parmesan cheese

¼ cup sour cream
¼ cup chopped green olives
½ pound *tagliatelle*

Sauté steak in butter in a skillet until lightly browned. Add onion and cook until soft; add Worcestershire, pepper, basil, marjoram and tomatoes. Bring to a boil and simmer until most of water has evaporated, about 20 minutes. Blend cheeses, sour cream and olives. Cook *tagliatelle al dente*; drain. Spread half of the *tagliatelle* in a buttered baking dish; top with cheese mixture. Spread another layer of *tagliatelle* and cover with the meat sauce. Bake, uncovered, in a preheated 400° F. oven for 20 minutes. Serves 4 to 6.

PORK "NEW LIFE"

1 cup heavy cream
4 ounces fontina or Bel Paese cheese
4 ounces ricotta cheese
4 tablespoons butter
1 tablespoon olive oil
4 mushrooms, sliced
1 cup diced leftover lean pork or other leftover meat
½ teaspoon salt
1 pound spaghetti
⅓ cup grated Parmesan cheese

In a double boiler, stirring constantly, blend cream, fontina or Bel Paese and ricotta cheese, working mixture into a smooth sauce. Heat butter and oil in saucepan and sauté mushrooms in it for 5 minutes. Stir in the pork, sprinkle

lightly with salt, and simmer for 5 minutes. Blend this into the cream-and-cheese sauce, stirring well. Cook spaghetti *al dente*, drain, and place in hot soup bowls. Spoon pork-and-cheese sauce atop, sprinkle lightly with Parmesan, and serve immediately. Serves 4 to 6.

LAST-OF-THE-HAM AND SPAGHETTI CASSEROLE

When your leftover is just a fragment, such as the very last of a baked ham, use it for its flavor, added here to what is really a lamb's tongue mixture.

2 cups leftover spaghetti
3 tablespoons butter, melted
3 tomatoes, peeled and diced
¼ cup Madeira wine
1 cup chopped leftover ham
1 small canned lamb tongue, cut into strips
2 mushrooms, sliced
2 tablespoons grated Swiss cheese

Blend spaghetti, melted butter and tomatoes; simmer for 20 minutes. Add wine, ham, tongue and mushrooms. Blend well and cook for 10 minutes. Off fire, add grated cheese and mix; place combination into buttered casserole; bake at 475° F. for 10 minutes. (If you have no leftover pasta, cook ½ pound *al dente,* then blend with butter and tomatoes.) Serves 4 to 6.

STUFFED PEPPERS PASQUALE

3 large green peppers
4 white onions, minced
2 tablespoons butter
2 cups chopped leftover beef or pork
1 cup leftover pasta (*al dente!*)
½ teaspoon salt
4 cups Marinara Sauce (page 69)
½ cup dry white wine
¼ pound pepato cheese, grated

Split green peppers lengthwise into halves. Remove seeds and stems and wash peppers. Drop them into a large pot of boiling salted water; turn off heat and let stand for 8 minutes. Drain peppers and place them in a casserole. Sauté onions in butter until soft. Blend onions, chopped meat, pasta, salt and half of the marinara sauce. Fill peppers with this meat mixture. Stir the wine into the remaining marinara sauce. Spoon this over the peppers. Bake in 400° F. oven for 20 minutes. Sprinkle with grated cheese; bake for another 10 minutes. Serves 6.

VEAL CANNELLONI

As with the ravioli *recipe in this chapter, the filling for* cannelloni *can be nearly any meat (or vegetable) you have left over in the refrigerator— chicken, turkey, duck, ham, beef or pork, or a mixture of some of these.*

4 cups twice-ground leftover veal
¼ teaspoon grated nutmeg
½ teaspoon salt
Milled black pepper
3 tablespoons heavy cream
1 tablespoon minced parsley
5 cups Filetto di Pomodoro (page 68)
1 recipe Pasta Fresca all'Uovo (page 42)
¼ cup grated Asiago cheese

In a bowl blend veal, nutmeg, salt, pepper, cream, parsley and 2 tablespoons of the *filetto* sauce; mix well. Prepare the pasta dough, cut into squares (page 43), and dry. Cook and drain the squares. Spoon some veal filling along the bottom edge of each pasta square; roll into a tight tubular shape. Into a large flat baking dish spoon enough sauce to cover the bottom; arrange the *cannelloni* on it so the rolls do not touch one another. Cover with the rest of the sauce and sprinkle with Asiago. Bake in a preheated 400° F. oven for 30 minutes. Serves 6.

CHICKEN CROQUETTES

Here's one I had in Milan, as an appetizer with cocktails, but it can be served with Mornay sauce as a luncheon dish.

1 cup finely diced leftover chicken
1 small canned lamb tongue, diced finely
4 large mushrooms, minced
¼ pound small elbow macaroni, cooked *al dente* and drained

402

¼ cup grated Parmesan cheese
1 tablespoon heavy cream
3 eggs, beaten
1 teaspoon salt
Milled black pepper
¼ cup bread crumbs
2 tablespoons olive oil
1 recipe Mornay Sauce (page 73)

Mix chicken, tongue, mushrooms, macaroni, cheese, cream and one of the eggs; season with salt and pepper. Shape mixture into croquettes. Dip croquettes into remaining eggs, then into bread crumbs; sauté in the oil until golden, turning once; drain on paper towels. Prepare Mornay sauce; serve croquettes hot with a spoonful of Mornay sauce over each. Or shape very small croquettes and serve them crisp and hot with cocktails; omit the sauce. Serves 6.

FETTUCCELLE TETRAZZINI

10 small mushrooms, quartered
4 tablespoons butter
2 cups diced leftover chicken (or veal, turkey or duck)
½ teaspoon salt
1 teaspoon flour
½ cup heavy cream
1½ cups milk
2 egg yolks
½ pound *fettuccelle* ("little ribbons" or narrow *fettuccine*)
½ cup grated Parmesan cheese

Sauté mushrooms in 2 tablespoons of the butter for 5 minutes; add chicken and continue to sauté. Sprinkle in the salt and flour; blend. Add the cream and ½ cup of the milk and simmer, stirring, until well blended. Beat egg yolks with remaining 1 cup milk and add to chicken mixture. Stir quickly (don't boil) until sauce is slightly thickened, about 5 minutes. Stir steadily so the egg doesn't curdle.

Cook *fettuccelle al dente*; toss with 1 tablespoon of the butter and ¼ cup of the Parmesan. Place in 4 buttered ramekins. Pour the chicken mixture over the noodles. Sprinkle with remaining Parmesan and dot with remaining butter. Place under broiler until brown. Serves 4.

FETTUCCINE WITH CHICKEN

1 pound *fettuccine*
4 tablespoons butter
1 cup diced leftover chicken
1 carrot, diced
2 tablespoons fresh peas, cooked
6 small mushrooms, sliced thin
1½ cups heavy cream
⅓ cup grated Romano cheese
⅓ cup grated Parmesan cheese

Cook *fettuccine* less than *al dente*; drain. Butter a glass casserole. Arrange the noodles evenly across the bottom. Sauté the chicken and carrot in 2 tablespoons of the butter for 5 minutes; then add peas and mushrooms and sauté for 5 minutes more. Pour this over the noodles, then pour the cream over all. Sprinkle generously with the cheeses, which have been mixed. Fleck with the remaining butter; place in broiler for 10 minutes, or until brown. Serves 4 to 6.

TAGLIOLINI AND CHICKEN

1 tablespoon olive oil
2 white onions, chopped
1 garlic clove, minced
4 cups (one 2-pound can) Italian tomatoes, put through food mill
6 black olives, sliced
6 mushrooms, sliced
½ cup strips of green pepper
1 teaspoon salt
Freshly milled black pepper
¼ teaspoon dried sweet basil
1 pound *tagliolini*
5 cups Chicken Broth (page 84)
3 cups large pieces of leftover chicken or turkey

Place olive oil, onions and garlic in a heavy skillet; simmer over low heat until onions are soft. Add tomatoes, olives, mushrooms, green pepper, salt, pepper and basil. Cook over low heat until moisture has evaporated, about 20 minutes. Drop *tagliolini* into the boiling broth; stir with a wooden fork so they won't stick; cook until less than *al dente*. Drain, and place in a shallow 2-quart casserole. Spread chicken over noodles; pour sauce over all. Bake in 350° F. oven for 30 minutes. Serves 4 to 6.

SLICED BREAST OF TURKEY WITH VERMICELLI

This is a good one for that tired lunch three days after Thanksgiving.

12 slices (3 inches long) of left-over turkey breast
4 tablespoons butter
Liberal amount of milled black pepper
½ cup grated Parmesan cheese
1 pound *vermicelli*

Sauté the slices of turkey in 2 tablespoons of the butter; mill black pepper over turkey as it warms in the butter. Just before removing from fire sprinkle half of the Parmesan over the meat. Cook *vermicelli al dente*, drain, and place in a warm bowl with remaining butter and cheese. Mill in black pepper and toss. Bring to table in individual dishes with the turkey slices arranged on top of the pasta. Serves 4 to 6.

CHITARRA WITH SPINACH

1 small white onion, chopped
1 tablespoon butter
1 cup cooked spinach (or whatever amount you have left in the refrigerator)
2 eggs
½ cup freshly grated Parmesan cheese
Liberal amount of milled black pepper
1 pound *chitarra* ("guitar strings")

Sauté onion in butter until soft; slowly add the spinach and stir it in. Beat eggs in bowl, add the cheese and much black pepper, and blend well. Cook *chitarra al dente;* fork from boiling water directly into the egg bowl and toss well. Now add spinach and onion to the pasta in the bowl and toss again. Serve in very hot bowls. Serves 4 to 6.

TAGLIOLETTE WITH SPINACH

(*or with Broccoli or Cauliflower*)

- 1 cup leftover cooked spinach
- 2 leftover chicken legs or thighs
- 1 recipe Mornay Sauce (page 73)
- 1 pound *tagliolette*
- 2 tablespoons butter
- 4 tablespoons grated Parmesan cheese

Place the spinach in a strainer and drain liquid off. Slice meat from chicken legs or thighs into julienne strips. Prepare Mornay sauce; stir in the sliced chicken and the spinach. Cook *tagliolette al dente,* drain, and toss with half of the sauce. Butter ramekins; spoon in the pasta mixed with sauce; spoon remaining sauce over and sprinkle with Parmesan. Dot with remaining butter. Place in broiler and brown. Serves 4 to 6.

RAVIOLI WITH SPINACH

- 1 recipe Pasta Fresca for Ravioli (page 44)
- 1 cup finely chopped leftover cooked spinach
- 1 cup ricotta cheese, drained
- ½ cup grated Parmesan cheese
- 2 tablespoons bread crumbs
- 1 egg, beaten
- 1 teaspoon salt
- Milled black pepper
- 6 tablespoons butter, melted

Prepare fresh pasta dough. In a large bowl blend spinach, ricotta, half of the Parmesan, the bread crumbs, egg, salt and pepper; mix well. Roll out dough. On one sheet place 1 tablespoon of the filling every 2 inches, cover with second sheet of dough, seal, and cut with a pastry wheel. Cook in gently simmering salted water; water should not be boiling vigorously or the *ravioli* will open. Remove one *ravioli* with a slotted spoon as they float to the top. Test; if it is done, remove the others, and drain. Serve immediately, drenched with the melted butter and sprinkled with remaining Parmesan. Serves 6.

Note: This versatile recipe can be varied in many ways. Chopped leftover meat of any kind can be substituted for the bread crumbs; the amount of meat may be increased to 2 cups; also the ricotta may be omitted. Mushroom sauce or any of the tomato sauces in the sauce chapter can be substituted for butter.

MACARONI MEDLEY

Here is one designed to utilize an assortment of whatever leftovers are in the refrigerator.

> 3 white onions, chopped
> 2 small green peppers, chopped
> 2 small red peppers, chopped
> 2 celery ribs, chopped
> 3 tablespoons olive oil
> 1 or more tablespoons leftover cooked peas, corn, or string beans
> Chopped tag-end pieces of pork, ham, veal, chicken, beef
> 1 pound macaroni (elbow, or *maccheroncelli*)
> Salt
> Milled black pepper
> 1 cup buttered bread crumbs

Sauté onions, peppers and celery in oil until soft. Add the leftover vegetable and meat. Cook the macaroni *al dente;* drain. Place in a baking dish, stir in the vegetable-meat sauce, sprinkle with salt and black pepper to taste, and stir. Top with the buttered bread crumbs; place under broiler for 7 minutes. Serves 4 to 6.

PASTA OMELETTE

This is a popular luncheon dish in Naples (which has much better food than is credited) and is one of my favorites. I use leftover pasta, usually spaghetti, that has been cooked al dente, of course, and which has had only a butter or a white sauce added to it, if any.

> 5 eggs
> Leftover spaghetti (no more than 2 cups)
> ¼ cup grated Romano cheese
> 1 teaspoon salt
> Liberal amount of milled black pepper
> 1 tablespoon olive oil
> 1 tablespoon butter

Beat the eggs well in a bowl; stir in the pasta, cheese, salt and pepper. Fry in oil and butter in large frypan, either folding as an omelette or just turning straight over, pancake style. It should be golden and fluffy, not rubbery or overcooked; 3 minutes at the most on each side should be enough. If you have any leftover tomato sauce, this is excellent served hot on the side. Serves 4.

Index to Photographs

FLORENCE, *detail of the Church of Santa Croce—Tuscany*

Index

SIENA, *doorway adjoining the Duomo—Tuscany*

417

427

About the author . . .

JACK DENTON SCOTT has spent most of his life traveling to far and un-usual places, as a war correspondent, as a columnist, and to write ten books and innumerable articles for major American magazines.

Jack Scott and his wife, Maria Luisa Limoncelli Scott, have logged 700,000 miles of international travel since 1959. Needless to say, they have spent a good portion of that time in Italy. He has been cooking since he was fourteen and establishing fast friendships with leading chefs and restaurateurs all over the world ever since he first started to travel. His particular passion for pasta he attributes to the influence of his wife and of his mother-in-law, Maria Limon-celli, both accomplished cooks, and to a conviction that Italian cuisine is the world's best. The many Italian chefs Jack Scott knows have taught him the technique of pasta cookery as few amateurs could ever know it, and several of them have honored him by sitting back and letting him do the cooking when he has visited them, or they him.

The Scotts live in Washington, Connecticut.

About the photographer . . .

SAMUEL CHAMBERLAIN, artist, photographer, and author, has written and illustrated some 50 books about New England, European architecture, and food and travel in Europe. An architect by training, he started his career as an etcher. Among his best-known books are *The New England Image,* the autobi-ographical *Etched in Sunlight—Fifty Years in the Graphic Arts,* and *Bouquet de France, Italian Bouquet,* and *British Bouquet,* three gastronomic travel epics illustrated with his drawings, prints, and photographs. The Chamberlains live in Marblehead, Massachusetts.